LETTERS

AND

ORATIONS

THE
OTHER VOICE
IN
EARLY MODERN
EUROPE

A Series Edited by Margaret L. King and Albert Rabil, Jr.

OTHER BOOKS IN THE SERIES

Cassandra Fedele

LETTERS
AND
ORATIONS

৵

Edited and translated by
Diana Robin

THE UNIVERSITY OF CHICAGO PRESS
Chicago and London

Cassandra Fedele (1465–1558)

Diana Robin is professor of classics and director of comparative literature and cultural studies at the University of New Mexico. She is author of *Collected Letters of a Renaissance Feminist* (University of Chicago Press).

The University of Chicago Press, Chicago 60637
The University of Chicago Press, Ltd., London
© 2000 by The University of Chicago
All rights reserved. Published 2000
Printed in the United States of America
09 08 07 06 05 04 03 02 01 00 1 2 3 4 5

ISBN: 0-226-23931-4 (cloth)
ISBN: 0-226-23932-2 (paper)

Library of Congress Cataloging-in-Publication Data

Fedele, Cassandra, 1465?–1558.
  [Selections. English]
  Letters and orations / Cassandra Fedele ; edited and translated by Diana Robin.
    p. cm.—(The other voice in early modern Europe)
  Includes bibliographical references (p.) and index.
  ISBN 0-226-23931-4 (alk. paper)—ISBN 0-226-23932-2 (pbk. : alk. paper)
  1. Fedele, Cassandra, 1465?–1558—Translations into English. 2. Speeches,
addresses, etc., Latin (Medieval and modern)—Italy—Venice—Translations
into English.   3. Authors, Latin (Medieval and modern)—Italy—Venice—
Correspondence.   4. Fedele, Cassandra, 1465?–1558—Correspondence.   5.
Humanists—Italy—Venice—Correspondence.   6. Feminists—Italy—Venice—
Correspondence.   I. Robin, Diana Maury.   II. Title.   III. Series.

PA8520.F392 A27 2000
875'.04—dc21   99-051321

This translation was supported by a generous grant from the NEH.

CONTENTS

THE OTHER VOICE IN EARLY MODERN EUROPE: INTRODUCTION TO THE SERIES

Margaret L. King and Albert Rabil, Jr.

THE OLD VOICE AND THE OTHER VOICE

In western Europe and the United States women are nearing equality in the professions, in business, and in politics. Most enjoy access to education, reproductive rights, and autonomy in financial affairs. Issues vital to women are on the public agenda: equal pay, child care, domestic abuse, breast cancer research, and curricular revision with an eye to the inclusion of women.

These recent achievements have their origins in things women (and some male supporters) said for the first time about six hundred years ago. Theirs is the "other voice," in contradistinction to the "first voice," the voice of the educated men who created Western culture. Coincident with a general reshaping of European culture in the period 1300 to 1700 (called the Renaissance or early modern period), questions of female equality and opportunity were raised that still resound and are still unresolved.

The "other voice" emerged against the backdrop of a three-thousand-year history of misogyny—the hatred of women—rooted in the civilizations related to Western culture: Hebrew, Greek, Roman, and Christian. Misogyny inherited from these traditions pervaded the intellectual, medical, legal, religious, and social systems that developed during the European Middle Ages.

The following pages describe the misogynistic tradition inherited by early modern Europeans, and the new tradition which the "other voice" called into being to challenge reigning assumptions. This review should serve as a framework for the understanding of the texts published in the series "The Other Voice in Early Modern Europe." Introductions specific to each text and author follow this essay in all the volumes of the series.

THE MISOGYNIST TRADITION, 500 B.C.E.—1500 C.E.

Embedded in the philosophical and medical theories of the ancient Greeks were perceptions of the female as inferior to the male in both mind and body. Similarly, the structure of civil legislation inherited from the ancient Romans was biased against women, and the views on women developed by Christian thinkers out of the Hebrew Bible and the Christian New Testament were negative and disabling. Literary works composed in the vernacular language of ordinary people, and widely recited or read, conveyed these negative assumptions. The social networks within which most women lived—those of the family and the institutions of the Roman Catholic Church—were shaped by this misogynist tradition and sharply limited the areas in which women might act in and upon the world.

GREEK PHILOSOPHY AND FEMALE NATURE. Greek biology assumed that women were inferior to men and defined them merely as childbearers and housekeepers. This view was authoritatively expressed in the works of the philosopher Aristotle.

Aristotle thought in dualities. He considered action superior to inaction, form (the inner design or structure of any object) superior to matter, completion to incompletion, possession to deprivation. In each of these dualities, he associated the male principle with the superior quality and the female with the inferior. "The male principle in nature," he argued, "is associated with active, formative and perfected characteristics, while the female is passive, material and deprived, desiring the male in order to become complete."[1] Men are always identified with virile qualities, such as judgment, courage, and stamina; women with their opposites—irrationality, cowardice, and weakness.

The masculine principle was considered to be superior even in the womb. Man's semen, Aristotle believed, created the form of a new human creature, while the female body contributed only matter. (The existence of the ovum, and the other facts of human embryology, were not established until the seventeenth century.) Although the later Greek physician Galen believed that there was a female component in generation, contributed by "female semen," the followers of both Aristotle and Galen saw the male role in human generation as more active and more important.

In the Aristotelian view, the male principle sought always to reproduce itself. The creation of a female was always a mistake, therefore, resulting from an imperfect act of generation. Every female born was considered a "defective" or "mutilated" male (as Aristotle's terminology has variously been translated), a "monstrosity" of nature.[2]

For Greek theorists, the biology of males and females was the key to their psychology. The female was softer and more docile, more apt to be despondent, querulous, and deceitful. Being incomplete, moreover, she craved sexual fulfillment in intercourse with a male. The male was intellectual, active, and in control of his passions.

These psychological polarities derived from the theory that the universe consisted of four elements (earth, fire, air, and water), expressed in human bodies as four "humors" (black bile, yellow bile, blood, and phlegm) considered respectively dry, hot, damp, and cold, and corresponding to mental states ("melancholic," "choleric," "sanguine," "phlegmatic"). In this schematization, the male, sharing the principles of earth and fire, was dry and hot; the female, sharing the principles of air and water, was cold and damp.

Female psychology was further affected by her dominant organ, the uterus (womb), *hystera* in Greek. The passions generated by the womb made women lustful, deceitful, talkative, irrational, indeed—when these affects were in excess—"hysterical."

Aristotle's biology also had social and political consequences. If the male principle was superior and the female inferior, then in the household, as in the state, men should rule and women must be subordinate. That hierarchy did not rule out the companionship of husband and wife, whose cooperation was necessary for the welfare of children and the preservation of property. Such mutuality supported male preeminence.

Aristotle's teacher, Plato, suggested a different possibility: that men and women might possess the same virtues. The setting for this proposal is the imaginary and ideal Republic that Plato sketches in his dialogue of that name. Here, for a privileged elite capable of leading wisely, all distinctions of class and wealth dissolve, as do consequently those of gender. Without households or property, as Plato constructs his ideal society, there is no need for the subordination of women. Women may, therefore, be educated to the same level as men to assume leadership responsibilities. Plato's Republic remained imaginary, however. In real societies, the subordination of women remained the norm and the prescription.

The views of women inherited from the Greek philosophical tradition became the basis for medieval thought. In the thirteenth century, the supreme scholastic philosopher Thomas Aquinas, among others, still echoed Aristotle's views of human reproduction, of male and female personalities, and of the preeminent male role in the social hierarchy.

ROMAN LAW AND THE FEMALE CONDITION. Roman law, like Greek philosophy, underlay medieval thought and shaped medieval society. The ancient belief that adult, property-owning men should administer house-holds and make decisions affecting the community at large is the very fulcrum of Roman law. Around 450 B.C.E., during Rome's Republican era, the community's customary law was recorded (legendarily) on the Twelve Tables, erected in the city's central forum. It was later elaborated by profes-sional jurists whose activity increased in the imperial era, when much new legislation, especially on issues affecting family and inheritance, was passed. This growing, changing body of laws was eventually codified in the *Corpus of Civil Law* under the direction of the emperor Justinian, generations after the empire ceased to be ruled from Rome. That *Corpus*, read and commented upon by medieval scholars from the eleventh century on, inspired the legal systems of most of the cities and kingdoms of Europe.

Laws regarding dowries, divorce, and inheritance most pertain to women. Since those laws aimed to maintain and preserve property, the women concerned were those from the property-owning minority. Their subordination to male family members points to the even greater subordina-tion of lower-class and slave women, about whom the laws speak little.

In the early Republic, the *paterfamilias*, "father of the family," possessed *patria potestas*, "paternal power." The term *pater*, "father," in both these cases does not necessarily mean biological father, but householder. The father was the person who owned the household's property and, indeed, its human members. The *paterfamilias* had absolute power—including the power, rarely exercised, of life or death—over his wife, his children, and his slaves, as much as over his cattle.

Male children could be "emancipated," an act that granted legal auton-omy and the right to own property. Males over the age of fourteen could be emancipated by a special grant from the father, or automatically by their father's death. But females never could be emancipated; instead, they passed from the authority of their father to a husband or, if widowed or orphaned while still unmarried, to a guardian or tutor.

Marriage under its traditional form placed the woman under her hus-band's authority, or *manus*. He could divorce her on grounds of adultery, drinking wine, or stealing from the household, but she could not divorce him. She could possess no property in her own right, nor bequeath any to her children upon her death. When her husband died, the household prop-erty passed not to her but to his male heirs. And when her father died, she had no claim to any family inheritance, which was directed to her brothers or more remote male relatives. The effect of these laws was to exclude women from civil society, itself based on property ownership.

In the later Republican and Imperial periods, these rules were significantly modified. Women rarely married according to the traditional form, but according to the form of "free" marriage. That practice allowed a woman to remain under her father's authority, to possess property given her by her father (most frequently the "dowry," recoverable from the husband's household in the event of his death), and to inherit from her father. She could also bequeath property to her own children and divorce her husband, just as he could divorce her.

Despite this greater freedom, women still suffered enormous disability under Roman law. Heirs could belong only to the father's side, never the mother's. Moreover, although she could bequeath her property to her children, she could not establish a line of succession in doing so. A woman was "the beginning and end of her own family," growled the jurist Ulpian. Moreover, women could play no public role. They could not hold public office, represent anyone in a legal case, or even witness a will. Women had only a private existence, and no public personality.

The dowry system, the guardian, women's limited ability to transmit wealth, and their total political disability are all features of Roman law adopted, although modified according to local customary laws, by the medieval communities of western Europe.

CHRISTIAN DOCTRINE AND WOMEN'S PLACE. The Hebrew Bible and the Christian New Testament authorized later writers to limit women to the realm of the family and to burden them with the guilt of original sin. The passages most fruitful for this purpose were the creation narratives in Genesis and sentences from the Epistles defining women's role within the Christian family and community.

Each of the first two chapters of Genesis contains a creation narrative. In the first, "God created humankind in his image, in the image of God he created them; male and female he created them" (NRSV, Genesis 1:27). In the second, God created Eve from Adam's rib (2:21–23). Christian theologians relied principally on Genesis 2 for their understanding of the relation between man and woman, interpreting the creation of Eve from Adam as proof of her subordination to him.

The creation story in Genesis 2 leads to that of the temptations in Genesis 3: of Eve by the wily serpent, and of Adam by Eve. As read by Christian theologians from Tertullian to Thomas Aquinas, the narrative made Eve responsible for the Fall and its consequences. She instigated the act; she deceived her husband; she suffered the greater punishment. Her disobedience made it necessary for Jesus to be incarnated and to die on the cross. From the pulpit, moralists and preachers for centuries conveyed to women the guilt that they bore for original sin.

The Epistles offered advice to early Christians on building communities of the faithful. Among the matters to be regulated was the place of women. Paul offered views favorable to women in Galatians 3:28: "There is neither Jew nor Greek, there is neither slave nor free, there is neither male nor female; for you are all one in Christ Jesus." Paul also referred to women as his coworkers and placed them on a par with himself and his male coworkers (Philippians 4:2–3; Romans 16:1–3; 1 Corinthians 16:19). Elsewhere Paul limited women's possibilities: "But I want you to understand that the head of every man is Christ, the head of a woman is her husband, and the head of Christ is God" (1 Corinthians 11:3).

Biblical passages by later writers (though attributed to Paul) enjoined women to forego jewels, expensive clothes, and elaborate coiffures; and they forbade women to "teach or have authority over men," telling them to "learn in silence with all submissiveness" as is proper for one responsible for sin, consoling them, however, with the thought that they would be saved through childbearing (1 Timothy 2:9–15). Other texts among the later Epistles defined women as the weaker sex, and emphasized their subordination to their husbands (1 Peter 3:7; Colossians 3:18; Ephesians 5:22–23).

These passages from the New Testament became the arsenal employed by theologians of the early church to transmit negative attitudes toward women to medieval Christian culture—above all, Tertullian ("On the Apparel of Women"), Jerome (*Against Jovinian*), and Augustine (*The Literal Meaning of Genesis*).

THE IMAGE OF WOMEN IN MEDIEVAL LITERATURE. The philosophical, legal, and religious traditions born in antiquity formed the basis of the medieval intellectual synthesis wrought by trained thinkers, mostly clerics, writing in Latin and based largely in universities. The vernacular literary tradition that developed alongside the learned tradition also spoke about female nature and women's roles. Medieval stories, poems, and epics were infused with misogyny. They portrayed most women as lustful and deceitful, while praising good housekeepers and loyal wives, or replicas of the Virgin Mary, or the female saints and martyrs.

There is an exception in the movement of "courtly love" that evolved in southern France from the twelfth century. Courtly love was the erotic love between a nobleman and noblewoman, the latter usually superior in social rank. It was always adulterous. From the conventions of courtly love derive modern Western notions of romantic love. The phenomenon has had an impact disproportionate to its size, for it affected only a tiny elite, and very few women. The exaltation of the female lover probably does not reflect a higher evaluation of women, or a step toward their sexual liberation.

More likely it gives expression to the social and sexual tensions besetting the knightly class at a specific historical juncture.

The literary fashion of courtly love was on the wane by the thirteenth century, when the widely read *The Romance of the Rose* was composed in French by two authors of significantly different dispositions. Guillaume de Lorris composed the initial four thousand verses around 1235, and Jean de Meun added about seventeen thousand verses—more than four times the original—around 1265.

The fragment composed by Guillaume de Lorris stands squarely in the courtly love tradition. Here the poet, in a dream, is admitted into a walled garden where he finds a magic fountain in which a rosebush is reflected. He longs to pick one rose but the thorns around it prevent his doing so, even as he is wounded by arrows from the God of Love, whose commands he agrees to obey. The remainder of this part of the poem recounts the poet's unsuccessful efforts to pluck the rose.

The longer part of the Romance by Jean de Meun also describes a dream. But here allegorical characters give long didactic speeches, providing a social satire on a variety of themes, including those pertaining to women. Love is an anxious and tormented state, the poem explains, women are greedy and manipulative, marriage is miserable, beautiful women are lustful, ugly ones cease to please, and a chaste woman is as rare as a black swan.

Shortly after Jean de Meun completed *The Romance of the Rose*, Mathéolus penned his *Lamentations*, a long Latin diatribe against marriage translated into French about a century later. The *Lamentations* sum up medieval attitudes toward women, and they provoked the important response by Christine de Pizan in her *Book of the City of Ladies.*

In 1355, Giovanni Boccaccio wrote *Il Corbaccio*, another anti-feminist manifesto, though ironically by an author whose other works pioneered new directions in Renaissance thought. The former husband of his lover appears to Boccaccio, condemning his unmoderated lust and detailing the defects of women. Boccaccio concedes at the end "how much men naturally surpass women in nobility"[3] and is cured of his desires.

WOMEN'S ROLES: THE FAMILY. The negative perceptions of women expressed in the intellectual tradition are also implicit in the actual roles that women played in European society. Assigned to subordinate positions in the household and the church, they were barred from significant participation in public life.

Medieval European households, like those in antiquity and in non-Western civilizations, were headed by males. It was the male serf, or peasant, feudal lord, town merchant, or citizen who was polled or taxed or who succeeded to an inheritance or had any acknowledged public role, although his wife or widow could stand on a temporary basis as a surrogate for him. From about 1100, the position of property-holding males was enhanced further. Inheritance was confined to the male, or agnate, line—with depressing consequences for women.

A wife never fully belonged to her husband's family or a daughter to her father's family. She left her father's house young to marry whomever her parents chose. Her dowry was managed by her husband and normally passed to her children by him at her death.

A married woman's life was occupied nearly constantly with cycles of pregnancy, childbearing, and lactation. Women bore children through all the years of their fertility, and many died in childbirth before the end of that term. They also bore responsibility for raising young children up to six or seven. That responsibility was shared in the propertied classes, since it was common for a wet nurse to take over the job of breastfeeding, and servants took over other chores.

Women trained their daughters in the household responsibilities appropriate to their status, nearly always in tasks associated with textiles: spinning, weaving, sewing, embroidering. Their sons were sent out of the house as apprentices or students, or their training was assumed by fathers in later childhood and adolescence. On the death of her husband, a woman's children became the responsibility of his family. She generally did not take "his" children with her to a new marriage or back to her father's house, except sometimes in artisan classes.

Women also worked. Rural peasants performed farm chores, merchant wives often practiced their husbands' trades, the unmarried daughters of the urban poor worked as servants or prostitutes. All wives produced or embellished textiles and did the housekeeping, while wealthy ones managed servants. These labors were unpaid or poorly paid, but often contributed substantially to family wealth.

WOMEN'S ROLES: THE CHURCH. Membership in a household, whether a father's or a husband's, meant for women a lifelong subordination to others. In western Europe, the Roman Catholic Church offered an alternative to the career of wife and mother. A woman could enter a convent parallel in function to the monasteries for men that evolved in the early Christian centuries.

In the convent, a woman pledged herself to a celibate life, lived according to strict community rules, and worshiped daily. Often the convent offered training in Latin, allowing some women to become considerable scholars and authors, as well as scribes, artists, and musicians. For women who chose the conventual life, the benefits could be enormous, but for numerous others placed in convents by paternal choice, the life could be restrictive and burdensome.

The conventual life declined as an alternative for women as the modern age approached. Reformed monastic institutions resisted responsibility for related female orders. The church increasingly restricted female institutional life by insisting on closer male supervision.

Women often sought other options. Some joined the communities of laywomen that sprang up spontaneously in the thirteenth century in the urban zones of western Europe, especially in Flanders and Italy. Some joined the heretical movements flourishing in late medieval Christendom, whose anticlerical and often antifamily positions particularly appealed to women. In these communities, some women were acclaimed as "holy women" or "saints," while others often were condemned as frauds or heretics.

Though the options offered to women by the church were sometimes less than satisfactory, sometimes they were richly rewarding. After 1520, the convent remained an option only in Roman Catholic territories. Protestantism engendered an ideal of marriage as a heroic endeavor, and appeared to place husband and wife on a more equal footing. Sermons and treatises, however, still called for female subordination and obedience.

THE OTHER VOICE, 1300–1700

Misogyny was so long established in European culture when the modern era opened that to dismantle it was a monumental labor. The process began as part of a larger cultural movement that entailed the critical reexamination of ideas inherited from the ancient and medieval past. The humanists launched that critical reexamination.

THE HUMANIST FOUNDATION. Originating in Italy in the fourteenth century, humanism quickly became the dominant intellectual movement in Europe. Spreading in the sixteenth century from Italy to the rest of Europe, it fueled the literary, scientific, and philosophical movements of the era, and laid the basis for the eighteenth-century Enlightenment.

Humanists regarded the scholastic philosophy of medieval universities as out of touch with the realities of urban life. They found in the rhetorical discourse of classical Rome a language adapted to civic life and public speech. They learned to read, speak, and write classical Latin, and eventually classical Greek. They founded schools to teach others to do so, establishing the pattern for elementary and secondary education for the next three hundred years.

In the service of complex government bureaucracies, humanists employed their skills to write eloquent letters, deliver public orations, and formulate public policy. They developed new scripts for copying manuscripts and used the new printing press for the dissemination of texts, for which they created methods of critical editing.

Humanism was a movement led by men who accepted the evaluation of women in ancient texts and generally shared the misogynist perceptions of their culture. (Female humanists, as will be seen, did not.) Yet humanism also opened the door to the critique of the misogynist tradition. By calling authors, texts, and ideas into question, it made possible the fundamental rereading of the whole intellectual tradition that was required in order to free women from cultural prejudice and social subordination.

A DIFFERENT CITY. The other voice first appeared when, after so many centuries, the accumulation of misogynist concepts evoked a response from a capable female defender, Christine de Pizan. Introducing her *Book of the City of Ladies* (1405), she described how she was affected by reading Mathéolus's *Lamentations*: "Just the sight of this book . . . made me wonder how it happened that so many different men . . . are so inclined to express both in speaking and in their treatises and writings so many wicked insults about women and their behavior."[4] These statements impelled her to detest herself "and the entire feminine sex, as though we were monstrosities in nature."[5]

The remainder of the *Book of the City of Ladies* presents a justification of the female sex and a vision of an ideal community of women. A pioneer, she has not only received the misogynist message, but she rejects it. From the fourteenth to seventeenth century, a huge body of literature accumulated that responded to the dominant tradition.

The result was a literary explosion consisting of works by both men and women, in Latin and in vernacular languages: works enumerating the achievements of notable women; works rebutting the main accusations made against women; works arguing for the equal education of men and women; works defining and redefining women's proper role in the family, at court, and in public; and works describing women's lives and experiences. Recent monographs and articles have begun to hint at the great range of this phenomenon, involving probably several thousand titles. The protofeminism of these "other voices" constitutes a significant fraction of the literary product of the early modern era.

THE CATALOGUES. Around 1365, the same Boccaccio whose *Corbaccio* rehearses the usual charges against female nature wrote another work, *Concerning Famous Women*. A humanist treatise drawing on classical texts, it praised 106 notable women—100 of them from pagan Greek and Roman antiquity, and 6 from the religious and cultural tradition since antiquity— and helped make all readers aware of a sex normally condemned or forgotten. Boccaccio's outlook, nevertheless, was misogynist, for it singled out for praise those women who possessed the traditional virtues of chastity, silence, and obedience. Women who were active in the public realm, for example, rulers and warriors, were depicted as suffering terrible punishments for entering into the masculine sphere. Women were his subject, but Boccaccio's standard remained male.

Christine de Pizan's *Book of the City of Ladies* contains a second catalogue, one responding specifically to Boccaccio's. Where Boccaccio portrays female virtue as exceptional, she depicts it as universal. Many women in history were leaders, or remained chaste despite the lascivious approaches of men, or were visionaries and brave martyrs.

The work of Boccaccio inspired a series of catalogues of illustrious women of the biblical, classical, Christian, and local past: works by Alvaro de Luna, Jacopo Filippo Foresti (1497), Brantôme, Pierre Le Moyne, Pietro Paolo de Ribera (who listed 845 figures), and many others. Whatever their embedded prejudices, these catalogues of illustrious women drove home to the public the possibility of female excellence.

THE DEBATE. At the same time, many questions remained: Could a woman be virtuous? Could she perform noteworthy deeds? Was she even, strictly speaking, of the same human species as men? These questions were debated over four centuries, in French, German, Italian, Spanish, and English, by authors male and female, among Catholics, Protestants, and Jews, in ponderous volumes and breezy pamphlets. The whole literary phenomenon has been called the *querelle des femmes*, the "woman question."

The opening volley of this battle occurred in the first years of the fifteenth century, in a literary debate sparked by Christine de Pizan. She exchanged letters critical of Jean de Meun's contribution to *The Romance of the Rose* with two French humanists and royal secretaries, Jean de Montreuil and Gontier Col. When the matter became public, Jean Gerson, one of Europe's leading theologians, supported de Pizan's arguments against de Meun, for the moment silencing the opposition.

The debate resurfaced repeatedly over the next two hundred years. *The Triumph of Women* (1438) by Juan Rodríguez de la Camara (or Juan Rodríguez del Padron) struck a new note by presenting arguments for the superiority of women to men. *The Champion of Women* (1440–42) by Martin Le Franc addresses once again the misogynist claims of *The Romance of the Rose,* and offers counterevidence of female virtue and achievement.

A cameo of the debate on women is included in *The Courtier,* one of the most read books of the era, published by the Italian Baldassare Castiglione in 1528 and immediately translated into other European vernaculars. *The Courtier* depicts a series of evenings at the court of the duke of Urbino in which many men and some women of the highest social stratum amuse themselves by discussing a range of literary and social issues. The "woman question" is a pervasive theme throughout, and the third of its four books is devoted entirely to that issue.

In a verbal duel, Gasparo Pallavicino and Giuliano de' Medici present the main claims of the two traditions—the prevailing misogynist one, and the newly emerging alternative one. Gasparo argues the innate inferiority of women and their inclination to vice. Only in bearing children do they profit the world. Giuliano counters that women share the same spiritual and mental capacities as men and may excel in wisdom and action. Men and women are of the same essence: just as no stone can be more perfectly a stone than another, so no human being can be more perfectly human than others, whether male or female. It was an astonishing assertion, boldly made to an audience as large as all Europe.

THE TREATISES. Humanism provided the materials for a positive counterconcept to the misogyny embedded in scholastic philosophy and law, and inherited from the Greek, Roman, and Christian pasts. A series of humanist treatises on marriage and family, on education and deportment, and on the nature of women helped construct these new perspectives.

The works by Francesco Barbaro and Leon Battista Alberti, respectively *On Marriage* (1415) and *On the Family* (1434–37), far from defending female equality, reasserted women's responsibilities for rearing children and managing the housekeeping while being obedient, chaste, and silent. Nevertheless, they served the cause of reexamining the issue of women's nature by placing domestic issues at the center of scholarly concern and reopening the pertinent classical texts. In addition, Barbaro emphasized the companionate nature of marriage and the importance of a wife's spiritual and mental qualities for the well-being of the family.

These themes reappear in later humanist works on marriage and the education of women by Juan Luis Vives and Erasmus. Both were moderately sympathetic to the condition of women, without reaching beyond the usual masculine prescriptions for female behavior.

An outlook more favorable to women characterizes the nearly un-known work *In Praise of Women* (ca. 1487) by the Italian humanist Bartolom-meo Goggio. In addition to providing a catalogue of illustrious women, Goggio argued that male and female are the same in essence, but that women (reworking from quite a new angle the Adam and Eve narrative) are actually superior. In the same vein, the Italian humanist Mario Equicola asserted the spiritual equality of men and women in *On Women* (1501). In 1525, Galeazzo Flavio Capra (or Capella) published his work *On the Ex-cellence and Dignity of Women*. This humanist tradition of treatises defending the worthiness of women culminates in the work of Henricus Cornelius Agrippa, *On the Nobility and Preeminence of the Female Sex*. No work by a male humanist more succinctly or explicitly presents the case for female dignity.

THE WITCH BOOKS. While humanists grappled with the issues per-taining to women and family, other learned men turned their attention to what they perceived as a very great problem: witches. Witch-hunting manu-als, explorations of the witch phenomenon, and even defenses of witches are not at first glance pertinent to the tradition of the other voice. But they do relate in this way: most accused witches were women. The hostility aroused by supposed witch activity is comparable to the hostility aroused by women. The evil deeds the victims of the hunt were charged with were exaggerations of the vices to which, many believed, all women were prone.

The connection between the witch accusation and the hatred of women is explicit in the notorious witch-hunting manual, *The Hammer of Witches* (1486), by two Dominican inquisitors, Heinrich Krämer and Jacob Sprenger. Here the inconstancy, deceitfulness, and lustfulness traditionally associated with women are depicted in exaggerated form as the core fea-tures of witch behavior. These inclined women to make a bargain with the devil—sealed by sexual intercourse—by which they acquired unholy pow-ers. Such bizarre claims, far from being rejected by rational men, were broadcast by intellectuals. The German Ulrich Molitur, the Frenchman Ni-colas Rémy, the Italian Stefano Guazzo coolly informed the public of sinis-ter orgies and midnight pacts with the devil. The celebrated French jurist, historian, and political philosopher Jean Bodin argued that, because women were especially prone to diabolism, regular legal procedures could properly be suspended in order to try those accused of this "exceptional crime."

A few experts, such as the physician Johann Weyer, a student of Agrip-pa's, raised their voices in protest. In 1563, Weyer explained the witch phe-nomenon thus, without discarding belief in diabolism: the devil deluded foolish old women afflicted by melancholia, causing them to believe that they had magical powers. His rational skepticism, which had good credibility in the community of the learned, worked to revise the conventional views of women and witchcraft.

WOMEN'S WORKS. To the many categories of works produced on the question of women's worth must be added nearly all works written by women. A woman writing was in herself a statement of women's claim to dignity.

Only a few women wrote anything prior to the dawn of the modern era, for three reasons. First, they rarely received the education that would enable them to write. Second, they were not admitted to the public roles— as administrator, bureaucrat, lawyer or notary, university professor—in which they might gain knowledge of the kinds of things the literate public thought worth writing about. Third, the culture imposed silence upon women, considering speaking out a form of unchastity. Given these conditions, it is remarkable that any women wrote. Those who did before the fourteenth century were almost always nuns or religious women whose isolation made their pronouncements more acceptable.

From the fourteenth century on, the volume of women's writings increased. Women continued to write devotional literature, although not always as cloistered nuns. They also wrote diaries, often intended as keepsakes for their children; books of advice to their sons and daughters; letters to family members and friends; and family memoirs, in a few cases elaborate enough to be considered histories.

A few women wrote works directly concerning the "woman question," and some of these, such as the humanists Isotta Nogarola, Cassandra Fedele, Laura Cereta, and Olympia Morata, were highly trained. A few were professional writers, living by the income of their pen: the very first among them Christine de Pizan, noteworthy in this context as in so many others. In addition to *The Book of the City of Ladies* and her critiques of *The Romance of the Rose*, she wrote *The Treasure of the City of Ladies* (a guide to social decorum for women), an advice book for her son, much courtly verse, and a full-scale history of the reign of King Charles V of France.

WOMEN PATRONS. Women who did not themselves write but encouraged others to do so boosted the development of an alternative tradition. Highly placed women patrons supported authors, artists, musicians, poets, and learned men. Such patrons, drawn mostly from the Italian elites and the courts of northern Europe, figure disproportionately as the dedicatees of the important works of early feminism.

For a start, it might be noted that the catalogues of Boccaccio and Alvaro de Luna were dedicated to the Florentine noblewoman Andrea Acciaiuoli and to Doña María, first wife of King Juan II of Castile, while the

French translation of Boccaccio's work was commissioned by Anne of Brittany, wife of King Charles VIII of France. The humanist treatises of Goggio, Equicola, Vives, and Agrippa were dedicated, respectively, to Eleanora of Aragon, wife of Ercole I d'Este, duke of Ferrara; to Margherita Cantelma of Mantua; to Catherine of Aragon, wife of King Henry VIII of England; and to Margaret, duchess of Austria and regent of the Netherlands. As late as 1696, Mary Astell's *Serious Proposal to the Ladies, for the Advancement of Their True and Greatest Interest* was dedicated to Princess Anne of Denmark.

These authors presumed that their efforts would be welcome to female patrons, or they may have written at the bidding of those patrons. Silent themselves, perhaps even unresponsive, these loftily placed women helped shape the tradition of the other voice.

THE ISSUES. The literary forms and patterns in which the tradition of the other voice presented itself have now been sketched. It remains to highlight the major issues about which this tradition crystallizes. In brief, there are four problems to which our authors return again and again, in plays and catalogues, in verse and in letters, in treatises and dialogues, in every language: the problem of chastity, the problem of power, the problem of speech, and the problem of knowledge. Of these the greatest, preconditioning the others, is the problem of chastity.

THE PROBLEM OF CHASTITY. In traditional European culture, as in those of antiquity and others around the globe, chastity was perceived as woman's quintessential virtue—in contrast to courage, or generosity, or leadership, or rationality, seen as virtues characteristic of men. Opponents of women charged them with insatiable lust. Women themselves and their defenders—without disputing the validity of the standard—responded that women were capable of chastity.

The requirement of chastity kept women at home, silenced them, isolated them, left them in ignorance. It was the source of all other impediments. Why was it so important to the society of men, of whom chastity was not required, and who, more often than not, considered it their right to violate the chastity of any woman they encountered?

Female chastity ensured the continuity of the male-headed household. If a man's wife was not chaste, he could not be sure of the legitimacy of his offspring. If they were not his, and they acquired his property, it was not his household, but some other man's, that had endured. If his daughter was not chaste, she could not be transferred to another man's household as his wife, and he was dishonored.

The whole system of the integrity of the household and the transmission of property was bound up in female chastity. Such a requirement pertained only to property-owning classes, of course. Poor women could not expect to maintain their chastity, least of all if they were in contact with high-status men to whom all women but those of their own household were prey.

In Catholic Europe, the requirement of chastity was further buttressed by moral and religious imperatives. Original sin was inextricably linked with the sexual act. Virginity was seen as heroic virtue, far more impressive than, say, the avoidance of idleness or greed. Monasticism, the cultural institution that dominated medieval Europe for centuries, was grounded in the renunciation of the flesh. The Catholic reform of the eleventh century imposed a similar standard on all the clergy, and a heightened awareness of sexual requirements on all the laity. Although men were asked to be chaste, female unchastity was much worse: it led to the devil, as Eve had led mankind to sin.

To such requirements, women and their defenders protested their innocence. Following the example of holy women who had escaped the requirements of family and sought the religious life, some women began to conceive of female communities as alternatives both to family and to the cloister. Christine de Pizan's city of ladies was such a community. Moderata Fonte and Mary Astell envisioned others. The luxurious salons of the French *précieuses* of the seventeenth century, or the comfortable English drawing rooms of the next, may have been born of the same impulse. Here women might not only escape, if briefly, the subordinate position that life in the family entailed, but they might make claims to power, exercise their capacity for speech, and display their knowledge.

THE PROBLEM OF POWER. Women were excluded from power: the whole cultural tradition insisted upon it. Only men were citizens, only men bore arms, only men could be chiefs or lords or kings. There were exceptions that did not disprove the rule, when wives or widows or mothers took the place of men, awaiting their return or the maturation of a male heir. A woman who attempted to rule in her own right was perceived as an anomaly, a monster, at once a deformed woman and an insufficient male, sexually confused and, consequently, unsafe.

The association of such images with women who held or sought power explains some otherwise odd features of early modern culture. Queen Elizabeth I of England, one of the few women to hold full regal authority in European history, played with such male/female images—positive ones, of course—in representing herself to her subjects. She was a prince, and manly, even though she was female. She was also (she claimed) virginal, a condition absolutely essential if she was to avoid the attacks of her opponents. Catherine de' Medici, who ruled France as widow and regent for her sons, also adopted such imagery in defining her position. She chose as one symbol the figure of Artemisia, an androgynous ancient warrior-heroine, who combined a female persona with masculine powers.

Power in a woman, without such sexual imagery, seems to have been indigestible by the culture. A rare note was struck by the Englishman Sir Thomas Elyot in his *Defence of Good Women* (1540), justifying both women's participation in civic life and their prowess in arms. The old tune was sung by the Scots reformer John Knox in his *First Blast of the Trumpet against the Monstrous Regiment of Women* (1558), for whom rule by women, defects in nature, was a hideous contradiction in terms.

The confused sexuality of the imagery of female potency was not reserved for rulers. Any woman who excelled was likely to be called an Amazon, recalling the self-mutilated warrior women of antiquity who repudiated all men, gave up their sons, and raised only their daughters. She was often said to have "exceeded her sex," or to have possessed "masculine virtue"— as the very fact of conspicuous excellence conferred masculinity, even on the female subject. The catalogues of notable women often showed those female heroes dressed in armor, armed to the teeth, like men. Amazonian heroines romp through the epics of the age—Ariosto's *Orlando Furioso* (1532), Spenser's *Faerie Queene* (1590–1609). Excellence in a woman was perceived as a claim for power, and power was reserved for the masculine realm. A woman who possessed either was masculinized, and lost title to her own female identity.

THE PROBLEM OF SPEECH. Just as power had a sexual dimension when it was claimed by women, so did speech. A good woman spoke little. Excessive speech was an indication of unchastity. By speech women seduced men. Eve had lured Adam into sin by her speech. Accused witches were commonly accused of having spoken abusively, or irrationally, or simply too much. As enlightened a figure as Francesco Barbaro insisted on silence in a woman, which he linked to her perfect unanimity with her husband's will and her unblemished virtue (her chastity). Another Italian humanist, Leonardo Bruni, in advising a noblewoman on her studies, barred her not from speech, but from public speaking. That was reserved for men.

Related to the problem of speech was that of costume, another, if silent, form of self-expression. Assigned the task of pleasing men as their primary occupation, elite women often tended to elaborate costume, hairdressing, and the use of cosmetics. Clergy and secular moralists alike condemned these practices. The appropriate function of costume and adornment was to announce the status of a woman's husband or father. Any further indulgence in adornment was akin to unchastity.

THE PROBLEM OF KNOWLEDGE. When the Italian noblewoman Isotta Nogarola had begun to attain a reputation as a humanist, she was accused of incest—a telling instance of the association of learning in women with unchastity. That chilling association inclined any woman who was educated to deny that she was, or to make exaggerated claims of heroic chastity.

If educated women were pursued with suspicions of sexual misconduct, women seeking an education faced an even more daunting obstacle: the assumption that women were by nature incapable of learning, that reason was a particularly masculine ability. Just as they proclaimed their chastity, women and their defenders insisted upon their capacity for learning. The major work by a male writer on female education—*The Education of a Christian Woman: A Sixteenth-Century Manual*, by Juan Luis Vives (1523)—granted female capacity for intellection, but argued still that a woman's whole education was to be shaped around the requirement of chastity and a future within the household. Female writers of the following generations—Marie de Gournay in France, Anna Maria van Schurman in Holland, Mary Astell in England—began to envision other possibilities.

The pioneers of female education were the Italian women humanists who managed to attain a Latin literacy and knowledge of classical and Christian literature equivalent to that of prominent men. Their works implicitly and explicitly raise questions about women's social roles, defining problems that beset women attempting to break out of the cultural limits that had bound them. Like Christine de Pizan, who achieved an advanced education through her father's tutoring and her own devices, their bold questioning makes clear the importance of training. Only when women were educated to the same standard as male leaders would they be able to raise that other voice and insist on their dignity as human beings morally, intellectually, and legally equal to men.

THE OTHER VOICE. The other voice, a voice of protest, was mostly female, but also male. It spoke in the vernaculars and in Latin, in treatises and dialogues, plays and poetry, letters and diaries and pamphlets. It battered at the wall of misogynist beliefs that encircled women and raised a banner announcing its claims. The female was equal (or even superior) to the male in essential nature—moral, spiritual, intellectual. Women were capable of higher education, of holding positions of power and influence in the public realm, and of speaking and writing persuasively. The last bastion of masculine supremacy, centered on the notions of a woman's primary domestic responsibility and the requirement of female chastity, was not as yet assaulted—although visions of productive female communities as alternatives to the family indicated an awareness of the problem.

During the period 1300 to 1700, the other voice remained only a voice, and one only dimly heard. It did not result—yet—in an alteration of social patterns. Indeed, to this day, they have not entirely been altered. Yet the call for justice issued as long as six centuries ago by those writing in the tradition of the other voice must be recognized as the source and origin of the mature feminist tradition and of the realignment of social institutions accomplished in the modern age.

We would like to thank the volume editors in this series, who responded with many suggestions to an earlier draft of this introduction, making it a collaborative enterprise. Many of their suggestions and criticisms have resulted in revisions of this introduction, though we remain responsible for the final product.

PROJECTED TITLES IN THE SERIES

Giuseppa Eleonora Barbapiccola and Diamante Medaglia Faini, *The Education of Women*, edited and translated by Paula Findlen and Rebecca Messbarger

Marie Dentière, *Prefaces, Epistles, and History of the Deliverance of Geneva by the Protestants*, edited and translated by Mary B. McKinley

Isabella d'Este, *Selected Letters*, edited and translated by Deanna Shemek

Marie de Gournay, *The Equality of Men and Women and Other Writings*, edited and translated by Richard Hillman and Colette Quesnel

Annibale Guasco, *Discussion with D. Lavinia, His Daughter, concerning the Manner of Conducting Oneself at Court*, edited and translated by Peggy Osborn

Olympia Morata, *Complete Writings*, edited and translated by Holt N. Parker

Isotta Nogarola, *Selected Letters*, edited by Margaret L. King and Albert Rabil, Jr., and translated by Diana Robin, with an introduction by Margaret L. King

Christine de Pizan, *Debate Over the "Romance of the Rose,"* edited and translated by Tom Conley

François Poulain de la Barre, *The Equality of the Sexes and The Education of Women*, edited and translated by Albert Rabil, Jr.

Olivia Sabuco, *The New Philosophy: True Medicine*, edited and translated by Gianna Pomata

Maria de San Jose, *Book of Recreations*, edited and translated by Alison Weber and Amanda Powell

Madeleine de Scudéry, *Orations and Rhetorical Dialogues*, edited and translated by Lillian Doherty and Jane Donawerth

Sara Copio Sullam, *Apologia and Other Writings*, edited and translated by Laura Stortoni

Arcangela Tarabotti, *Paternal Tyranny*, edited and translated by Letizia Panizza

Lucrezia Tornabuoni, *Sacred Narratives*, edited and translated by Jane Tylus

ENDNOTES

1.   Aristotle, *Physics*, 1.9 192a20–24, in *The Complete Works of Aristotle*, ed. Jonathan Barnes, rev. Oxford translation, 2 vols. (Princeton, 1984), 1:328.

2.   Aristotle, *Generation of Animals*, 2.3 737a27–28 (Barnes, 1:1144).

3.   Giovanni Boccaccio, *The Corbaccio or The Labyrinth of Love*, trans. and ed. Anthony K. Cassell (Binghamton, N.Y.; rev. paper ed., 1993), 71.

4.   Christine de Pizan, *The Book of the City of Ladies*, trans. Earl Jeffrey Richards; foreword by Marina Warner (New York, 1982), 1.1.1., pp. 3–4.

5.   Ibid., 1.1.1–2, p. 5.

ACKNOWLEDGMENTS

I would like to express my gratitude to the friends, colleagues, and institutions that made it possible for me to complete this project. My thanks go to the Newberry Library in Chicago and the Gladys Krieble Delmas Society for the fellowships they awarded me in the summer of 1991, and to the National Endowment for the Humanities for two years of support from 1993 to 1995. I owe a special debt of gratitude to Margaret King and Albert Rabil for the years of pep talks, gentle prodding, and excellent advice (which I often, fortunately, tried unsuccessfully to reject). I also wish to thank a few friends who generously provided me with suggestions and good cheer over the years it has taken me to finish this manuscript: Beverly Burris, David Marsh, Paul Gehl, Barbara Gold, Ken Gouwens, Nancy Jaicks, Minrose Gwin, Judy Hallett, Dale Kent, Patricia Labalme, John Marino, Tom Mayer, Letizia Panizza, Shane Phelan, Amy Richlin, Ruth Salvaggio, and Nina Wallerstein. And finally, and most importantly, my thanks go to the amazing editorial group who worked with me at the University of Chicago Press: Susan Bielstein, Paige Kennedy-Piehl, Maia Rigas, and Anita Samen, for their fine work at every stage of the process and for their patience with me, beyond the call of duty.

Diana Robin

LETTERS
AND
ORATIONS

Ætatis An. XVI

CASSANDRA FIDELIS VENETA
LITERIS CLARISSIMA.

EDITOR'S INTRODUCTION

Stronger than a strong man, more constant than any human soul, a
marvelous example of honesty and virtue; nature has made no other woman
like her [Queen Isabella of Spain].

Pedro Martir de Angeleria, *Epistolario*

If no woman is able to explore the truth hidden in God's mind and bosom
or bring divine inspiration to nature, then you [Cassandra Fedele] never
were a woman; but you were a man.

Julius Caesar Scaliger

By the end of the fifteenth century, Cassandra Fedele was perhaps the best-known female scholar and humanist living in Europe. Kings and queens courted her. Poets, university professors, and churchmen sought her imprimatur for their work. Celebrity came to her before she was twenty-five, yet by the time she was thirty-three her days in the limelight were over. Early modern biographical encyclopedias document her fame and productivity as a writer, though little of her work survives.[1] Her book *Ordo scientiarum* (*The Order of the Sciences*) and her Latin poetry, though well attested in the biographical tradition,[2] are no longer extant. Only one of her books saw publication during her lifetime: a fourteen-page volume containing her *Oratio pro Bertucio Lamberto* ("Oration in Honor of Bertucio Lamberti"), a speech she delivered at the University of Padua on the occasion of her cousin's graduation.[3] Her book of collected letters—the obligatory humanist oeuvre—survives only in a single printed edition of two-hundred-some pages published in 1636 in Padua under the title *Clarissimae Feminae Cassandrae Fidelis venetae. Epistolae et orationes* (The Letters and Orations of the Illustrious Venetian Woman, Cassandra Fedele), edited by Jacopo Filippo Tomasini.[4]

BIOGRAPHY

Cassandra Fedele was born in Venice in 1465 to a family of professional men. She counted among her living kin a physician, a bishop, a lawyer, and a banker who was sent to prison for forgery.[5] No detailed information has come down to us about her mother Barbara Leoni's family or her father Angelo Fedele's position in Venice. They were not members of the Venetian patriciate, though the seventeenth-century historian Sansovino wrote that Angelo was "respected" by the nobility, suggesting that he may at some point have been employed by members of the patriciate.[6] Cassandra was proud of her uncle Balthassare's claim that the Fedeli had been courtiers of the Visconti lords in Milan before emigrating to Venice at the turn of the fifteenth century.

Fedele was one of five children. She had three sisters and a brother, none of whom pursued a scholarly career. She speaks fondly of her siblings in her letters, though never of her mother, who may have died when the children were young. In any case, Fedele's silence on the subject is consonant with her distancing of herself from women as a group throughout her letters, with the exception of her wealthy female patrons. Her father Angelo, who saw Cassandra's fame as a child prodigy as a vehicle to further his own career,[7] first taught her Greek and Latin. And when at the age of twelve, Fedele was proficient in those languages and thoroughly knowledgeable in Roman literature, she was sent to Gasparino Borro, a Servite monk and noted scholar of classical literature and rhetoric. With Borro, she studied Greek, philosophy, the sciences, and dialectics, struggling in particular with Aristotle, whose language and ideas she found more difficult than any other author she had read. By the age of sixteen she was frequently invited to appear before groups of learned men who tested her knowledge and were amazed by her erudition.

Yet her intellectual training and aspirations and the virtual prohibition of women's publication of their work or entrance into the professions (law, medicine, university teaching, and the church) in the fifteenth century could not help but put Fedele on a collision course.[8] Although she never held a university appointment, from 1487 to 1497 she was very active among a circle of prominent humanists associated with the University at Padua. This circle included the leading Aristotelian scholar in Venice Niccolò Tomeo, the Rimini-born scholar Giovanni Aurelio Augurello, the Brescian theologian Bonifacio Bembo, Panfilo Sasso from Modena, Gianfrancesco Superchio of Pesaro (known as Filomuso), and the Paduan painter, sculptor, and philosopher Girolamo Campagnola. With such men, whom she clearly considered her peers, she publicly debated philosophical and theological questions at the University of Padua. The most celebrated of her public appearances was her delivery in 1487 of an oration in honor of her cousin Bertuccio Lamberti on the completion of his baccalaureate in philosophy at Padua.[9] She delivered two other public orations before the doge and the Venetian Senate, one at the behest of the distinguished scholar and philosopher Giorgio Valla and the other on the occasion of the state visit of Bona Sforza, queen of Poland, to Venice.[10]

Aided by her uncle Niccolò Franco, the papal envoy to the Spanish court who also served as her go-between, Fedele came close to accepting a position as a courtier with Queen Isabella and King Ferdinand of Spain during the years 1487–95 when the royal couple issued repeated invitations to her to join their entourage in Spain. For almost a decade she corresponded with the queen and her representatives in hopes of arranging to leave Italy for Spain. The threat of imminent war with France put an end to Fedele's travel plans in the fall of 1494 when Charles VIII crossed the Alps with an army of 31,000 men and occupied Florence, Rome, and Naples while menacing Venice and Milan. In Fedele's last published letter to Isabella, dated 1495, she told the queen that with Italy at war she could not leave Venice. She promised that when the war was over, she would go to her. But peace did not come to Italy in the 1490s, nor would Fedele have another opportunity to accept an appointment outside Venice. Tomasini and her subsequent biographers believed that the doge himself had in 1492 issued a decree that referred to Fedele as an "ornament to the state" and forbade her removal to Spain,[11] though no such decree has come to light.

Early in her career as a writer, Fedele established close ties by letter with the leading patrons of humanism and the arts and with many intellectuals outside her circle of Paduan, Brescian, Venetian, and Veronese humanists. From among Lorenzo de' Medici's circle, she corresponded with the chancellor of Florence Bartolomeo Scala and his daughter Alessandra, the philosopher Pico della Mirandola, and the brilliant poet and Greek scholar Angelo Poliziano with whom Fedele had met and conversed at length when he visited Venice in 1494. Through her connections to the Aragonese court in Spain, Fedele entered into correspondence with the two daughters of King Ferrante of Naples and Aragon: Eleonora, the duchess of Ferrara; and Beatrice, the queen of Hungary. In Milan she maintained cordial ties with Eleonora's daughter Beatrice d'Este and her husband Lodovico (Il Moro) Sforza, the duke of Milan, who intervened to recommend that the doge increase Fedele's state stipend. The many letters exchanged between the Sforza, their circle, and Fedele suggest that the duke and duchess of Milan may at least have been weighing the possibility of offering Fedele a court appointment or an annual stipend.

Leading writers and academicians who corresponded with Fedele praised her mind, her letters and orations, and the polish of her Latin style in extravagant terms. Yet Poliziano and certain other influential men of letters described her physical appearance with more relish—reporting on the "simple elegance" of her gowns, her gestures, and the natural beauty of her face unspoiled by makeup—than what she said or thought. When Fedele reached her early thirties and was no longer looked upon as a child prodigy or a pretty young girl, she found the road to further success full of obstacles.

In 1492 Fedele went on record as saying that an educated woman could not have both her profession and marriage: she could either choose a career of scholarship and writing or she could marry and settle for a life of domestic servitude. Sometime in 1499, blocked in her professional aspirations at thirty-four, she married Gian-Maria Mappelli, a physician from Vicenza. Her warnings about the incompatibility of marriage and a commitment to research and writing proved to be well-founded; few of her works from the years after 1500 survive. Little is known about her relationship with Mappelli, nor does she write about him except in one lamentory letter in the collection. The couple sailed to Retima, Crete, in the summer of 1515, where Mappelli practiced medicine. By the time Fedele and her husband sailed back to Venice in 1520, her father, brother, and one of her sisters were dead. That same year Mappelli also died leaving her a widow, childless, and almost penniless since the couple lost all their worldly possessions in a shipwreck on their return to Venice.

Long before her marriage, Fedele had complained intermittently of a malady that she could not name; it was sapping her of the will to work, and she felt she could not read, write, or concentrate for any length of time.[12] Despite her bouts of illness and the relative poverty in which she lived, Fedele continued to lead an active life until her ninety-third year, when she died. The last forty years of her life were marked by particular hardship. After her marriage she no longer received the invitations to lecture and dine that poured in during her twenties, nor was her state stipend renewed after she was widowed. For a time, she lived with her sister Polissena and her family. In 1547, she wrote to Pope Paul III begging him to assist her. He responded by securing an appointment for her as the prioress of an orphanage on the premises of the church of San Domenico di Castello in Venice. Visible once again to the citizenry, Fedele received one last invitation from the doge, to deliver an oration in honor of the queen of Poland, Bona Sforza, in 1556.

When Fedele died on March 24, 1558, the Venetian Republic honored her with a state funeral in the church of San Domenico. Her body was placed on a marble bier, her white hair was bound with laurel, and her favorite books rested in her hands.[13]

WOMEN AND HUMANISM BEFORE FEDELE

A century of Italian women humanists preceded Fedele and the learned female writers of her era. These learned women were educated in the classics of Greco-Roman antiquity under the auspices of their fathers, brothers, and their brothers' tutors.[14] Coming almost exclusively from the ruling classes, none of these women—among whom were Maddalena Scrovegni of Padua (1356–1429), Cecelia Gonzaga of Mantua (1425–51), Battista Montefeltro Malatesta of Urbino (1383–1450), Caterina Caldiera (d. 1463), Ippolita Sforza of Milan (1445–88), and Costanza Varano of Pesaro (1428–47)—represented herself as separate from her family or wrote for causes unconnected to its interests.

A second generation of women humanists came typically from the urban citizen classes rather than the nobility. These women, who received at least some of their humanist schooling from a teacher beyond the range of the panoptic gaze of the father, were the first female writers in Italy to mobilize their talents to advance their own interests rather than those of their families. But they were working against the grain. Influential humanists such as Leonardo Bruni and Francesco Barbaro intimated that no virtuous woman should seek to publish her work or express her views in public.[15] The response from this second wave of women humanists was a relentless pairing in their writings of the theme of feminine eloquence with that of chastity. The emergence of this theme in the letters of the Veronese writer Isotta Nogarola (1418–66) suggests an attempt on the part of a new generation of women scholars to counter Bruni's and Barbaro's pronouncements barring women from the literary arena with the new paradigm of the *chaste* female orator.[16] But while both Isotta and her sister Ginevra Nogarola (1417–61/8) collected their Latin letters for publication, neither was able to sustain her career as a writer for very long. Ginevra abandoned her career when she married; Isotta retreated from the public forum to a life of private study.

Antonia Pulci (1452–1501), wife of the poet and humanist Bernardo Pulci, wrote religious plays in the vernacular; chief among her supporters were Ficino's patron Lorenzo de' Medici and the humanist scholar and poet Angelo Poliziano.[17] Also closely connected to the literati who gravitated to the circle of "Il Magnifico" was the brilliant young Hellenist and pupil of

Poliziano, Alessandra Scala (fl. 1490), who was much admired by the Florentine humanists for her Greek intonation and accent when she played the role of Sophocles' Electra at a salon performance of the play. She was also much admired for the original Greek epigrams she composed.[18]

The only second-generation woman humanist who rivals Fedele in importance, although she lacked her notoriety, was the Brescian writer Laura Cereta (1469–99). Cereta's Latin letterbook differed from Fedele's and represented a radical departure from any other work of her time in that she mingled in her epistolary essays themes anticipating modern feminism with those characteristic of humanist discourse. Unlike Fedele who aimed her letters at influential scholars and wealthy patrons, most of them male and many of them royal, Cereta primarily addressed family members and friends, an unusual proportion of them women. Her letters dealt with private matters such as her relationships with her mother, sisters, and husband. Other of her letters squarely confronted the problem of the slavery (she uses the term *servitus*) of women in marriage. She argued for women's right to higher education in literature, philosophy, and the sciences. Rejecting the Ciceronian elegance of Fedele and other humanists, Cereta blended diction from Juvenal, Pliny the Elder, Apuleius, and her native Italian to produce a hybrid Latin.

HUMANIST AND NONHUMANIST THEMES
IN FEDELE'S LETTERS

Fedele's themes are largely those of the humanists of her period. Her major work in print, the *Epistolae et orationes*, exemplified the kind of publication that was expected of a fifteenth-century intellectual. Such letter collections were the most popular form of autobiography in the Renaissance. Like other humanist works, Fedele's letters are written in the mannered Latin of Cicero, Seneca, and Pliny the Younger, and the letters included in her letterbook were selected to showcase her learning and social connections. Her letters feature the stock themes of her era: the exaltation of reason as a quasi-divine faculty unique to the human race; the supremacy of eloquence among human achievements; the importance of a liberal arts education; the role of the writer as cultural critic, prophet, and high priest (the Romans called such a poet-seer a *vates*); and perhaps most important in her pantheon of topoi, the sublime nature of friendship (*amicitia*) between intellectual and moral peers, and others themes that idealize the patronage relationship.

The chief feature that distinguishes Fedele's rhetorical style from that of male contemporaries is her self-consciously gendered voice. In male humanist letters gender is not an issue since the "natural" superiority of the male over the female is a given. In the writings of Fedele, the theme of a client's exaggerated deference to his patron is sexualized.[19] Three groups of themes are salient in her patronage letters: those concerned with her sexual identity; those defining her in terms of her female lack, deficiency, weakness, and diminution of mind, talent, physical stature; and those that praise the purity of her body.

In a programmatic letter to the *Epistolae* addressed to Francesco Gonzaga, marquis of Mantua, she explains that she has put aside woman's work in order to devote herself to "manly pursuits."[20] In the speech she delivers on the occasion of her cousin Bertuccio Lamberti's graduation she apologizes for daring to speak in public since she is only a woman; in other letters and orations she writes that she has studied literature despite the weakness of her sex.[21] To a friend from the University of Padua she apologizes again for having only "a girl's mind." In taking on the role of a writer she pursues "manly work"; she oversteps gender borders and thus presents a self that is "daring." In the many eulogies written for Fedele that are included in her *Epistolae*, her praisers frequently position her within a Boccaccian-style catalog of famous women[22]—a history of earlier gender transgressors.

A second theme in her patronage letters concerns her minimizing of traits that could be seen as masculine—or less than feminine. She is only a scholar "to the extent that our sex permits such a thing," she writes to one of Louis XII's courtiers. In order to appear less menacing to both her male and female patrons, Fedele uses the privative force of diminutives to represent her own insufficiency of talent, mind, learning, and work. The superfluity of diminutives found in her patronage letters—her relentless use of the suffixes *olus*, *ulus*, and *culus*—represents a departure from both classical and humanist usage and suggests, if not a comic tone, at least a degree of irony in her letters. She is not a writer; she is only a pushy little woman (*audacula*), she assures her readers. Her letters are insignificant; they are little notes (*literulae*); her voice (*vocula*) is small and ineffectual, and her talent is slight (*ingeniolum*). She herself is only a diminutive man in a woman's skin (*homuncula*), a little client (*servula* in the language of patronage), and a very small maiden (*virguncula*). Such diminutives are designed not only to circumscribe her attributes and thus allay male fears; they are meant to stress her youthful sexual innocence and to arouse male desire. The compliment often paid to her, and regularly to male humanist courtiers as well, is that she is an ornament (*decus*, *ornamentum*) to her city and country, and her sex is diminishing of her significance and substance, reducing her to that which is superfluous and decorative.

Poor health and fragility add a further dimension to the defensive figure that Fedele crafts for herself. Ravaged physically, she is too weak to pursue her career and thus represents a threat to no one. Her illness is the subject of several letters to patrons. At the age of thirty-two Fedele complains that she finds herself stricken with an "infirm mind, a frail body, and a trembling hand."

A third constellation of themes concerning her virginity and her saintly removal from the world is evinced in both her letters and Renaissance catalog articles on her life. Her own sense of distance from the social world of her patrons is apparent from her frequent professions of fear that she will displease them with her awkward writing style. She worries in her letters to Queen Isabella and other friends that she may be too fearful of the separation from her family to accept the queen's invitation to join her court. She sometimes lacks the courage even to go walking in her own city.

Among the dominant humanist themes in Fedele's letters and orations is the power of eloquence. In Fedele's writing, eloquence takes precedence over reason and dialectics. While only the power of reason separates us from animals and makes us like the gods (oration no. 2, "In Praise of Letters"), without eloquence reason and the mind lie dormant. These faculties must be exercised through the vehicle of eloquence, for only eloquence can form and refine our capacity to reason (oration no. 2). Although philosophy is the greatest of all disciplines, for it enables us to pursue the truth, without eloquence it is empty. Fedele writes that she has labored to master dialectics and the philosophy of Aristotle, but she fears that the quality of her writing is being harmed by these studies.

At the close of the *Epistolae et orationes*, Fedele's panel of three orations represents a kind of variation on Thucydides' encomium for Athens in Pericles' funeral oration. The study of the liberal arts, as exemplified in Greco-Roman antiquity, is what ennobles the Venetian citizenry and distinguishes them from the residents of other cities. Innate intelligence, talent, and material advantages are useless unless they are cultivated and properly utilized through education.[23] Public affairs cannot be conducted by the uneducated.[24] The city of Venice is the great marketplace of the world because of the splendor and variety of its goods, but its university at Padua offers the best education in the world.[25] While Fedele clearly alludes to Thucydides' formulation of the city as a school for the world, she departs from his exclusion of women from this school. If not explicitly, Fedele's public presentation of her own orations implicitly suggests that educated women can play a role in civic affairs. The threefold tradition of Plato, the Peripatetics, and Cicero teaches us all (read women as well as men) that while there are many kinds of goods worthy of seeking, only the goods of the intellect and soul, which must be cultivated through education and study, are lasting.[26]

Other stock humanist themes are notably missing in Fedele's extant work. The typical philosophical excursions on fate, the will, and virtue certainly present in her contemporary Laura Cereta's work are not found in Fedele's letters. Also missing are the stinging invectives with which the humanists lambasted their adversaries and the intimate, chatty letters they sent to their friends and advocates, although Fedele's warm, joking, familiar notes to Bonifacio Bembo, Gianfrancesco Superchio (Filomuso), Girolamo Campagnolo, and Giovanni Scita are exceptions. With the exception of Alessandra Scala, the daughter of the Florentine chancellor Bartolomeo Scala, Fedele's female correspondents are patrons and not peers. Apart from her suggestion that women, too, could benefit from education, one looks in vain for feminist themes in her letters.

EARLY MODERN WOMEN WRITERS AFTER FEDELE

In the sixteenth century a new literary woman emerged in the northern Italian cities. No longer dependent on the circulation of their works in handwritten manuscripts, women writers in Italy reached a wide audience in the first era of the machine-made book. Though classically educated, the women writers in the generation that followed Fedele wrote in Italian, not Latin. They composed love songs and dialogues, not erudite letters. The thriving commercial presses in Venice and Lucca, Ferrara, and Naples enabled the leading women writers of the period—Isabella Andreini, Tullia of Aragon, Laura Battiferri Ammanati, Vittoria Colonna, Veronica Franco, Veronica Gambara, Lucrezia Marinella, Chiara Matraini, Isabella di Morra, Moderata Fonte (Modesta da Pozzo), Gaspara Stampa, Laura Terracina, and many others—to achieve fame through a wide circulation of their books, which included collections of *rime* and *stanze*, essays, epic poems, dialogues, and pastoral plays, all of them in Italian.[27]

A few learned women continued to publish translations and commentaries of classical texts and to write and publish in Latin and Greek after 1500. But for ambitious women writers, the age of humanism and humanist letters was over. Olympia Morata (1526–55), the daughter of a classical scholar at the ducal court in Ferrara, was the most prolific of the last of the women humanists. The Protestant-leaning Morata, who had already written hundreds of letters, dialogues, and poems in Greek and Latin by the time the Roman Inquisition came to Ferrara, fled in 1550 to Germany. Her humanist writings never saw the light of day in Italy; but her works found a publisher in Basel in 1558, after her death.[28] Another northern Italian woman humanist, Tarquinia Molza (1542–1617) wrote both poetry in her native Modenese dialect and translated Plato's *Charmides* and selections from the *Crito* into Italian.

The long-term influence of humanism on the literary culture of women was significant. It would be a mistake to confine its impact solely to writers who published in Greek or Latin. Most sixteenth-century women writers, though not humanists themselves, were profoundly influenced by humanism. The vernacular love poet Tullia d'Aragona (1506–66) composed an Italian prose work in which she gave new life and meaning to a Neoplatonic theme that had become a humanist trope—the infinity of love. And although both d'Aragona's *On the Infinity of Love* and Moderata Fonte's (1555–92) *The Worth of Women* were written in Italian, each of these women chose to frame her discourse in the most characteristic of all humanist genres, the dialogue. The sixteenth-century women poets Vittoria Colonna, Veronica Gambara, Veronica Franco, and others wrote volumes of humanist-inflected letters in Italian, and their lyric poetry was as much indebted to Ovid, Propertius, and Catullus as it was to Petrarch.

While Fedele was perhaps the first public intellectual of her sex in Europe, her fame was short-lived. A woman humanist extraordinaire, she failed despite her early promise to keep pace with the new literary trends that print culture promoted, with its emphasis on the vernacular and marketability. When scores of women in the 1530s, 1540s, and 1550s were publishing popular books of poetry featuring love lyrics with suggestive erotic imagery and were at the same time gaining visibility as the subjects of their own writings, Fedele no longer wrote or spoke publicly.[29] Whether or not she knew the works of this new breed of women writers or, for that matter, the vernacular treatises of male contemporaries such as Goggio, Vespasiano, and Sabadini who praised women as a class, her letters show no sign that she foresaw better times coming for female authors. And although a call for institutional changes in the status of women would not come until the end of the sixteenth century in the writings of the Italian feminists Moderata Fonte, Lucrezia Marinella, and Arcangela Tarabotti, it was Cassandra Fedele who first paved the way for women in the republic of letters.

NOTES TO INTRODUCTION

1.   Giacomo Alberici, *Catalogo breve degli illustri et famosi scrittori venetiani* (Bologna: Heredi di Giovanni Rossi, 1605); Jacopo Filippo Bergamo [J. F. Foresti, pseud.], *De claris mulieribus* (Ferrara: Laurentius de Rubeis, 1497); Guiseppe Betussi, *Libro di M. Giovanni*

Boccaccio delle donne illustri tradotto per Messer Giuseppe Betussi (Venice: n.p., 1545); Giovanni Battista Egnazio, *De exemplis illustrium virorum venetae civitatis atque aliarum gentium* (Venice: Nicolaum Tridentinum, 1554); Battista Fregosa [Campofgregosa, Baptista Fulgosius, pseuds.], *Factorum dictorumque memorabilium libri IX* (Venice, 1483); Jean Tixier de Ravisius, ed., *De memorabilibus et claris mulieribus aliquot diversorum sciptorum opera* (Paris: S. Colin, 1521); Jacopo Filippo Tomasini, *Elogia literis et sapientia illustrium ad vivum expressis imaginibus exornata* (Padua: S. Sardi, 1644).

2.   See the early modern biographical catalog listed above in n. 1.

3.   *Oratio pro Bertucio Lamberto* was published three times in Fedele's lifetime: in Modena (1487), Venice (1488), and Nuremberg (1489). In addition to the oration, it also contains one letter of hers and three testimonial epistles and two poems from other scholars who praise her eloquence and learning.

4.   *Clarissimae feminae Cassandrae Fidelis, venetae. Epistolae et orationes* (Padua: Franciscus Bolzetta, 1636); sources are cited hereafter as "Tom." followed by letter or oration number and page number. All citations to Fedele's letters here refer to Tomasini's 1636 edition of the letters and orations.

   Five letters not contained in this edition have been published in the following sources: Adriano Capelli, "Cassandra Fedele in relazione con Lodovico Il Moro," *Archivio Storico Lombardo* 3, no. 4 (1895): 387–91; Cesira Cavazzana, "Cassandra Fedele erudita veneziana del Rinascimento," *Ateneo Veneto* 29, no. 2 (1906): 73–79, 249–75, 361–97; G. Pesenti, "Alessandra Scala, una figurina della Rinascenza fiorentina," *Giornale storico della letteratura Italiana* 85 (1925): 241–67; and Maria Petrettini, *Vita di Cassandra Fedele* (Venice: Giuseppe Grimaldo, 1852). I have translated and retained Tomasini's descriptive letter titles but have disregarded Tomasini's ordering of the letters and instead grouped them thematically.

   Tomasini, bishop of Ischia, client of Queen Anne of Austria (mother of Louis XIV) and her counselor Cardinal Mazarin, was a prolific biographer of women. He reports in his preface to her *Epistolae* that he received her correspondence from three different sources: from Evangelista Zagalia of Padua and Battista Fichetti of Venice he received bundles of letters in loose leaves and from Alessandro d'Este he got a bound codex of her letters. We might well question the authenticity of a posthumous edition of Fedele for which no manuscript copies and no exemplar exist, were we not fortunate enough to have another woman's letterbook edited by Tomasini with which we can compare the Fedele edition: Tomasini's edition of the collected letters of Fedele's contemporary Laura Cereta, *Laurae Ceretae brixensis feminae clarissimae epistolae iam primum e MS in lucem productae* (Padua: Sebastiano Sardi, 1640). It is clear to me that Tomasini faithfully and painstakingly redacted his Cereta edition from two nearly complete late fifteenth-century or early sixteenth-century manuscripts of her letters that now survive in the Vatican Library's Vat. lat. 3176 and the Marcian Library in Venice's Marc. lat. 4186.

5.   The only full-length study of Fedele that deals with archival sources is Cavazzana, "Cassandra Fedele," see esp. 82–84; see also (the very rare) Maria Petrettini, *Vita di Cassandra Fedele.* On Fedele manuscripts see also Capelli, "Cassandra Fedele," 387–91; Henry Simonsfeld, "Zur Geschichte der Cassandra Fedele," in *Studien zur Literaturgeschichte. Michael Bernays Gewidmet* (Hamburg: Leopold Voss, 1893). See also Margaret L. King, "Thwarted Ambitions: Six Learned Women of the Italian Renais-

sance," *Soundings* 59, vol. 3 (1976): 295–99; Franco Pignatti, "Cassandra Fedele," in *Dizionaro biografico degli Italiani [DBI]* (Rome: Instituto della enciclopedia italiana, 1995), vol. 45, 566–68; Diana Robin, "Cassandra Fedele's *Epistolae* (1488–1521): Biography as Ef-facement," in Thomas Mayer and Daniel Woolf, eds., *The Rhetorics of Life-Writing in Early Modern Europe: Forms of Biography from Cassandra Fedele to Louis XIV* (Ann Arbor: University of Michigan Press, 1995), 187–203; Robin, "Cassandra Fedele," in Rinaldina Russell, ed., *Italian Women Writers: A Bio-Bibliographical Sourcebook* (Westport, Conn.: Greenwood Press, 1994), 119–27. See further, Giovanni Pesenti, "Lettere inedite del Poliziano," *Athenaeum* 3 (1915): 284–304; and Pesenti, "Alessandra Scala."

6.   Cavazzana, "Cassandra Fedele," 80.

7.   King, "Thwarted Ambitions."

8.   Margaret L. King, "Book-Lined Cells: Women and Humanism in the Early Italian Renaissance," in Patricia H. Labalme, ed., *Beyond Their Sex: Learned Women of the European Past* (New York: New York University Press, 1980), 66–90; esp. 77.

9.   The text for this oration (no. 1) is provided below in chapter 7.

10.   The texts for these two orations (nos. 2 and 3) are provided below in chapter 7

11.   Tomasini, "Vita," in *Epistolae et orationes,* 30. Fedele's biographers follow Tomasini's assertion: see Pettrettini, *Vita,* 25; Cavazzana, "Cassandra Fedele," 265; Capelli, "Cassandra Fedele," 393ff.

12.   The majority of her letters about her mysterious illness are in chapter 6 under the heading "Letters Excusing Her Lateness."

13.   Petrettini, *Vita,* 33.

14.   Margaret L. King and Albert Rabil, Jr., eds., *Her Immaculate Hand: Selected Works by and about the Women Humanists of Quattrocentro Italy* (Binghamton, N.Y.: Medieval & Renaissance Texts & Studies), 16–25.

15.   King and Rabil, *Her Immaculate Hand,* 11–30; Benjamin G. Kohl and Ronald G. Witt, eds., *The Earthly Republic: Italian Humanists on Government and Society* (Philadelphia: University of Pennsylvania Press, 1978), 177–228; Gordon Griffiths, James Hankins, and David Thompson, eds., *The Humanism of Leonardo Bruni. Selected Texts* (Binghamton, N.Y.: Medieval & Renaissance Texts & Studies, 1987), 240–50.

16.   Margaret L. King, "The Religious Retreat of Isotta Nogarola (1418–1466): Sexism and Its Consequences in the Fifteenth Century," *Signs* 3 (1978): 807–22; Lisa Jardine, "Isotta Nogarola: Women Humanists—Education for What?" *History of Education* 12 (1983): 231–44.

17.   Bernard Toscani, "Antonia Pulci (1452–1501)," in R. Russell, ed., *Italian Women Writers. A Bio-Bibliographical Sourcebook* (Westport, Conn.: Greenwood Press, 1994), 344–52.

18.   Alison Brown, *Bartolomeo Scala, 1430–1497, Chancellor of Florence: The Humanist as Bureaucrat* (Princeton: Princeton University Press, 1979), 226–29; G. Pesenti, "Lettere inedite," 299–301.

19.   Robin, "Cassandra Fedele," in R. Russell, ed., *Italian Women Writers;* Robin, "Cassandra Fedele's Epistolae (1488–1521): Biography as Ef-facement."

20. See chapter 3, letter XX. Tom. 1, 1–3 leads off his edited volume with this letter to Gonzaga, which exemplifies the patronage themes in her letter collection.

21. See letter XX to Gonzaga in chapter 3 and oration nos. 1 and 2 in chapter 7.

22. Boccaccio's misogynistic Latin catalog of 104 women's lives, *Concerning Famous Women* [*De claris mulieribus*], trans. Guido A. Guarino (New Brunswick: Rutgers University Press, 1963), completed in 1355, was the single most important influence in the subsequent stereotyping of women in European literature.

23. See oration no. 2 in chapter 7 below.

24. See oration no. 1 in chapter 7 below.

25. See oration no. 1 in chapter 7 below.

26. See oration no. 1 in chapter 7 below.

27. Russell, *Italian Women Writers;* Margaret L. King, *Women of the Renaissance* (Chicago: University of Chicago Press, 1991); P. O. Kristeller, "Learned Women of Early Modern Italy: Humanists and University Scholars" in *Beyond Their Sex. Learned Women of the European Past,* ed. Patricia H. Labalme (New York: New York University Press, 1980), 91–116.

28. Her *Omnia opera* is published in four separate editions: Basel (1558), (1562), (1570), and (1580).

29. It is important to note that the sixteenth-century boom of women vernacular writers also ends by the end of the century and that women's voices again fall silent.

I

WOMEN PATRONS

Cassandra Fedele corresponded with women who occupied thrones in Spain, Hungary, and the Italian city-states. All these royal women were related by blood or marriage to the Aragonese monarchy of Spain.[1] The most powerful of these monarchs, Isabella of Castile, queen of Spain and wife of King Ferdinand II of Aragon, was introduced to Cassandra Fedele by her uncle, the Venetian Niccolò Franco, the pope's ambassador to the Spanish court in the 1480s–90s. Isabella and Ferdinand, who were frequent visitors to the court of their cousin King Ferrante of Aragon, in Naples recommended Fedele to the king's daughters: Beatrice of Aragon, who became a queen through her marriage to Mattias Corvinus, king of Hungary; and Eleonora of Aragon, who became the duchess of Ferrara when she married Duke Ercole I d'Este. In the early 1490s, Fedele began corresponding with Eleonora's daughter, Beatrice d'Este, who became duchess of Bari and Milan though her marriage to Lodovico (Il Moro) Sforza.

Fedele's letters to these queens and duchesses resemble in many ways the typical fifteenth-century male humanist's correspondence with his patrons. She praises her patrons' greatness and generosity and apologizes for her own lack of knowledge and talent. She also invokes the humanist trope of the menace from Islam and praises her queen as the defender of the Christian faith against the infidel Turks. For at least a century after the fall of Constantinople in 1453, the humanists continue to advocate the city's recapture as the last bastion of classical and Christian civilization in the face of the westward advance of the Turks. Like her male humanist colleagues, Fedele praises her women patrons as role models for the female sex. Only Fedele's foregrounding of the recurrent illness that plagued her and of her fear of intellectual inadequacy distinguishes her letters as different from those of male humanists and as self-consciously feminine.

At the end of this chapter I have included a set of three letters that Fedele sent to the accomplished young Hellenist and student of Poliziano, Alessandra Scala. Though too young to have been a patron of Fedele's herself, as the daughter of the Florentine chancellor Bartolomeo Scala, who had long been a member of Lorenzo de' Medici's inner circle, Alessandra represented for Fedele a possible path to Medici patronage.[2]

᠅

I–V

Letters I–V represent the ten-year courtship between Fedele and Queen Isabella of Spain, which culminated in Fedele's decision to accept the queen's invitation to join her entourage in Spain and ended with Fedele's hopes of finding employment outside Italy being dashed. Letter V suggests Fedele's tacit understanding (articulated more clearly in letters to other friends in this collection) that now in 1495, given the French invasion of the previous year, her family and friends would hardly support her move to Spain and the possibility that she might somehow be used as political capital in the struggle between the two great powers, France and Spain, for hegemony in the Italian peninsula. With the court appointments that were extended to humanist scholars such as the one Isabella and her deputies offered to Fedele generally came the expectation that the appointee would perform a variety of tasks. These might include the establishment and administration of a small humanist school for the classical education of children of the king and queen and their courtiers; the composition of letters for the king and queen in Ciceronian Latin; the writing of eulogistic poems, letters, and orations for the royal couple; the writing of occasional letters and essays to celebrate birthdays and weddings or to supply condolences in case of illness or death; and, last, the scholar might be offered a chair of rhetoric or Greek at the local university.

I

To Isabella, by the grace of God, the invincible queen of Castile, Aragon, and Sicily[3]

*I*f anyone should perchance be surprised that I write to you, invincible queen, and if he should call me a bold little woman,[4] then he can— unless I err—be criticized for his opinion since your divine rather than human virtues and your extraordinary deeds would invite, entice, and seduce not just literary men into describing them but even me who am fired up by the study of literature: especially since I hear that your goodness is continually celebrated by the Magnificent and Honorable Pietro Superanzio,[5] our Illustrious Senate's ambassador to you and the Prince, and by another admirer who in his praises of your prince tells me much about you and extols your virtues everywhere, namely your ambassador Pedro Martir,[6] who conducts his consulship with modesty, prudence, and grace in all things. Nor, O Queen, could I adequately describe his proclamations in which he sang your praises and those of your prince, about which he admits he is most concerned because of the many kindnesses he has received from you and your household: indeed, he is the tireless eulogist of your name. He would pour out his life, no less his fortune, for the slightest reason regarding your realm, but really on your account, Princess. And so, since I have now witnessed so many of your qualities, I would seem to have deserved blame myself for my own ingratitude and neglect, if I had merely glossed over your innumerable virtues in my meager notes, which are certainly unworthy of you. For it can easily be agreed that because of your virtues, whose fame has spread far and wide not only by the testimony of Christians but by infidels as well,[7] our sex[8] has been defended, recuperated, and renewed. For in whom, not only among the living but among all those who ever lived in past ages, has there been the great power, the greatness of soul, and the generosity that no one can deny are in you?[9] For everyone unanimously agrees that you were sent down from heaven to put down insurrection and to suppress the enemies of the Christian faith, whom no mortal men were ever able to contain, and if any had ever dared to do so, all their attempts were futile. You alone through your leadership and the armed forces under you have led the fiercest army against a savage nation of barbarians. With what flourish and, finally, to what end shall we speak of other campaigns conducted under your auspices? You and your great regiments and companies have gravely shaken and harassed the most well-armed enemy troops, and you have laid siege to innumerable cities. Thus all men declare that the task of defending the faith belongs to you alone: there is no one who either surpasses you in prudence and wisdom in battle nor is there anyone superior to you in the administration of justice in your empire. O holy, blessed, happy, and fortunate is the age in which you who are endowed with so strong a faith and such piety happened to be born. Therefore all things on the earth itself seem to obey you, who rule with justice, integrity, and faith. Ah, but why did I say "seem"? They absolutely do obey and are willingly subservient to you, and they ready and curb themselves to do your bidding. Not only is it certain that the men of every age but also that fortunes and city walls and the houses and temples of cities rejoice in you. All that is left to say is that I shall show you that I am wholly devoted to you in heart and mind and that I think continually of you and your virtues. But why are words necessary? If I were to sacrifice my life for your friends, not to mention you, still I would seem to have expressed not even a part of my love and desire to serve you. I would like you to know that in serving you and the fame of your reign I shall never be wanting in acclaiming the greatness of your deeds. Therefore, may the almighty and greatest God protect and defend you, O glory of our sex and salvation of the Christian faith. Venice. October 1487.

II

Isabella, queen of Sicily, to Cassandra[10]

*H*onorable young woman, dedicated to us and much beloved, we have read your letters with pleasure, and from those as well as from our Aurelio[11] we have learned of your extraordinary learning and your heart wholly devoted to us. We trust in two things: one is that because of you our sex and era will win just as much praise for its literary achievements as the Amazons won in olden times for their military glory because of Penthesilea;[12] the second thing is that you, whom we can and should love for the simple gifts of your mind, have found favor with us. Come, then, at our urging, since you have received it so wholeheartedly, so that the goodwill that we have begun to extend to you will grow as your virtue and ability increase, and proceed as your devotion to us, which you will always be able to make use of, and your studies in the liberal arts, by which we are moved, demand. Farewell. From the Castello Nuovo in Naples. September 1488.

III

To the invincible queen of Sicily, Isabella[13]

*A*lthough I am accustomed to writing to the greatest and most distinguished men, I was afraid to send my numerous letters to Your Highness lest I should seem to weary her whose chief and most important concern is her great empire and its army. But when the orator of our Illustrious Senate, the magnificent Girolamo Leone,[14] a man devoted to Your Majesty, approached me concerning Your Highness's command, he carefully and eloquently related many pleasing and delightful things regarding your kindness toward me. Afterward I was so overcome with joy that I was unable to express myself in words—even in the longest of letters—now that I had been summoned and thus saluted by the most powerful queen on the entire earth: she, the punisher of infidels and the bestower of the name Christian. And so I confess that I am in your debt and would be perpetually thanking you, were it not that the magnanimity of your mind and your kindness to me have kept me from performing such acts. You will therefore know that I have paid some homage to your renown when you learn that I have resolved to serve you with the utmost deference, with undying constancy, and with intense loyalty.[15]

In addition to this and inspired by your most distinguished accomplishments, I am more and more inflamed each day by the most worthy papal legate and most excellent bishop from Treviso to whom I am related by blood.[16] O immortal gods, with what love does he honor your brilliance, what service, loyalty and constancy; finally, with what declarations does he sing your praises! Since I have always obeyed his loyal and loving plans, I am now determined to obey him with an even more ready and more joyous heart as you will easily see from my letters to you and indeed from your magnificent ambassador and humble servant, Pedro Martir.[17] Therefore, I shall abandon my kin, friends, and my native city. All these I shall relinquish so that I may enjoy the happiness I have long desired, under the shade of your wings. I believe I can render myself immortal and happy in this life in two ways: one, through the dedication of my life to literature, a goal to which I have devoted myself from a tender age on; the other, through my complete commitment to you, mind and soul, to the end that I may admire and contemplate your fortitude and the rest of your magnificent virtues and in your very presence. And through the agency of my eulogy, may the gathering together of all the virtues continue to abide in your incomparable breast. All that remains for me to say is that it is yours to command in your prudence when and how the plans for the journey of my companions should be carried out. In the meantime I entrust myself to you as your servant again and again. Farewell. [Undated.]

IV

To Isabella, queen of Sicily, Castile, and Aragon[18]

*S*ince I often think on the highest gifts of your mind and your invincible power, to which nothing on this globe can be compared, nor is it said that such power will ever exist, I would not dare to send my frequent letters to Your Highness unless your kindness and clemency had invited—no really, compelled—me to do so. On this account, you have thought it worthwhile to listen to everyone with the utmost courtesy, and especially to me since (as you have often heard from my friends) I am devoted to Your Grace. The message that I am to come to you has been relayed to me by the Magnificent Knight Girolamo Leone, Orator to Your Highness most humbly serving at the aforesaid time Your Majesty and the very great distinction of this most glorious City.

When I heard this, I immediately carried a letter addressed to you to my uncle Niccolò Franco, the distinguished bishop of Treviso and a man dedicated to Your Highness. That letter—perhaps due to the very great distance as well as because of many other hindrances—was never delivered. Therefore I decided to write again, and from this letter you will learn that I, who am devoted to the study of literature, wish only to serve Your Majesty. This is very much my hope, even if I should admit that it is hard for me to leave my family, those near to me, and my sweet native city, still I prefer to be your subject, O Queen, who are the emblem of all the virtues, the guarantor of the Christian faith, and the protectress of the entire earth. Therefore it is yours to command, mine to follow your commands, and when I have received your orders, still I will not come to you—I will fly.[19]

In the meantime know that I am your devoted servant. July 1492.

V

To the queen of Spain[20]

ow that I know, through the agency of your very devoted servant the reverend brother Agostino, that I should come to Your Highness, I would indeed have flown to you, were I not to have been impeded by serious illness from which I have not yet completely recovered. Still, with the help of God, I hope to be free of it in a very short time.

But when I do regain my former health and when I see that there is peace, tranquility, and serenity in Italy (for in these turbulent times and particularly with Italy preparing to go to war it is not advisable for me, a young maiden, to take so much as a stroll, nor could even you, most prudent one, persuade me to do so) then I promise I shall come to Your Highness and I shall serve you with the deepest loyalty and love. I have always thought this would be the happiest place for me, ever since I learned from men of every kind of your generosity, your noble mind, and your almost divine wisdom. It is difficult to imagine how pleasing and delightful it will be for me to be loved and known by you face-to-face and, likewise, how pleasing it will be for you to be continually praised, celebrated, and venerated as a goddess by me. In the meantime, I shall pray to God that your greatness, your family, all your reigning years may be vouchsafed by Him to whom I also entrust and commend myself. Farewell. 1495.

᠅

VI–VII

Letters VI and VII to Beatrice d'Este, duchess of Milan and Bari and wife of Duke Lodovico (Il Moro) Sforza, taken together with Fedele's letters to the duke, suggest that Fedele hoped that she might be offered a stipend or even a scholarly appointment of some sort at the ducal court in Milan.[21] The kinds of labors Fedele would perform in exchange for such an appointment would be the same as those I have described above.

VI

To Beatrice, duchess of Bari and later of Milan

Fedele congratulates her on the birth of her son.[22]

*I*t seems right to me to imitate the custom of the Egyptians, the Persians, and all the ancients, who were accustomed to declare their happiness publicly and privately with gifts when a prince was born. On this account, lacking such things I shall retreat to what is mine so that I may express my delight at your letter about your new offspring being born.

I hope you will not think me an improperly bold little woman[23] because I have not hesitated to write you, a princess known for your justice, fortitude, beauty, and innumerable other noble gifts—especially since all things, animate and inanimate,[24] rejoice that you have given birth to a son of divine lineage who is the hope of the whole world. What therefore could all your subjects hope for more than a prince born of parents unsurpassed in their natures and power? What could occur that would be more pleasing or more delightful to your friends and the rest of your kingdom than the birth of an heir, O wisest of Sovereigns? All men should then rejoice and exult in this divine gift, and I pray again and again that the Almighty God will protect him as long as you wish. Finally, may I wish that your noble gifts may gladden you, though if I were able to speak to you I would say more than a letter allows.

That is all, except that you should know I am bound to Your Highness in perpetual service, and I commend myself to you as your little servant. Farewell.

VII

Beatrice Sforza, viscountess d'Este, duchess of Bari and later of Milan, to Cassandra Fedele

She thanks her for her letter.[25]

*N*ot only do I not think you should be blamed for daring to write me, but I thank you instead, as I ought. For you, whom I respect for your great virtue and because you alone have ennobled the female sex in our time through your great knowledge of literature, have shown that you are equally desirous that I should both know you and know that I am loved by you. And this is something that I consider not only pleasing, but I think it marvelous. Indeed, your desire is even more pleasing to me because in congratulating me on the birth of my newborn son you so easily and simply expressed the magnitude of your love for me. And although I do not see those things in myself that you with too much love attribute to me, still I rejoice that you, not content to love me merely with eulogies, have taken care to make your love felt in a more direct way.[26] Such a tribute at the very beginning of a friendship is more pleasing to me than all the treasures in the world. If it was your wish to imitate the custom of the Persians, then I think you have surpassed them with your gift. Milan. April 1493.

﹏

VIII–X

Letters VIII, IX, and X to Beatrice d'Este's aunt and namesake, Beatrice, queen of Hungary, indicate that Fedele spread a wide net in her attempt to win support and employment for her humanist activities and skills.[27] Even the court of King Mattias and Queen Beatrice at Buda was not beyond her dreams for herself. In letter IX, Fedele employs the typical Renaissance device of supplying a series of exemplary characters from myth or history with whom she compares the subject of her encomium. In fifteenth- and sixteenth-century encomia of women, the examples, as is the case in this letter, are almost always drawn from Boccaccio's popular book, *Concerning*

Famous Women. Fedele's exemplary women synthesize two character traits that, according to male humanist discourse, could not be combined in women: chastity and rhetorical skill. The open mouth signified the open womb.[28] In Fedele's encomium, the queen of Hungary is more chaste than three famous examples of sexual purity in ancient Rome: Lucretia, Sulpicia, and the Sabine women; at the same time she is more eloquent than three masters of Roman oratory: Veturia, Calpurnia, and Hortensia.

VIII

To the queen of Hungary, Beatrice of Aragon[29]

Even if I feel that the duty of writing to you, most generous and exalted Princess,[30] weighs heavy on my shoulders, still I preferred to obey the wishes of your most honorable consort and illustrious Prince[31] for my uncultivated letters though they are unworthy of the royal honors of princes rather than to seem obstinate or expose myself to accusations of procrastination. For the prince, when he came to see me, demanded and insisted very urgently that I give him some sort of letter for you, and I thought I should obey him. For what he asked for was fair: that my respect[32] for him should be wisely and best displayed, by whatever means,[33] especially since I have been so desirous of showing my affection for you. And even if I cannot capture your magnanimity, munificence, and your other character traits (in which you surpass everyone—as is only right to say), still you should understand that this failing ought not to be attributed to me but rather to your innumerable and ineffable virtues. For who could tell your praises so fully, so elegantly, and beautifully and who could meet the standards of your virtues all told? Do not men of letters praise, exalt, and glorify you as pure, just, and an emblem of every virtue in elegant commemorations and lucid and lucubracious speeches?[34] The telling or proclaiming of this information is of very great import to your orator, Sigismondo, a man of the highest probity and virtue since he has praised[35] you assiduously in a long and marvelous oration. From this speech, by Hercules, I know that you came to us not by chance, as others have come into the world, but as some divine sign from heaven. And even if the race of your people has been sufficiently illuminated already by the distinction of its own excellent deeds, still you render it even more renowned and celebrated. Indeed, I would like to follow those deeds so worthy of praise and celebration with more words, were I not afraid that I would seem inept and that I might hurt your ears with my uncultivated oration. For this reason I would prefer to learn from you rather than from my own letters how powerfully bound I am by ties of love and loyalty to the majesty of your mind and to your illustrious Prince.

I greet you most warmly. Seven days before the first of May.

IX

To the queen of Hungary, Beatrice of Aragon

Cassandra dedicates praises to her.[36]

 $\mathcal{I}$ f in earlier days I was determined to write a letter that would pay homage to the greatness of your mind, even though I was not given the privilege even to utter a few syllables[37] or to open my heart to you in your presence, nonetheless I never abandoned my great esteem for you and my desire to demonstrate it in my meager writings.[38] And even if it should seem that I might be deterred from writing by the limitations of my intellect, my lack of suitable material for oratory, and the unsuitability of my ideas, for fear that my awkward words might hurt your erudite ears and the magnitude of a mind so schooled in prudence, wisdom, and the use of many things, still the sublimity of your intellect prevented me from being afraid to write, particularly when I heard that you were favorably disposed toward literary people and especially those of our sex.[39]

I became more and more inspired to write when I heard that you should be considered superior not only to all living women but to all those who ever have lived or ever will live. For you surpass Lucretia, Sulpicia, and the Sabine women in chastity; Roman Veturia in gravity and charm; and in eloquence and ornateness of speech, you far exceed Calpurnia and even Hortensia.[40] And what else shall I say? For who can deny that you[41] equal the gods, not mere mortal men, determined that you should be guardian[42] over the safety of the people in all these lands? Nor can anyone be found who in intellect, religious piety, and invincible power is more suited to be their protector. Therefore not just princes, kings, and the populace but even the very walls and inanimate things rejoice, delight, and celebrate your name with the greatest joy.

I shall pass over in silence[43] your royal family, whose power, fortitude, and justice, which you yourself have embellished, strengthened, and increased with your talent, are known not only throughout Italy but the whole world. It remains for me only to extol the virtues of your invincible consort who surpasses all other regents not only of the present age but of past ages as well in power, equity, courage, and all the heroic gifts. The rhetorical skills not just of a little newcomer[44] like myself but those of a consummate orator are insufficient to do justice to his praises. And so, though I have omitted eulogizing all the members of your family, you should *persuade* yourself that my respect for the greatness of your mind increases each day—a thing I thought was not possible—since your stepmother or your mother, the most Serene Queen, and your most illustrious sister, the duchess of Ferrara,[45] have thought it worthy to respond with kindness and extraordinary benevolence to my little letters.[46]

Therefore, it is difficult for me to express how lovingly and loyally I honor Your Highness. May Almighty God attend you. Venice. January 1488.

X

To Beatrice, queen of Hungary[47]

*I*ll health, with which I have been afflicted for a long time now, has deterred me from the duty of writing, although I have wanted to write to Your Highness, most Holy Queen. Nor am I in fact at the moment so strong of body or mind that I should be writing to you whose letters are so polished and ornate, were it not that otherwise I would be afraid I would seem either neglectful or forgetful. But when Sigismondo, a man of great integrity, approached me, he inspired me—though it was not the first time—with such love for you that I decided that I had to write as much as my limited physical strength would allow, though I was still feeling somewhat sluggish from this chronic illness of mine, so that even if I had already lost my grace as a writer and had none, still I would leave you this testimony of my affection and devotion to you. Certainly I would seem to myself ungrateful were I not to respond in whatever way I can to you by whom I am so dearly loved and esteemed.

Therefore since everyone knows you are a unique example and model of all the virtues, I embrace you with all my heart and mind; and I venerate, respect, and admire you as though you were a deity most divine. But now with a weak mind, a frail body, and a trembling right hand, I am not strong enough to write more. When I am well, if I ever am, I shall repair this brevity with many long letters. May you in the meantime, most happy Queen, be well and blessed, and may you know that your little servant has been dedicated and devoted to you for a long time now.

Farewell again. Venice. October 1497.

XI

Letter XI presents an unusual instance of a eulogy honoring a prominent woman writer that was composed by an important woman patron of arts and letters in Italy.

Eleonora of Aragon, duchess of Ferrara, to Cassandra Fedele

A singular encomium of Cassandra sent by Eleonora of Aragon.[48]

We have read your sweetest letters, which are exemplary, Cassandra, of the eloquence and learning not of a young woman but of an old man and seasoned orator. For they are filled with elegance of diction and gravity of sentiment and thought. They have also been burnished with the sheen of chastity. We should praise[49] those festive gardens in which lilies, violets, roses, and different kinds of fruits are located, each in their proper place, and which delight us with their variety in appearance, fragrance, and taste. In the same way we admire and love you, a maiden pure in your unaffected manners, graced with remarkable eloquence, and endowed with extraordinary virtues. We judge you worthy of every praise. You are fortunate and blessed because you are filled with such heavenly and sacred graces and gifts that you are, even at so tender an age, an ornament to our sex. From those who nursed you at their breasts you received sweet milk and the beautiful honey they say the bees brought drop by drop to Plato's lips while he slept, which caused speech sweeter than honey to flow from him. Your letters in themselves were a delight to us. But all the more pleasing were the qualities that our Laura[50] made abundantly clear to us: the honor of your life, the splendor of your virtues, your maidenly manners, and the brilliance of your learning. We urge you to conserve these qualities in your study of the good arts and letters diligently and carefully, as you now do, and apply yourself again and again in this effort. Farewell, and persuade yourself that you are very dear to us. Ferrara. November 1488.

࿔

XII–XIV

Fedele addressed three letters to Alessandra Scala, the daughter of the Florentine chancellor Bartolomeo Scala. Poliziano, who taught Alessandra to write Greek epigrams and to read the Athenian tragedians, introduced his student to Fedele. In letter XIII, Fedele warns Alessandra that marriage and the life of a scholar don't go together. Both women chose marriage in spite of warnings to the contrary.

XII

To Alessandra Scala and her father Bartolomeo Scala[51]

Those who sing your praises have come to us, and so now your name is held in the highest esteem here in this city. Marvelous and almost incredible things are reported to us about your genius, your learning, and your character. Therefore I congratulate and thank you because you adorn not only our sex but this age of ours as well. Farewell. October 1492.

XIII

To Alessandra Scala[52]

When I read your letter so full of charm and grace, I would have admired[53] your having praised my letter had I not feared that I was not so much offering an opinion about you as I appeared to be thanking you for your words about me. Still, your letter pleased me very much. For from it I have come to know you. I would like to pursue this with the greatest goodwill, and I also want you to know that I will do much more and that you are very dear to me. I will not fail, moreover, to celebrate your name to the best of my ability. Farewell. [Undated.]

XIV

To Alessandra Scala

Should an erudite woman prefer marriage to her studies?[54]

From your very lovely letters I have learned something that pleases me very much: namely, that you by no means considered our friendship an ordinary thing since you wanted not only to know everything about me but also to consult with me on these matters. And so, my Alessandra, as to your being undecided whether to dedicate yourself to the Muses or to a husband, I think you must choose the path for which nature has suited you. For Plato says that every road taken is taken for the sake of the traveler's ease.[55] This therefore will be an easy choice for you to make, since nothing violent in its nature is ever lasting.[56] Farewell. January 1492.

NOTES TO CHAPTER 1

1.   Isabella (1451–1504), queen of Castile and daughter of Juan II of Castile, married Ferdinand II of Aragon in 1469, thereby becoming queen of Spain, Aragon, and Sicily. Ferdinand II was the son of Juan II of Aragon, Sicily, Navarre, and Sardinia and the nephew of Alfonso V (1396–1458), king of Naples, Aragon, and Sicily. King Alfonso V was father of Ferrante I, who reigned over the kingdom of Naples (1458–94) and whose daughters, in turn, were Eleonora of Aragon (1450–93) and Beatrice of Aragon (1457–1508). Eleonora's daughter, Beatrice d'Este (1475–97) married Lodovico Sforza (1452–1508), duke of Milan until 1500.

2.   The chief patrons and members of Marsilio Ficino's (1433–99) Platonic academy were Lorenzo (Il Magnifico) de' Medici (1449–1492), Angelo Poliziano (1454–94), and Giovanni Pico della Mirandola (1463–94). Bartolomeo Scala (1428–96) served as chancellor of the Florentine Republic for thirty years; his chief patron was Lorenzo de' Medici; Scala's daughter Alessandra (d. 1500) studied Greek with Poliziano and performed the role of the female protagonist in a salon performance of Sophocles' *Electra* in ancient Greek. Poliziano introduced Fedele to Alessandra.

3.   Tom. 13, 20–22. I have translated and retained Tomasini's descriptive letter titles. I have disregarded Tomasini's ordering of the letters throughout this edition in order to group the letters thematically.

4.   "Audaculam": a neologism in its feminine form from *audax* (daring, bold) and the first of a series of diminutives that characterize Fedele's style.

5.   I have retained Tomasini's capitalization of adjectives and titles to capture the formality and stilted quality of Fedele's language in her letters to royalty.

6.   "Petro Martinez" in Tomasini's text. Fedele refers clearly to Pedro Martir d'Anghiera (Pedro Martir or Peter Martyr), a native of Milan who was called to Isabella's court in Spain in 1487 to serve as a humanist teacher. Martire remained in Spain as the queen's ambassador to Italy and Egypt until Isabella's death in 1504. His letters are famed for their detailed descriptions of Columbus's voyage to America.

7.   "Infidelium" (infidels): an epithet generally assigned to the Turks.

8.   "Nostrum sexum" (our sex): "sexus" (the sex) is regularly used to denote the members of the female gender.

9.   Tomasini erroneously reads: "Cuinam mortalium [understand here: *fuit*]—non modo e viventibus verum etiam ex iis qui unquam fuerun—tanta potentia, *magnanimitate* [changed in my text to the nominative form *magnanimitas*], munificentia, quae tibi esse a nullo inficias [changed to *infitias*] iri potest." *Fuit* or a form of *esse* should be assumed as the verb for the triple collective subject (*potentia, magnanimitas, munificentia*), which in both main and relative clauses (*fuit . . . tanta potentia . . . quae . . . potest*) should take singular verbs. The triplet subject *potentia, magnanimitas*, and *munificentia* cannot be anything but the subject nominative. The medieval Latin *c* in *inficias* has been modernized to a *t*. It should also be noted that incidences of the verb *infitias ire* in the text are rare in the passive.

10.   Tom. 12, 19.

11.   In 1485 G. Aurelio Augurello (b. 1440 in Rimini) served Niccolò Franco, the pope's ambassador to Queen Isabella and Cassandra Fedele's uncle, as his secretary. Giuseppe Pavanello in *Un Maestro del Quattrocento (Giovanni Aurelio Augurello)* (Venice: Emiliana, 1905) writes that Aurelio was transformed into an ardent humanist at Padua in the 1470s and that in the late 1480s or early 1490s he fell under the spell of Cassandra Fedele. Regarded as one of the leading poets of his generation, Aurelio was a frequent correspondent of Fedele's.

12.   Penthesilea, queen of the Amazons, is famed for having been slain in battle by Achilles, the greatest of the Greek warriors in the Trojan War. Even as he pierced her with his sword Achilles is said to have fallen in love with her.

13.   See Tom. 11, 16–18. On Queen Isabella's titles see n. 1 above.

14.   Tomasini identifies Girolamo Leone (Hieronymus Leo) as a member of the Venetian patriciate and of a family still flourishing in the seventeenth century, see Tomasini, *Epistolae et orationes*, 214. None of my sources has further information on him.

15.   Fedele's promise to her patron of service full of "summa observantia, constantia perenni, ac singulari fide" constitutes a formulaic yet completely obligatory pledge within the patronage relationship. Such a phrase could be read verbatim from any fifteenth-century handbook for humanists on how to address patrons.

16.   She refers here to her uncle Niccolò Franco, bishop of Treviso and papal legate.

17.   On Pedro Martir, see n. 6 above.

18. See Tom. 60, 87–89.

19. The text reads "ad te volabo": literally, "I will fly to you."

20. See Tom. 66, 93–94.

21. The lineage of Beatrice d'Este is described above in n. 1.

22. See Tom. 57, 84–85.

23. "Me auda*culam* iudices homun*culam*": note the rare and striking doubling of diminutives here, both of them in the feminine gender. See again my introduction to the volume on Fedele's use of diminutives in her self-fashioning.

24. "Inanimata" (cf. inanimantia) is not attested in the *Oxford Latin Dictionary* (hereafter *OLD*).

25. See Tom. 58, 85–86.

26. "Amorem cognosci illustrius": literally, "for your love to be known more brightly." I wanted to bring out the contrast between the paleness of words and the vividness of concrete action.

27. See n. 1 above for Beatrice's genealogy.

28. See King and Rabil, "Introduction to the Series," xxi–xxiv.

29. See Tom. 78, 108–109.

30. Tomasini reads "ad te excelsum, munificentissimum Principem"; I have emended this to "excelsam, munificentissimam" since "te . . . Principem" clearly refers to Fedele's addressee, Queen Beatrice.

31. Beatrice's consort is King Mattias (Mátyás) Corvinus. See n. 1 above.

32. I have emended Tomasini's erroneous accusatives "meam . . . observantiam" to nominatives: "mea . . . observantia."

33. I have deleted the preposition "a" before "quodam" from Tomasini's text.

34. "Luculento atque *lucubrato* sermone" (my emphasis): I wanted to capture Fedele's vivid alliteration here in my translation by a near transliteration of the peculiarly classical and Renaissance Latin trope involving the act of *lucubratio:* the burning of midnight oil to compose literary works.

35. I have emended the erroneous "amplectantur" in the Tomasini edition to "amplectatur."

36. See Tom. 21, 33–35.

37. "Meis voculis": literally, "with my little words or with my tiny voice."

38. "Literulis meis": literally, "my little writings." Fedele's characteristic tendency to add a diminutive suffix (-*ulus*) to descriptors in order to emphasize her insufficiency and slightness of talent, intellect, and so on.

39. "Nostrum sexum": the usual Renaissance Latin signification for the female gender.

40. Lucretia's desire for chastity was so extreme that she preferred to commit suicide rather than live on after the Roman tyrant Tarquin raped her. Sulpicia was memorialized by Martial as a poetess of honorable love. The chaste Sabine women bravely fought their rapists to no avail. Only Coriolanus's mother Veturia's elo-

quence could soften her son's rage when he lay siege to Rome. Julius Caesar's wife Calpurnia almost succeeded by her eloquence in dissuading him from going to the senate where he died. Hortensia, the daughter of the famous orator Hortensius, moved the entire Roman senate with her eloquent speech.

41. Add: "te" with the infinitive "aequare."

42. Tomasini has "tutela," which I have emended to "tutelam."

43. This typical classical and Renaissance trope, in which a speaker first regrets that he lacks the time to fully describe his subjects' virtues and then proceeds to do so anyway, is called *praeteritio.*

44. "Tyrunculae": a typically Fedelian turn: a diminutive neologism in a feminine form, from the noun *tiro* (beginner, novice).

45. Her mother was Joanna, queen of Aragon; her sister Eleonora, wife of Ercole I d'Este, duchess of Ferrara.

46. "Literulis" (little letters): Fedele's signature diminutive again.

47. See Tom. 71, 99–101.

48. Ibid., 161–62. See n. 1 above for the genealogy of Eleonora.

49. I have emended Tomasini's reading "laudare" to "laudaremus."

50. The person referred to as "Nostra Laura" is unknown to me.

51. See Tom. 107, 163–64. On Scala and her circle see n. 2 above.

52. See Tom. 108, 164.

53. In Tomasini the text reads "admirata sum"; I have emended the verb in the apodosis, since a contrary to fact condition is clearly indicated to "admirata essem."

54. See Tom. 111, 167.

55. The text here reads "omne consilium quod recipitur pro recipientis facilitate recipi" (literally, "every plan which is received is received for the sake of the receiver's ease") is best translated via a metaphor. I chose the metaphor of the road because it is a favorite image of Plato's. Fedele appears to be noncommittal in her advice. On the other hand the line with which she concludes the letter "cum violentum perpe- tuum" (literally, "since nothing is perpetually violent") seems to suggest that the mar- riage option may prove risky; in any case the line isn't a warning against choosing a life of scholarship and writing.

56. See n. 55.

II

FAMILY MEMBERS

True to the tradition of the humanist letterbook, Cassandra Fedele's published collection *Epistolae* includes no letters to her parents, siblings, or other immediate family members.[1] The book of autobiographical letters was the humanist's curriculum vitae. It displayed her (or his) social and academic connections, her classical erudition and Latin style; and it showcased both her publications and the offices, honors, and invitations bestowed on her by the rich and famous. It was the de rigeur humanist vehicle for self-fashioning. Fedele took special pride in her correspondence with her successful maternal uncle, Niccolò Franco, the bishop of Treviso and the pope's ambassador to the king and queen of Spain; and with Balthassare Fedele, the archbishop of Modena and Mutina, who if only remotely related to her branch of the Fedeli, nonetheless reinforced the image she projected of herself as a scholar descended from an ancient and noble line. Balthassare's letter to Cassandra with its numerous references to Roman history is especially interesting for its elevation of the Fedeli to a mythological plane and its firm placement of the family and its name within the context of antiquity.

The last two letters included in this chapter show an unusual warmth and tenderness of feeling. They are addressed to an unnamed physician who had either so closely insinuated himself into the good graces of Cassandra and her family that she speaks to him as though he were a family member, or he is in fact the older man she would marry a year or so after the date of this letter, in 1498 or 1499, who was himself a physician. There is no other trace of her husband, Gian-Maria Mappelli, in her epistolary.

XIV

To Niccolò Franco, papal legate to the king of Spain

Cassandra wishes to have her greetings to the queen of Spain relayed to her.[2]

I could not fail to express my allegiance to you in this letter, and I hoped to speak with you face-to-face, although I was not able to gratify my wish because of the important matters that have kept you busy right up to the day of your departure. For this reason, it seemed best to me to tell you in this brief letter that I urgently hoped that your excellency would convey my greetings again and again to the invincible queen of Spain. For I recently heard from her magnificent golden knight Girolamo Leone that the queen herself had addressed many questions to the same orator about me and had said that she hoped I would soon be with her at her court. I would gladly have gone were the distance not such an obstacle and had travel arrangements been provided for this very long journey. Therefore, I beg and ask you, ambassador par excellence, to see to it that my wish be expedited. This will be very easy to do, I think, if you commend me to the queen herself with a pleasing oration. I shall be brief about the matter since it has been written in an old proverb, "Send me a philosopher and say nothing." In closing: please do not forget to write me about this matter, which I hope I shall bring to pass. Indeed, you are capable of doing a great deal if you wish. I am putting myself in your hands. [Undated.]

XV

To Balthassare Fedele

She invites him to honor their bond of kinship.[3]

*W*hen I realized that I had discovered family ties that made us blood relations, which came as a surprise to me, I felt that we should not dismiss this bond but rather embrace it wholeheartedly. For not only does nature itself prompt us to protect this bond, but also almost all ancient writers have warned that the kinship relationship is the strongest of all bonds because of its role in the preservation of the human race. Thus your messenger . . . ,[4] a good man, so it seems to me, who has carefully laid out your instructions to us in an unadorned speech of his own, has attested to our both descending, according to your ancient testimonials, from the same long lineage, ancient in its origins. And it has brought us all great happiness since we know that our common lineage has derived from you and your forbears, men of learning and great authority. This will be clearly established by our common surname and a great deal of additional evidence, if we are able to discuss these matters in person.

Moreover, the gravity and the sanctity of our eminent uncle, the canon, are included in our kinship; your eloquence of speech and learning, and all those things that should be loved and cherished summon and draw us all to you, whether we wish it or not, and because of this you not only equal but have surpassed by far our forebears. From the coming time onward, I too am putting a lot of work, for a member of my sex, into my studies in the liberal arts, so that I may not seem unworthy of our great-great-grandfather, our grandfather, and our most preeminent forebears. For what better thing could have happened to me than this recent discovery of our kinship. On hearing about this, I would have rushed to Modica immediately had I not considered the principle of my honor. For I am scarcely allowed, being both a woman and a naive young girl, to go out of my little schoolhouse, much less to go wandering around the country.

Therefore, since I am not allowed to come to you myself, I think it only right that you should hasten to us, commending my parents and all the rest of us to our most worthy uncle. O pleasing and blessed day when we shall be able to join hands and learn the origin of our kinship. We have the greatest desire to see you, and you ought not to disappoint us. Farewell. [Undated.]

XVI

From Balthassare Fedele, archbishop of Modena and Mutina, to Cassandra Fedele

On the history of the Fedele family.[5]

I am finally in the process of unraveling the information I promised I would write you about concerning the genealogy of Fedeli. In this one offers, though rather late, a document that has never existed. It is agreed that the Visconti surpassed all others in Latium in the opulence of their wealth and the glory of their deeds. Many of the Visconti grew to be excellent men for whom there would be no point in hoping or striving for more or greater things. But one of these stands out, Otho by name, whom I might have rightly called the father of both war and peace. When something had to be done about the issue of the Church, the armed forces chose him as their commander in chief to make war on the perpetrators of schism in the east and to bring Jerusalem back under Christian authority. During this time in the city of Milan, there were three brothers who excelled in popular favor and authority. In ancient times their ancestors had been called the Magi, the name of the kings who brought gifts to Christ, as though they possessed something unique. Thus it was that when Otho was on the point of death, he summoned the brothers to him and in a meeting he appointed Balthassare, a doctor eminent in Roman law and the best of them, to act as counselor to his adolescent son Andreas; he made Melchior the guardian of the citadel, and Sigismondo he inducted into the army as his Achates.[6] He also did the following: the loyalty of the Magi was established for our ancestors and me; Otho's sons relied on their counsel. Finally, since Otho was a man of keen intellect, in a grave and elegant oration he urged the people of Milan to carry out his commands and heed his warnings. The three brothers accomplished everything with such zeal, constancy, and moderation that everyone judged them exemplary of the appellation "fidelity." The people said, "Our prince has rightly called these wonderful men the 'Fideles.'"[7]

And so it was done. They were said to be the "Fedeli,"[8] and their descendants bore that name. However, the name Fedele was conferred on the heroes of the Visconti at such a cost that Andreas avenged the death of one of his kinsmen by plundering the well-fortified city of Como, publicly avowing that it was a lesser injury for a city to lose its authority than it was for a man to lose his honor and his name. But why did the fortunes of the Fedeli decline? As to how the family was dispersed hither and thither, now hear. When the emperor Frederick had completely gutted the city of Milan and had taken Andreas's son Galvaneo captive, he destroyed all the most beloved members of the Visconti family by plundering their estates and murdering them. And the citizens of Milan paid an even harsher penalty for the popularity and honor of the Visconti in the city. The first was the tragedy of our ancestors. Afterward, when Galvaneo died without an heir, the fickle rabble spurned the rule of a prince and instead put tyrants at the head of state, and these they obeyed and supported. But the tyrants, fearing that the Visconti again would seize the principate, every day charged them with a thousand crimes. And so there ensued proscriptions, exiles, murders, and when the Visconti themselves were cut down, the best citizens and the nobility abandoned the city and established settlements in the countryside; some of them founded Fidelium, others Vicomercatum (Vimercate), still others Modoetia (Modica). Many citizens made their way to Santa Columba, a beautiful town; others fled to the valleys near Bergomo and Mantua, since they sought hiding places. The cruel reign of the tyrants lasted more than fifty-five years. No wonder few sought their fathers', or rather, their grandfathers', Lares.[9] You cannot imagine the sweetness with which every person's native city calls to him, or how she does not allow him to forget her.

There are still some Fedele families in Milan, though by no means cohesive ones. We still survive and are not entirely devoid of honor, if one can say that. The marquis of Mantua, Lodovico Gonzaga, having adopted as his own the name of the renowned soldier of the golden militia of Andreas and having claimed for the Gonzaga family the cognomen Fedele, provides proof of a noble lineage. I am convinced, however, that your ancestors, divine Cassandra, who settled Vicomercatum, brought the Fedele lineage to me. For my father, who is in his eighties, told the story passed on to him by his father that one of his nearest kinsmen lived in a shop in Venice. I am wonderfully glad and, as long as the spirit moves these limbs of mine, I shall be glad that I will spend my life in an era when you, a girl more rare than the phoenix,[10] are alive. What could be more marvelous? What more glorious gift could this age or nature have given? You alone suffice for an eternity of Fedeli. Antiquity lauds Sappho and Aspasia and extols Hortensia.[11] But to you, Cassandra, the whole of history gives praise. Future generations will marvel at the poet Cassandra. Eulogies of the virgin Cassandra will be handed down to posterity, nor will they ever be consigned to oblivion. For the purity of most chaste manners, the knowledge of things human and divine, and the skill and ability to speak appropriately—qualities that separate and define the sexes and divide men from good women—all these gathered together you alone possess. Farewell, O delight of the city, I beg all your kinsmen—your father, uncle, sisters, all yours and all mine—to speak out. Farewell all. From my house in Milan. September 1493.

XVII

To Balthassare Fedele

She thanks him for his letter and asks for his coat of arms.[12]

Even if I were to remain silent, you would easily know how much pleasure I had on reading your elegant letter, in which you treated so fully the subject of the Fedele family's origins.

For who would not enjoy this so excellent history of our history, especially when our forebears were men of the greatest gravity, virtue, and loyalty, who were everywhere celebrated with honor after honor.

And if I heard previously that when my grandfather was alive he often said that our stock derived from the greatest men of Milan, still I am glad to have been informed of the story more fully and in greater detail from you. I must confess, however, that now that you have recognized and confirmed our kinship, I care for you exceedingly. Although I always loved and honored you and your family previously, because of your extraordinary virtue and our consanguinity, my love has now grown greater. And so, no one could come before you in my regard, and few are your equal. This, by Hercules, is easy to see since men were so inflamed by the zeal of your praises that access to you became possible. We, then, want to see you and to drink in your virtues face-to-face. Your presence adorns our house wondrously. It is difficult for me to say whether this longing of mine for you can be satisfied.

What else? Since it is now established that we share the same lineage, can you send us information as to whether we bear the same coat of arms, and as soon as possible? Because it is my habit to ask in this way, I beg you to send the information, though I fear that you won't. Farewell, and see that you and all your family consider yourselves greeted by my parents and all my relations. Venice. September 14 [No year given.]

XVIII

To a physician extraordinary in his duties[13]

I pray that reading these letters won't fatigue you, for once you have read them they should give you great pleasure in every sense. For it is a very pleasing thing to reflect on a friendship that has endured for a long time, especially one that has been as unusual in its reciprocity as that between you and my uncle Giovanni Fedele, who is learned both in medicine and the liberal arts. For he urged me to love you and in the strongest possible terms, all the more because this longstanding friendship of yours prompted you to care for my sister when her entire body was wracked with pain, as if she were your own daughter. And so it is difficult to know whether it is this time-honored association between the two of you or the expression of your sense of duty toward us that encourages me to love you more.

For one thing, I trust you because you are an honorable man; for another, you have really proven yourself in this matter. But to tell the truth, even if I were to affirm that your kindnesses to us were of the most perfect sort, still I would have reason to count more important your longstanding and singular friendship than I do these other things, and so I would wish that you would be persuaded that I have more faith in you than I have in myself.

Besides, testifying that your kindness to us has been the result of a long friendship is what gives us reason to do even more than this. And since your wisdom and goodness are much celebrated by everyone, do not these qualities add even more love to my loyalty to you since your wisdom is much celebrated by everyone. I know this from my brother Matteo's letters, for he claims that all men of authority and dignity seek you with the greatest desire, particularly those who are ill and appear to be cured of their illness simply by your presence, and what is more, by your diligent care and learning. Because of all this, you ought to know that you are loved by me as a father and nothing would please me more, nor could anything more pleasant happen, than that I be allowed to contribute to your honor and utility.

If there is anything I can offer you in Venice you should let me know. If you do, I shall be extremely pleased. Farewell. January 1497.

XIX

To the same unnamed doctor[14]

I used to be sad that my brother and the others were absent. I really thought too much of the distance between places. But now a consolation by no means small softens this great sorrow. From the letters of my brother Matteo I have heard that he is very much loved by Pietro Superanzio, the great prefect, philosopher, and pride and glory of the Venetians to whom we are all obligated in perpetual service, and it is my understanding that my friends are so loved by you and so beloved among your friends that nothing could be dearer. And hearing this has brought me great happiness because you showed such vigilance in caring for my sister Christina and you have shown such kindness throughout this whole ordeal toward all my family that we seem to be connected by blood ties. Having seen and recognized these things, I am in such a state of mind that I feel I am very much indebted to you, and you should know that I shall lack neither spirit nor energy until I have given or relayed my thanks to you even though our friendship does not require us to thank one another. Our goodwill, which I ask you again and again to preserve toward me as long as you live, is a thing we share. And you will receive the most pleasure in this since all my kins-men will greatly surpass you in love, and I pray you to include me among their number. Then you will consider me included when you visit me in your letters, and there it will be yours to command whatever you think I can do for you. Farewell. December 25, 1497.

NOTES TO CHAPTER 2

1. On the humanist letterbook as a genre see Diana Robin, *Filelfo in Milan. Writings, 1451–1477* (Princeton: Princeton University Press, 1991), chapter 1.

2. See Tom. 67, 94–95. The title only of the addressee is provided. I have supplied Franco's name since he was papal legate to Isabella's court at the time and the only ambassador Fedele would have addressed in such familiar terms.

3. See Tom. 41, 62–64.

4. The ellipsis dots are in the Tomasini edition.

5. See Tom. 112, 168–72.

6. Achates is Aeneas's right-hand man in Virgil's *Aeneid*.

7. The "faithful ones."

8. Note the change from the ancient clan name—represented by the antique Latin *Fideles*—to the modern Italianized spelling, *Fedeli*.

9. The Lares are the Roman household gods; by metonymy they signify one's home or hearth.

10. The phoenix was a legendary bird that lived for five hundred years, burned itself to ashes, and then was reborn from its own ashes to live in another time.

11. Sappho, perhaps the most famous woman poet of all time, flourished c. 650 B.C.E. Aspasia of Miletus became Pericles' lifelong companion in c. 445 B.C.E.; she is said to have been highly educated and an eloquent speaker. Hortensia, famed for her oratory, was the daughter of the famous orator Hortensius.

12. Tom. 113, 172–73.

13. Tom. 68, 95–96.

14. Tom. 69, 97–98.

III

PRINCES AND COURTIERS

Fedele's correspondence with male royal patrons, like her epistolary friendships with royal women, spanned a broad geographical area. She maintained correspondence with the patriarchs of four powerful European dynasties and a male heir to a fifth kingdom: King Ferdinand II of Spain and Aragon; King Louis XII of France and Orleans; Duke Lodovico Sforza of Milan and Bari; Marquis Francesco Gonzaga of Mantua; and Prince Gaspare of Aragon, a grandson of King Ferrante II of Naples. The royal patronage letters fall into five family groups; they include two encomiastic epistles, one addressed to the marquis of Mantua, the other to the king of Spain; three letters to the king of France and his orator; six letters she exchanged with the duke of Milan; and six letters to and from the Aragonese prince and his courtiers. Some of these letters are condolences, but most are eulogies of their royal addressees, as is her letter to the marquis of Mantua, which stands first among this group of letters as it did in the 1636 edition. Here the letter to Gonzaga served as a program for the collection as a whole, introducing many of Fedele's major themes to her readers.

XX

To Francesco Gonzaga, marquis of Mantua

Cassandra celebrates his worthy virtues with a very worthy eulogy.[1]

It should by no means seem strange, invincible prince, that I have taken a great and weighty burden on my shoulders in not hesitating to direct my little letters[2] to you, though I at first—a very young girl[3] writing to a great prince—was terrified and shied away from the task of writing. But then, moved by your mercy and goodness toward everyone, I was persuaded, despite the meagerness of my talent, to write. At the beginning of my labors, when I had abandoned feminine concerns and turned to those pursuits that pertain not only to honor during this brief life but to the enjoyment of God's majesty, I considered that I would find immortal praise among men. And so my goal has been to exercise my virile, burning, and incredible—though not improper, I hope—desire for the study of the liberal arts so my name will be praised and celebrated by excellent men. Therefore, I have taken as my exemplar the Platonic saying that "one should live beautifully or die beautifully,"[4] and this I believe will be done when my little letters, even if they are of little importance and learning, are delivered to the excellence and greatness of so great a man as you. For, as all men agree, your excellence in the virtues of the mind and fortune as in other attributes I have called "the good," is such that all men unanimously affirm that no one is more distinguished, kindhearted, or just than you, nor is there anyone more just in cases of wrongdoing.

For there is such admiration for your genius in every area—in military prudence, justice, and the administration of your kingdom—that everyone follows and embraces you not only with love but a sort of veneration. What more should I wish to say about your physical strength? That you exceed Achilles in dexterity, Hercules in strength, and Paris in handsomeness?[5] Should I not mention your noble lineage and your great deeds because they call for another speaker and another occasion; certainly my ability is hardly equal to such a task. It is the very breadth of your gifts that makes the orator's task so very difficult and serious. Therefore I entrust and commend myself, O most illustrious prince, and all my efforts to your magnanimity. Farewell. [Undated.]

XXI

To the king of Spain, Ferdinand

A consolation on the death of his son.[6]

When I persuaded myself to write you, it occurred to me that I could be accused of audacity, and justly so, since I, though only a girl, am audacious enough to write to you, a very great king. But it was this same audacity—which at first warned me against writing—that persuaded me to write once I thought it over. First of all, the bitter tragedy and death of your most excellent son must be mourned by all of us, and so my job now is to excuse myself since I have declared my profound grief too late. For I confess that I have been guilty of procrastination. But it has been fitting for me to console Your Highness before assuaging my own deepest sadness, which can scarcely be done easily. And I have shown many people, with my tears and sighs, this cruel and bitter wound of human nature, and I have urged them to mourn so that this burden will not be left to me alone.

But let us spend every season in unending weeping and lamentation. For it is this light that has been extinguished by day, in whose prudence and divine wisdom not only your great city and peoples but also foreign nations and princes all over the earth had placed their hopes and expectations. And it occurred to me as I pondered this bitter loss for a long time and with continuous weeping that coping with this seemed hardest and most troublesome not rationally but emotionally for humans. For there is nothing at this time which he would find inviting with the exception of your magnanimity, since neither felicity nor tranquility is offered to mortals, for everywhere anxiety prevails.

Therefore, let us admit that Epicurus[7] hit on the truth when he asserted that in no way could happiness be found in this epoch. O most excellent thought! For nature is subject to mortal corruption. Why, then, are you so moved by grief when the death of your son has brought glory and perennial praise to your parents and your ancient clan? Because of this, it can easily be conjectured that he is loved above all other men by God, the supreme being. For just as your son was chosen from a multitude of many men to be the most perfect of all, so he decided to reveal his perfection to all, just so was the most excellent gift of God in his goodness storm-tossed amid the turbulent waves; yet he was unwilling to subject himself to corruption. Therefore, you should now impose a limit on this constant mourning of yours so that men will not judge you all the more inconstant and so you will not regret your way of thinking. Now you grieve over the death of a child whom you engendered from diverse elements, from which God almighty welded together a soul. And now if God takes back to himself each one of these as likenesses of himself, I think it is indeed fitting.

Nor should you lament in such a way that you may be suspected of mourning not for your son but rather his property: you might appear to envy him because he won respect and dignity that exceeded your authority and because he was declared a king everlasting in his virtues though born from a mortal. For he had such gentleness, kindness, and love that, while neglecting his own advantages, he abandoned all effort, diligence, and anxiety for anything else. Is it not true that he thought whatever shunned religion, justice, piety, clemency, and compassion should be reviled? Finally, he located the highest good in the heavenly beings above us, from whom the most shining diadem now adorns his divine head. Here angels bring you glory, praising you as our highest good and singing in sonorous voices to God on high, from whom your clemency toward us comes, and this is the gift of supreme happiness, which has been given—a gift so sweet, delightful, and pleasing.

Perhaps it should be mourned, Your unhappy Highness, that your son has died in the flower of his youth, but truly we should rejoice, O glorious king. For in the long duration of this fragile life we find nothing at all except a pack of wrongs to bear, a burden too heavy for our shoulders. And who does not know that the longer a man's life is, the more calamity and hardship he faces? Who disputes this? If Xerxes the Persian king, Gnaeus Pompey, Julius Caesar,[8] and many others who won innumerable victories with almost the greatest triumphs, had died sooner, their enemies would not have witnessed their wretched deaths and, what is more, their desires would have been sated by the many disasters they had seen. On this account, one poet has said wisely, "Behold how death diminishes the glory of life."[9] Therefore, O most merciful king, weeping must be restrained, tears must be dried, and sighing, suppressed. But it may torment you all the more that a cruel and ignoble death, and one not worthy of a king's son, has befallen your son contrary to your expectations. For he was overcome by a senseless animal, a thing grievous to hear, O wisest king, for as Plato says, "We should either live beautifully or die beautifully."[10] But Greatest God, who decided that he should depart to heaven, recognized that he could only be killed by an unreasoning creature; human reason, even that of an enemy, would not have allowed him to be killed. Rather, anyone who looked upon his shining and splendid presence was compelled and induced to love, cherish, and fear him as though he were a god. So great was the beauty of his body, so handsome his proportions, so dignified the composure of his face and its features, that he seemed godlike in his majesty.

It is now appropriate to your wisdom to withdraw from this long grief and your lamenting. For it is enough that you have been sunk in sorrow and immersed in mourning for so long. Now may a natural tranquility of mind and pleasing serenity of expression return to the noble generosity of mind that belongs to Your Highness and your consort so that then your friends, your people, and all nations will no longer be tormented with suffering, since they are greatly saddened that you mourn and since your son has been released from all danger, care, and anxiety, and he rests with God in heaven, in the highest felicity and glory. Besides, your wisdom and magnanimity, in which you surpass the whole race, will keep you from this excess.

I would prefer to recount the many other most excellent and splendid deeds of you and your queen, especially since they have been told by many, foremost among these by Pietro di Silva,[11] a most excellent knight and a man wholly dedicated to your service. But these things exceed the capacity of my mind, and I seem more prolix in speaking than is right. All that is left is to signify to you with a loyal heart my perpetual service to Your Highness—I who desire nothing and seek nothing except to be protected under your wings, whose shelter I, like a little servant girl,[12] entrust myself to, again and again. May 1492.

XXII

To Louis XII, king of France[13]

Since I have always been full of admiration for your glory, your name, and your virtues, most renowned King, for a long time now I have hoped that some occasion would be given to me to write to you and to be able to show that my heart is already dedicated and devoted to Your Highness. I understood that as a woman, not sufficiently learned and of a humble family, it was a great thing that I was sending a letter to you, the wisest and most invincible king of France and the most unique and extraordinary source of distinction in the world. But still, since entire nations rejoice over your dignity and felicity, and in particular the Republic of Venice exalts you above all others, I was not able to restrain myself from rejoicing and exulting in the public jubilation. And that which I do in thought, I also wished to express to you in a letter. Therefore, Your Majesty, do not disdain my congratulations, adoration, and love for you since the Lord himself listens to the prayers of the lowliest people. May your most sacred majesty be well and receive my will and mind, which are devoted and committed to you. Venice. June 1498.

XXIII

To Accorsio Maynerio, orator to the most Christian Louis XII, king of France[14]

T was very happy to read your sweet letter, most excellent orator, and because it comes from you, Accorsio Maynerio—expert attorney, exceptional counselor, and consummate orator of the very Christian King—I was all the more glad to comply with your honorable request since, though my body is frail, my mind remains strong. If I return to my former health—and I hope this will be soon—I shall ask Your Excellency to grant me a favor, and I shall ask it though I feel guilty, namely, that you consider me worthy to visit with your colleague Magister de Bellomonte.[15] Though I am only a girl and not truly learned, I am nonetheless a student of erudite men and a lover of the liberal arts in so far as our sex permits such a thing. And because nothing more delightful could happen to me on that day, I beg that I, a very young maiden, be allowed to enjoy the conversation, full of erudition and exemplary of rectitude, of the very learned orators of the most Christian King. For though I thirst for this fertile and long hoped for spring, I would approach it without knowledge of its utility to those who are learned, and ignorant of the riches of its waters to those who are knowledgeable in what is to be studied and advised. I would come into your midst, most excellent ones, inserting some minor little question for the sake of speaking. This would for me be the greatest pleasure.

You, however, write that Coroebus[16]—a poet in love to no avail—scorned the weapons and fire of the Greeks and that many people have come from faraway places around the world to visit the city of the Paduan poet Livy.[17] I, a female warrior, trample those things under my feet and think them of little importance. For the former is a story about passion, and the latter truly has to do with your humanity, neither of which example pertains to me. Therefore, exceptional virtue and this alone, in which you wondrously surpass all other men, bind me to your kindness and will always make me feel indebted to you, no less to your most splendid colleague and to all those similar to you, to whom I wholly entrust myself. Farewell. July 1499.

XXIV

To the invincible king of France, Louis XII[18]

t has been necessary for me to bow to the wishes of Accorsio Maynerio, your most excellent orator, a man expert in the science of the
law, who has urged me to write to you, most invincible of all kings. For
desire is born of necessity, and even if I signified my readiness to serve you
in earlier letters that I gave to your orator and knight Girolamo Giorgio[19]
to deliver to Your Majesty, still I wanted to affirm my desire so that I could
congratulate you not only on your recent accession to power and your victory achieved without very great loss of life, but so I could testify to my
very great felicity of mind, since all Italy and, above all, the Republic of
Venice, rejoices and congratulates Your Majesty in your absence more than
can be said. For everyone says that your felicitous arrival, O most Christian
and prudent king, has liberated Italy from the constant turmoil of war and
the rapine and plunder of tyrants.

I, however, the true bard and prophet of Italy now pacified, rejoice that
Your Highness will now set forth against the barbarian nations and above
all against the truculent barbarity of Mohammed in order to exterminate
and destroy that dire and impious nation, which not being content to menace your borders now threatens the destruction of the name of Christianity
and the most holy faith unless you alone and the Venetian republic intervene as your ancestors did against impending ruin. It is this that I hope and
desire Your Majesty, to whom I give and devote myself as a humble servant,
will do. [Undated.]

XXV

To Il Moro, the illustrious duke of Bari

A singular encomium of the duke of Bari, into whose hands she entrusts herself.[20]

iven that I thought it necessary to beg pardon for my audacity right
in the opening sentence of my letter—if it can really be called audacity for a young girl to have written to the greatest prince in the world—
Your Highness cannot fail to accuse me of ignorance. For I seem to be shy
in the face of your generosity, kindness, and your natural gentleness—of
which there is no greater example in the whole world. Your lofty mind,

which in the beginning terrified me, now inspires me to write to you. And even if among the rest of chroniclers of the illustrious deeds of the Sforza house I may seem to be an unsightly little blot, still, in response to your kindness and at the same time induced by reason, I thought that pleasing heroic poetry would be proper, since I, Cassandra, have often been allowed to sing the praises of very distinguished men and princes and marquises in my orations, whom I (and though I am perhaps not very old, I am still not utterly devoid of reason and judgment) have called *demarchs*.[21]

Oh, stubborn audacity! Your Highness will perhaps say I am a wretched girl. I beg you not to impose this judgment on an innocent young girl. Ye gods, "Fidelis" did not wish for this. Ever since I decided to break my long period of silence with you and finally formed an image of you, I have wanted to produce a portrait, and at some point I will. Certainly it has been for me to define and delineate you who were sent down to this house by necessity. For you surpass and far exceed the memory not only of all men in recent history but the ancients as well (incredible to hear and not unjust!) For the rich and fertile virtue of Il Moro must not only be marveled at, but all foreign nations and shores sing your praises, and especially admirable is the paean by Fracasso Gaspare of Aragon,[22] the most illustrious, fiercest, and most committed defender of Il Moro. What else? When I have heard him speak, I seem to hear not Fracasso but Il Moro himself. So magnificently, reverently, and worthily does he sing his praises, by heaven. Certainly Il Moro can be compared with Camillus.[23] For he not only showed the greatest virtue in expelling the barbarian hoards from Italy with a startlingly small militia while the empire remained intact at Rome, but after recovering the insignia of the Roman people, he then slaughtered and put to flight the barbarian marauders. This man, so that those same barbarians would not overrun Italy again and lay waste its land, stood in the way of the barbarian menace and put down their arrogance with divine majesty. In addition, this same prince was one who inspired such fear, who acted with such swiftness in council, yet who governed with the most saintly clemency and justice toward all and ruled the most pleasing empire that not only all men but also all nature and the almighty God himself sing his praises.

They will say that you, who were born on this day, are the guardian of religion and the faith, that you give sanctuary to the wretched, and that you are the ornament of all virtues and the most venerable of men. Why has it not been assigned to me, Cassandra, to praise you while you are here, and to guard and venerate Your Majesty as I would my father, your sweetest and most devoted servant, who in the last few days has not shrunk from undertaking this huge journey so that he can contemplate your brilliance?

Now, however, I shall commemorate neither you nor your ancestors' innumerable and unparalleled deeds in my little letters. For a long time now this difficult task has been assigned to others more skilled and experienced than I.

Farewell, little wonder of our time. I pray that with the shade of your wings you will protect us, your servants, whose only hopes are for you. Venice. October 1490.

XXVI

To Lodovico Sforza, the duke of Bari and later Milan

She thanks Lodovico Sforza for commending her to the Venetian Senate, and she complains of her fortune and the envy that has arisen from her erudition. She congratulates him on the birth of his son.[24]

I am vexed that I can in no way answer to the magnanimity of your praises of me, most invincible Prince, for due to your greatness, the slenderness of my talent makes me fearful of thanking you. Since you have not thought it unworthy to commend me to the most honorable Senate so very kindly and indeed much more elaborately than is called for considering my inferior virtue, your commendation, by Pollux,[25] has done me the highest honor. For so great a prince to praise me, so very young a maiden, ought to be received as a thing of great significance. But you will learn this better from your own splendid orator Taddeo.[26] Therefore, with what words, what oration, what service shall I respond to your generous opinion of me?

The answer escapes me, by Hercules, but it consoles me not a little to be able to confess freely that no one is a more loyal, more steadfast, or a more faithful servant to you than I. And this will be all the more pleasing to me when I consider that I am so well esteemed by Your Highness that I am convinced that happiness will be mine and all things will proceed accordingly. And even if I must regret that fortune has determined that my lot is to suffer sorrow, still, relying on the divine will of Il Moro, I shall prostrate myself at your feet. Indeed, I confess to you alone that some men envy the novelty of my talent, not recognizing what is unusual in a mind. Even so, I am accustomed to laugh at these men, following the habit of the philosophers. As long as I dwelt on the whims of the malevolent, it slowed me down in my writing.

Finally, I have heard that a son has been born to Your Highness. When I heard the news, I was so overcome with happiness that I scarcely knew what I should do. I give thanks to the Almighty God and shall continue always to do so that in this age He has given so great a gift to mortal men that from so supreme and excellent a Prince a son should be born. And I pray the omnipotent God may keep safe this son and favor him in all things together with his wisest mother and father. Farewell. [Undated.]

XXVII

Duke Lodovico Maria Sforza to Cassandra Fedele

He responds to each item in the preceding letter.[27]

We have gladly commended you to the illustrious Venetian doge, and we are delighted to have learned from you that our praise was of use to your honor. Therefore, as often as you should need our commendation in future, you will not be without it. For not only do we desire that men should know we esteem you because of the virtue that exists in your most dear sex but also that you have been the beneficiary of our benevolence. That there are those, however, who are envious of your virtue should by no means worry you. For this is the true proof of virtue, and besides, you will conduct yourself wisely if you do not depart from your plan of studies on account of those men's slander. In this you should imitate not only the philosophers but also, since you are Christian, the author of our faith who commanded not only that we should not hate our enemies but love them as though they were seen as the means for practicing our virtue. Moreover, you have congratulated me on the birth of a child, the son of my most illustrious wife. I recognize your own mind and character in these most loving words, and I receive them as an omen that this son who is born of me will be no less a party to your interests than am I myself, whom you will know as ever solicitous on behalf of your virtue. Milan. April 1493.

XXVIII

To Lodovico Maria Sforza

Fedele praises the excellent gifts of the queen.[28]

It is clear that my unflagging devotion to you has come merely in response to your generosity and that of your illustrious consort. For this is a quality easy to recognize since you so humanely and kindly thought it worthy to answer each of my notes with the loftiest promises. Therefore I would be eternally grateful simply if your magnanimity and beneficence were to endure and my small talent were not to fail me, for it directs and indeed insists that my thoughts, allegiance, and service be devoted to you alone. Because of your goodness and your other innumerable gifts and the magnificence of your kingdom, your divine name grows strong throughout the entire globe. It gleams like the brightest ray of light and its lasting memory will continue to be illuminated by many, among whose number I hope to be remembered myself for my own readiness of mind.

You should know how very happy I am to have heard that in a very short time your wife, the duchess, will be arriving in Venice. And on her arrival, I trust that I shall attain a twofold benefit: one, I shall enjoy feelings of happiness and bliss from the gaze of her divine countenance, and I shall venerate her as though she were a goddess on earth; and two, I do not doubt that I shall obtain by the grace of her word alone from this most distinguished senate an opportunity I have long hoped for. And if her greatness of mind does not think me undeserving of such a thing, not only will she thus provide an increase to my courage (which is very slight indeed) but she will abundantly fulfill your most generous promises. In the meantime I beg you to consider me your little servant. May 1492.

XXIX[29]

Lodovico Maria Sforza to Cassandra

His magnificent opinion of her and his promise of every favor and interest.

D. Gaspar Sanseverino,[30] your advocate and the enthusiastic herald of your praises, delivered to us your letter that, together with a great deal of other testimony, convinced us of what we so often had heard before about your extraordinary virtue, your supreme cultivation, and erudition, Cassandra. For in this letter you showed not only how great your service to us would be, which we esteem highly because of your splendid virtue, but you also exhibited the force of your intellect and eloquence, which is so great that it should not only be counted among the rare gifts of nature, but judged a wondrous thing that as much erudition and eloquence as you have is found in a woman and a girl. Fortunate is your father, who chanced to procreate a daughter blessed with such gifts of mind and nature. Happiest is the city of Venice, which has obtained in its citizen Cassandra an ornament for the greatness of its empire and heroic deeds, because nature wanted to test in her what was possible in the female sex. So much happiness is owed and indeed given to you especially because you have brought such glory to your sex in our time—glory that the excellent men of the habitable world were scarcely able to achieve in their studies, a part of which we also receive through your attention to us. For you have gladly shown us what you would do if you were with us: were this to be, we think it would not only bring us honor but should it not be, it would to be hoped for in all our prayers. For we confess freely that virtue is dearer to our heart than anything else and that those who strive for virtue are uniquely valued by us; and we judge you to be foremost among such persons. You ought to know that both you and your father, on whose behalf you have sent us greetings, can hope for our goodwill toward you and offer gifts that the most excellent and extraordinary men cannot hope for. If you think that this response to your letters is rather slow in coming, know that your letters have only just now been delivered to us. Know also that we would not have been so tardy in our response to your letters had we received them sooner. Vigevano. January 1490.

XXX

To Gaspare of Aragon

She commends her teacher Gasparino Borro to the prince of Aragon.[31]

*E*ven if in the past few days I sent Your Grace a little letter to which there has been no answer, still this has not made me fear to write you again. I see this as my tribute to your magnanimity, your countless virtues, and your kindnesses to me. For, since Fortune has not given me the wherewithal to give you adequate thanks, I will at least give over to you that which has been left to me as a little legacy: so that my gentle mind—so grateful to you and about to be all the more so—may so dispatch its duty that your generous goodwill and kindness, which we partake of each and every day, will become even better known to me. For I have always known that you were the herald of my praises and a prince devoted to virtue (a quality of which I have been permitted to have a small measure). Your task is to pursue this: to keep the promises of a prince and his great mind. To conclude, you see here the theologian Brother Gasparino,[32] my former teacher, who is a man richly endowed in virtue and utterly devoted to Your Grace. Him I commend to you, and should he be in need of your assistance at any time, I pray you will treat him well. In the meantime, most illustrious prince, haven for human kindness and the virtues, I entrust myself to Your Grace, nor is life itself more dear to me than your most excellent wife, the princess. Farewell. [Undated.]

XXXI

To Gaspare, prince of Aragon

She admires his virtue, and predicts an increase in honor for him. She recommends the poet Leonardo to him, introduces the subject of her love of philosophy.[33]

"What are you doing, Cassandra? Ye gods! What do you want from me?"

You have not heard my plan, which is either to praise and celebrate your fame or to sympathize completely with whatever state you are in, be it one of sadness or happiness. You now enjoy happiness, and I am glad that you enjoy being firmly entrenched in a place of honor, though malicious people who bay like dogs oppose you. I want to add the following: because of your great and heroic virtues, I prophesy that you will attain still greater things. Believe me, fidelity influenced by reason speaks to me. For people say you are like a shining star on earth. Nor do I mouth empty words. For you have done all things not underhandedly but freely and in the open with a face full of virtue. Nor are you praised undeservedly in every empire— both the invincible doge of the Venetians and the peerless duke of Milan esteem you. But why should Cassandra dally with more talk? Perhaps you will say, "Tell me in a word what you want."

Certainly, I shall say this: my desire is that the poet Leonardo,[34] who is dearer to you than anyone else and who will protect you in every conflict and at every turn, should be taken on as your servant so that his own lord will not think him unworthy of your clemency, especially when he has scorned and abandoned so many princes and many excellent men for the sake of serving you.

I rejoice at one thing: even if you support him unstintingly with your magnanimity and generosity, still for my sake, as I see it, you will provide whatever he needs for his health with even more solicitousness. But I ask that I not be made fun of so that you can make a name for yourself. For I have stated publicly that I feel well among the pleasant crowd of people around you. I would there recount the great and noble praises of your ancestors and their glorious deeds.

However, I should speak frankly. My studies in philosophy are so exhausting me that I am unable to undertake the burden of praising you, a duty not to be taken lightly. Therefore, if you will allow it, I place a limit on myself. But first I would like you to know that my service and commitment to you could not possibly be greater. I place myself in your hands. Farewell. Venice October 1490.

XXXII

To Pietro of Aragon

A consolatory letter on the death of his son.[35]

*E*ven if it is hardly appropriate for me, knowing nothing of letters, to write to the most important duke in the world, I never could have dared to express my deep and heartfelt sorrow to Your Highness. For when I heard the news of the death of your son from your father, the invincible King Ferrante's splendid and most devoted orator, for whose loyalty and perennial service I am grateful, I moaned strangely in pain, and I have been unable to stop weeping, especially over the last few days, since when my letter was read, he issued the command that I be honored with the most learned poems. Therefore, I confess that painstaking and difficult material was offered to me so that I could console Your Highness. But I, who am wretched myself, am in need of consolation. What am I to do in my grief? Is it right to add sorrow to sorrow, tears to tears? Instead, let me follow the custom of the ancients, who mourned to an excessive degree, singing eulogies over the bodies of the dead and moving those at the funeral to vent their tears and sighs. For who is so hard-hearted that on hearing the innumerable virtues of your most excellent son he would not be moved to a flood of tears since he will no longer have his radiant presence?

As I pondered such thoughts, something came to mind that might bring some consolation to Your Highness. For even if you seem neither to need consolation nor to await the palliative of time, still you should not think it a waste of your time to hear this letter, in which you will be told that we must rejoice in your son's departure to another place. For who does not believe that he has departed to that place from which he once came? For not only the Christians but also almost all the ancient philosophers agree that the soul is immortal and abides among the gods after death. Did not Phaedo say that Socrates longed for death since through this release he would be able to enjoy immortality?[36] Who, then, doubts that your son resides in the bosom of the gods? For how pious, faithful, and religious he was from his earliest years on! And how beautifully and justly did he live his life, and not only was he admired by his own countrymen but by foreigners as well, for never did he do injury to anyone nor would he do so. Rather, he treated people with great concern and diligence: conduct admirable and almost unheard of at his tender age.

Therefore, we should rejoice rather than grieve, it seems, and now we must find moderation in mourning, most noble duke, lest you seem to grieve not so much for your son as you appear to envy his enjoying of eternal and everlasting life while you yourself are deprived of advantages. This indeed is not characteristic of this duke or of his magnanimous and liberal mind. Besides, it must be thought unjust if you, who surpass all the men of old in power, prudence, wisdom, and in every virtue and are far superior to them, should be allowed to be their inferior now. Have we not read that the Catos, the Brutuses, and almost all the heroes of antiquity were men of virtue and constancy no less in mourning than in war, and that Anaxagoras, who when told of the death of his son, said he had learned nothing new since he had never doubted that his son was born a mortal.[37] O words of great wisdom! For where now are the Athenians or Alexander or Caesar?[38] And where finally is Rome, most favored of cities and market for the whole world? Who has ever enjoyed such power and greatness, overthrown mountains and swam across seas, who has not suffered this scourge of death? How perfectly did Xerxes, the most preeminent of kings, know this when he surveyed from his lookout tower his massive army infinite in its numbers and scarcely was able to restrain himself from weeping because he knew that after a hundred years none of those at whom he was looking would survive. Since no one can escape the necessity of mortality, you can hardly experience it as troublesome that your son has been freed from this troublesomeness. For he himself came to know how long it was necessary for him to have lived since he covered himself sufficiently with virtues. For he was considered a man of the highest prudence and practically divine wisdom. He saw then his grandfather, a man of incredible power and the most serene of kings; his father, the most beloved and insuperable leader; your uncles, most illustrious princes; and his own sweetest brother, prince of Capua, and he saw them all triumphing. And content with these sights, he longed to return to the gods in heaven who had sent him into this world. Now he rejoices in the most splendid vision of God almighty. According to the apostle's testimony, "Him whom we now see reflected in a mirror, as in a mystery, we shall later see face-to-face."[39]

He, therefore, led by this longing, has gladly departed this life. And, with his happiest of prayers fulfilled, he has come from that wretched and unhappy way station and has arrived at the long-awaited homeland. He has been welcomed after a stormy trip by sea into a safe harbor. You, therefore, most gentle duke, should rejoice that your son has been removed from the darkness to this blessed life. Why all this from me, an insignificant girl? I seem to have added water to the sea. Therefore, invincible prince, in whatever way you use your prudence among others, I commit and hand myself over in perpetual service to you. Vale.

XXXIII

To Gaspare of Aragon, illustrious prince

She thanks him for his praise of her.[40]

Even if it embarrasses me to write to Your Honor, when I think of the extent of your assistance to me, for which I cannot thank you adequately, I am reminded that your generosity and kindness have not demanded any reciprocal service from me. Just within the last few days, the most eloquent letters, filled with wit and charm and addressed to me by the invincible duke Il Moro Sforza, were delivered to me by Lodovico degli Alberi,[41] a man of incomparable mental and physical vigor who is wholly dedicated to you, as everyone here attests.

From the duke's letters, it is very easy to see that my letters pleased and delighted His Highness, not on account of their eloquence, that being indeed slight, but because of the kindness of your extremely eloquent oration that celebrated me and my virtues—and more than is fair and just—at His

Highness, the illustrious Il Moro's palace, who in this age is superior by far to all other men because of his sublime wisdom, justice, and counsel, and finally, because he possesses every virtue of the mind.

I would have answered his letter had not I feared that my unsophisticated letters would be boring and tedious. But of your judgment we will stay clear in the future. In the meantime, I hope you will not think it a waste of your time to speak to him in my name if it seems appropriate to Your Highness that I should be engaged for perennial service. What else? You will do that which your judgment dictates, though it is not easy to say how much I owe you who have not ceased to extol and laud me day after day. I hope that you will do likewise hereafter, so that you can honorably pursue what you have promised. There is nothing further to say on that.

I commend my parents to you, who are most interested in your fame, and I commend all of us to your most excellent wife, a woman who is the greatest glory of our sex. Vale, light of the virtues.

XXXIV

Jacopo Bentivoglio of Aragon, viscount at the ducal court in Naples, to Cassandra

He thanks her for wanting to include him in the encyclopedia of illustrious men celebrated in her letters.[42]

Although I have long respected the high regard in which your learning is held, a regard few men and still fewer women in our own time enjoy, still I at least managed to impress you with the public declaration made by the men who came here from your city. But now that I have received your elegant letter telling me that you are planning to write something about me because you are going to include the lives of numerous famous men in your writings, so much increased is my affection for you that it is not possible for me to express how much I esteem and care for you. Nor is this wrong of me. For who is so devoid of all culture and learning that he does not love and cherish Cassandra Fedele, the most erudite and eloquent of women? Thus to you, whose erudition will cause us to be less in awe of those women of antiquity whose oratory was so distinguished that their fame was known and celebrated throughout the entire world, I pledge and promise my assistance and support, to the end that you may make use of such resources as these in whatever way you wish and at any time. Vale, glory of women. Know that you are very dear to me. Bologna. January 1487.

NOTES TO CHAPTER 3

1.   Tom. 1, 1–3. Francesco Gonzaga (1466–1519), marquis of Mantua and condottiere of the Venetian army, was married to Isabella d'Este, daughter of Eleonora of Aragon.

2.   "Literulis" (little letters): one of Fedele's trademark diminutives.

3.   "Virguncula" (little virgin): another of her signature diminutives.

4.   "Aut pulchre vivere, aut pulchre mori." Tomasini places this and all quotations from the ancient authors in roman type to distinguish them from the italic type. Fedele's paraphrasing of Plato emphasizes the Platonic conjunction of the good, the true, and the beautiful as the ultimate goals for humans. The goal of "living beautifully" is thus to be distinguished from the Stoic dictum of "living well."

5.   These are three standard Renaissance heroes, each endowed with his own characteristic virtues and faults. The pre–Trojan War hero Hercules represents brute strength and cunning. Achilles, the greatest of the Greek warriors in the Trojan War, as recounted in Homer's *Iliad* is known for his invincibility in battle and his pride. Paris, the son of King Priam of Troy who stole Helen from King Menelaus and thus initiated the Trojan War, is better known as a lover and lady's man than as a soldier.

6.   Tom. 48, 70–75. King Ferdinand of Aragon (1452–1516), husband of Queen Isabella of Castile (1451–1504).

7.   Born in Samos, Epicurus (341–270 B.C.E.) was the founder of the Epicurean school of philosophy.

8.   Three famous military leaders. Xerxes, king of Persia and famous for his bridge of ships across the Hellespont, was defeated by the Greeks in the Persian wars (479 B.C.E.). Gnaeus Pompeius (106–48 B.C.E.) was a member of the First Triumvirate with Caesar and Crassus and is remembered as one of Rome's greatest generals. Gaius Julius Caesar (102–44 B.C.E.) was at the time of his assassination the most powerful consul and military leader that Rome had ever known.

9.   "En vitae gloriam imminuit mors": this dictum is not identified in Tomasini's and its origin is unknown.

10.   See n. 4 above.

11.   "Di Silva" is unknown to me.

12.   "Servulam" (little servant or slave woman): this is another example of Fedele's characteristic use of diminutive forms.

13.   Tom. 72, 101–2. Louis XII of Orleans, king of France (1498–1515), took Milan by force in September 1499, claiming his right to it through his mother's Visconti lineage.

14.   Tom. 75, 104–5. Accorsio Maynerio was (as the heading indicates) the influential orator and counselor of King Louis XII of France.

15. "Bellomonte" is unknown to me.

16. *Aeneid* 2.341: Coroebus died at Troy. He had traveled to there to court King Priam's daughter Cassandra and to fight the Greeks.

17. The Roman historian Livy (59 B.C.E.–17 C.E.) was born in Padua. He wrote 142 books of history that covered from the founding of Rome to the rule of Augustus.

18. Tom. 76, 106–7.

19. "Girolamo" is unknown to me.

20. Tom. 29, 43–45. This letter bears the erroneous heading "Marco illustrissimo . . ." that is indicative of the errors that are common in Tomasini. It should read "Mauro . . ." Cassandra here addresses Lodovico Maria Sforza, "Il Moro," who was duke of Bari from 1479 to 1494. He was invested as duke of Milan in 1494. He married Beatrice d'Este in 1491, the daughter of the duchess of Ferrara, Eleonora of Aragon, who was the daughter of Ferrante of Aragon, king of Naples.

21. Fedele's use of the word *demarchos*, a Latin transliteration of the ancient Greek word for a head of state in the ancient Greek city, is meant to display her erudition and suggest her acquaintance with Aristotle and Plato. The word also suggests that these Italian nobles can be compared with leaders in democratic Athens. There is a problem with the Latin text since the adjective "antiquitus" is masculine singular rather than masculine plural or feminine singular, as it should be were it to modify either "principes," "marchiones," or "Cassandra," as I take it to do.

22. Fracasso Gaspare of Aragon is identified in the introduction to this chapter and the notes below.

23. Camillus was the great Roman general of the fourth century B.C.E. who defeated the Veii.

24. Tom. 55, 81–82. On Lodovico Sforza see n. 20 above.

25. "By Pollux" and "by Hercules" were popular oaths used by Latin-speaking peoples.

26. "Taddeo" is unknown to me.

27. Tom. 56, 83–84.

28. Tom. 59, 86–87.

29. Tom. 122, 187–88. The letter is misnumbered CVXII [sic] in Tomasini.

30. "Gaspar Sanseverino" is unknown to me.

31. Tom. 43, 65–66. Prince Gaspare of Aragon, grandson of King Ferrante I of Naples. See chapter introduction. Gaspare was the count of Aversa.

32. Gasparino Borro, a monk of the Servite Order, had taught Fedele Latin and Greek literature, history, and philosophy since she was a child.

33. Tom. 28, 41–42.

34. "Leonardo" is unknown to me. The Latin epithet Fedele used for Leonardo, *sacerdos* (priest) was also a sobriquet for poets in Roman poetry suggesting, as it does here, that a writer of verse was also a holy man of the Muses.

35. Tom. 36, 54–57. Pietro is the son of King Ferrante's orator.

36.   This idea appears throughout *Phaedo* but especially at the beginning and end of the dialogue. See 63B–C and 113D–114C.

37.   All three men, the two Romans (Cato and Brutus) and the ancient Greek philosopher, Anaxagoras (500–450 B.C.E.) were common Renaissance exempla for the Stoic facing of death. All of these men refused to allow mourning for their loved ones to overwhelm them but rather found consolation in philosophy.

38.   This whole paragraph in which Alexander, Caesar, and Xerxes are invoked— the greatest and most successful generals the world had ever known—Fedele uses a typical *ubi sunt nunc* trope. No matter how great humans may become, death comes for all; there is no escape.

39.   1 Cor 13:12.

40.   Tom. 32, 49.

41.   "Degli Alberi" is unknown to me.

42.   Tom. 106, 162–63.

IV

ACADEMICS AND LITERARY FRIENDS

Cassandra Fedele's correspondence produced a wide network of intellectual friendships, chiefly with men a generation older than she, through which she was able to enter into circles from which she would otherwise have been excluded as a woman.[1] In her book of letters, she fashioned an imaginary academic community that included faculty and students from Venice's university at Padua[2] and extended beyond that specific locale to Verona, Milan, Florence, Rimini, Pavia, and even Rome. For at least a decade Fedele exchanged letters with and acted as an intermediary between scholars and writers in those cities. She was a principal facilitator in an arterial system of social and intellectual relationships of which Venice and Padua were the primary nodes.

Rimini was the original home of two key networkers in Fedele's web: the Latin poet Giovanni Aurelio Augurello,[3] who came to the university in Padua to study Greek philosophy in the 1470s; and Paolo Ramusio, the author of two elegiac poems in Latin dedicated to Cassandra, who, after receiving his doctorate in law at Padua in 1481, remained to become a celebrated attorney in that city.[4] In the 1480s, Udine served as a way station for several of Fedele's correspondents including Ramusio; Marcantonio Sabellico, then the leading humanist historian in Venice; and a scholar and cleric known as Filomuso (Gianfrancesco Superchio), who after a three-year stint teaching at Udine returned to Venice.[5]

Another group of Fedele's correspondents was based in Verona. At the center of this circle Matteo Bosso presided. An alumnus of Padua, Bosso returned to Verona where he taught until 1492. That year he was named abbot of a monastery near Florence where he became part of Ficino's Neoplatonist circle.[6] Fedele's Veronese network also included the poet Panfilo Sasso, who was a close friend of Augurello's; the professor of literature,

Girolamo Bentacordo; and an envoy from Verona to the Venetian Senate, Lodovico Cendrata.[7]

Through Bosso's connections with Ficino's circle in Florence, Fedele entered into correspondence with the Florentine chancellor Bartolomeo Scala and his daughter Alessandra, who had played the leading role in a semipublic reading of Sophocles' *Electra* in Greek;[8] the philosopher Giovanni Pico della Mirandola; and the widely known Hellenist and tutor to Lorenzo de' Medici's sons, Angelo Poliziano. Poliziano visited Fedele in Venice in the summer of 1491, and, in a letter to Lorenzo de' Medici, he wrote a glowing account of their meeting.[9]

Fedele's core group of intellectual friends were residents of either Padua or Venice. Her Paduan "republic of letters"[10] included Giuseppe Gennari, the abbot at the Seminary in Padua; Angelo Tancredi of Lucca, a student of Francesco Negri,[11] a prominent Venetian Hellenist and admirer of Fedele; and Lodovico da Schio of Vicenza, rector of the College of Philosophy and Medicine at Padua.[12] Fedele's good friends Niccolò Leonico Tomeo, Aurelio Augurello, Paolo Ramusio, Girolamo Campagnola,[13] and her cousin Bertuccio Lamberti all studied under the great émigré scholar of Greek literature at Padua in the late 1470s–80s, Demetrius Chalcondylas. After 1497, Tomeo himself would occupy Padua's chair of Greek.[14] Fedele was able to parlay her longtime friendship with another key scholar from Venice, Bonifacio Bembo, by 1489 professor of philosophy at Milan's university in Pavia, into an introduction to Duke Lodovico Sforza of Milan and his wife Beatrice d'Este.[15]

The signal event in Fedele's academic life was her delivery of a formal oration in 1487, before the faculty and students at the University of Padua, on the occasion of the conferral of the baccalaureate on her cousin Bertuccio Lamberti. Many of the letters in this chapter reflect the respect and admiration she won as a result of her appearance that day. Reports of the elegant oration she presented at the university in Padua and of a second oration she presented before the doge and the Venetian Senate in praise of the liberal arts caused her fame to spread throughout Italy, northern Europe, and even eastward to Hungary and the Dalmatian coast. Fedele's *Oratio pro Bertuccio Lamberto* was published in Modena in 1487, in Venice in 1488, and in Nuremberg in 1489.

ॐ

THE PADUA CONNECTION

XXXV

Lodovico da Schio of Vicenza, rector of the faculty of philosophy and medicine, to Cassandra Fedele, most pure maiden and eloquent orator of the kindly Muses[16]

I used to think that the glory of the Muses, the eloquence of women, and every kind of rhetoric that was womanly (if one is allowed to use that word) had all but disappeared in our modern age, and I didn't believe that there was any woman now who could match either Hortensia's[17] skill at composition and her talent as an orator or, for that matter, any of the ancient Roman women orators. But when I think of your not simply human but divine eloquence, when I consider your physical gestures suitable to oratory, when I ponder your constantly ornate style, I don't know what else to say about you unless I may adapt the following passage from Virgil to describe you: "I believe—nor are these empty words—that you are descended from the race of the gods."[18] And do not think this is said without cause. For if anyone should ever think that the greatest talents in the art of oratory or the richest sources of inspiration or the enigmas of the dialectical method have been erased from the hearts of all mortal men, let him realize that this gift has been transmitted from the divinity to you and you alone. I therefore can rightly and justly say, "May Mantua cease to exalt its poet Virgil to the skies. May Verona keep silent about Catullus. Nor should Greece commemorate the great works of erudite Plato; and now Rome can pass over her eloquent Cicero in silence."[19] But if such a great oratorical power and such a talent for rhetoric are in you—a river of eloquence such as neither ancient nor future ages will have seen—why then should I not exalt with the highest reverence the name of a girl who is most perfect? This, then, has been done in praise of your character, chastity, elegance, and gentility, my most eloquent Cassandra, so that your Rector, whom you yesterday praised to the skies,[20] may confess he is deeply indebted to you. Vale, unique glory and jewel of the female sex. Again, farewell. "I have no gleaming gifts of golden ore. I therefore send you apples as a little gift."[21] [Undated.]

XXXVI

To Lodovico da Schio,
rector of the faculty of liberal arts

Fedele excuses herself for the lateness of her response on account of her debate
and the oration she delivered at the University of Padua.
She thanks Lodovico for his gift of fruit from Vicenza.[22]

I think I should excuse myself before I respond to your beautiful letter, which was so full of kindness. If you thought my answer was a bit slow in coming, you were aware that I had many obligations, as often happens with correspondence. After my departure, when I returned home, numerous men and women not only approached me to congratulate me but actually overwhelmed me. Besides, due to their pleasure at my appearance at the University of Padua, a city renowned for its flourishing studies, as many of my friends and family as could have participated in the meeting and its debates were there with me when I delivered my oration and argued my case—listening, questioning, and entering into the disputes themselves; and this removed me for three or four days not only from my little base of operations but from writing. And what else? My pen and ink have been thrust aside for eight days now. As soon as my doors were open and I was able to marshal the tools of my trade, I set about to respond to all the letters from your excellency that lay unanswered, and even though your eloquence, not only rich but overflowing with every sort of learning, would seem to require an orator or oratrix other than me to praise you, still, so that you won't accuse me of ingratitude or cowardice, which are the greatest human sins, and so that I may satisfy not only you but myself as well, I have written you a letter in which you will see that my mind and intelligence are indebted to you in everything that brings me honor. For from your letters, which are redolent of all antiquity, I have received a twofold profit: your kindness and your extraordinary verdict on me. I see that you have a very high opinion of me; moreover, to be honest, you surpass everyone else in your praises of me. Thus, our blessed friendship brings still more pleasure, by Castor, since it has strengthened your intention to praise and honor me.

For your most generous gift of apples from the garden of the Hesperides,[23] as I think of them, and for your praises of me, I give whatever thanks I can. Even though the extraordinary goodwill that exists between us does not seem to require the doing of favors, still you will not think it odd or strange to make use of my unharmonious oration in exchange for your very great praises of me. But I shall surpass your service and homage to me in my praises and celebrations of you.

Thus you should consider that one who is quite serious, loyal, and devoted has, in speech after speech, publicly praised not only you, though you are more distinguished, but all those who are dedicated to the study of the liberal arts and who are, above all, devotees of your school—of which I certainly confess myself a member. For I seem in no way able to respond to your kindness to me and your divine learning. Still, I promise never to tire of cherishing and respecting all of you, and I would like you to believe that my constancy will endure. It makes me truly ashamed when such matters are affected by fickleness. Above all else, you should consider this about me: that I wish to follow you with loyalty and single-mindedness; for I am not forgetful of our noble pledge when we promised to declare each other's praises and to engage in the mutual work of writing encomia. Farewell, you who are mindful of us: be the guardian of my reputation if I am deserving of this. Again, farewell. Venice. November 30. At the First Olympiad Convergence of the Elements. 1488.

XXXVII

Angelo Tancredi to Diva Cassandra, glory and blessing of Venice

He praises Cassandra's performance in the debate and her oration.[24]

Even if all men—for this is the lot nature has dealt us—live amid the harsh consequences of human frailty from which, as Fabius[25] has said, almost no mortal can escape, so that some wretched and intolerable calamity seems to befall each one of us, nonetheless I was able to return to the faculty of letters at the University of Padua after many cruel battles in debates with men, though in this deceitful world I might have perished in the perilous waters of Charybdis.[26] I returned also to that Favorinus[27] of yours, the very distinguished Francesco Negri (whom some said was a Platonist, and others, a Cyllenian),[28] as though to a common asylum for sick souls, since he allowed it and even thought it a good thing to enter into such friendship with me as scarcely could be believed or described. And why must one have many friends? In this one man were located for me all friendships, companionship, alliances, and when I was without him I felt that I was bereft of the one who was the other half of my soul. And thus it is that I approach this man most prudently, not only because I shall become more learned in conversation every day, but because, despite all our disasters, in him a safe haven and good weather always await me. But the day before, after your brilliant and tightly controlled oration, I went to him more hurriedly than I am accustomed to do to ask him what he thought of your eloquence. When I see him he is still singing hymns to your immortal praises. He sighs, grieves, and is ashamed of our times and our wretchedness, and shouts that he has had no peace or serenity. Nor did he speak wrongly, Cassandra, you are the one before whom the Roman writers and the Greeks would gladly bow. "I don't know whether anyone greater has been born in the whole world."[29] Surely you are divine, maiden, since your voice hardly sounds human, or you are related to the nymphs by blood.[30] For what directives have we had from history that could sow doubt about the ancient Sibyls[31] and other famous women? Who would ask whether writers praised or envied them? Let the matter rest: belief in these things must be maintained by those who tell of them. Indeed, we all gazed with rapt attention, as in the presence of a wonder, as you spoke and debated with the philosophers at this Antenorean[32] podium for the liberal arts. And we observed a face, expression, and the maidenly lines of your entire figure that were not human but divine. We listened to your plans and your principles fresh with all the flowers of the virtues, and all of it seemed greater than can be briefly told or comprehended. But why should I linger any longer on the superb gifts of your body and mind? But if I, a tongue-tied little man, wish to take up the burden of praising you, how can the most distinguished bards of our time refuse to assume this burden as well, be it as heavy as Mt. Aetna?[33] Accept, therefore, Cassandra, the poems of my Favorinus and likewise my meager missive. For we are giving you as much as we can possibly give; giving more would be as if I were to compete with Pliny[34]—if I were able to do so—if anything greater than glory, praise, and immortality could be given to you who are already immortal. Farewell from the Faculty of Letters at Padua, and with the remembrance of a Christian salutation. 1488.

XXXVIII

To the very learned Niccolò Leonico Tomei,
professor of Greek and philosophy
at the University of Padua

Cassandra Fedele invites him to cultivate their mutual friendship,
and she thanks him for his philosophical gift.[35]

I have resolved to respond to your ornate and charmingly eloquent letters, which I received on July 7. For (as you know) I have been bogged down with many matters. When I read your letters, I recognized all your affection for me, which was apparent in every part. Nor is this affection unfamiliar to me, but it is in any case pleasing, delightful, and long awaited. When I contemplate that to which one ought especially to attend during one's life, I think of the power of friendship. But since the first principle of friendship is that two persons come together in the service of honor, of the utmost importance is mutual goodwill. It is for the sake of virtue that this goodwill—this friendship—puts down deep roots that will continue to proliferate in the richest soil. It is to this virtue that good men are accustomed to summon one another, just as we read that Laelius and Scipio[36] did.

I must confess then that our delightful friendship, which we entered into for the sake of virtue, is true friendship. And so, because of your singular learning, goodness, integrity, I dedicate myself to you with no ordinary love and invite you to do the same. And if it should seem impossible that anything be added to your love for me, nonetheless I urge that we each should seek to maintain the goodwill we have for one another. If you do this, you could do nothing that would please me more.

How highly all men of letters esteem you is clear not only to me but to everyone. And lest I seem to dote on and adulate the brilliance of your mind and your magnitude of soul, I shall pass over these qualities in silence. For the completion of my lucubrations, I could receive nothing more pleasing than this philosophical gift.[37] Therefore, it is by no means easy to find the words to thank you. For I shall not only love you, I shall serve you. But why did I speak about serving? I pay my respects to you and wish to do so. May you not then think it unworthy to relay my greetings to Calphurnius,[38] a tutor in the liberal arts. August 1486.

XXXIX

To Girolamo Campagnola

She praises his family.[39]

I am distressed. Why, you ask? Because my brother and yours and my sister-in-law have, seemingly, in praising not only the probity and excellence of your wife, but also the beauty and honor of your daughters and the intellect, memory, and character of your sons, been beating a tattoo in my ears. What else do they say? They also insist that whatever good can be attributed to their natures was assigned to them by the gods, and they declare this with such constant oratory that a jury of good men would convict them of verbosity simply by virtue of their loquacity. And what is worse, they hardly allow me to study, saying, "Listen to the unheard of things Cassandra does!" I don't know what I should do. I do beg you to help me. For you can help a great deal; you should write to them asking them not to say these things until you return. For I am pained, I admit, not to be able to see such marvelous things and enjoy them. Finally, I am perennially grateful to you for your kindnesses to them and to me, and you have no friend who is more dedicated than I to you and your family. We'll talk about the rest of the situation and many other things—face-to-face, if possible. In the meantime I commend my brother and sister-in-law, and all the rest of us to your wife, your children—of both sexes—and to you, first and foremost. [Undated.]

XL

To Girolamo Campagnola

Concerning the same theme.[40]

Even if I may have nothing to write you, or anything worth your notice, still, to satisfy your compatriot and my brother, the ever loyal Matteo, who vehemently urges me to write you, I could not have refused to send you this as a token of my goodwill toward you. You will recognize in this letter that all of us are as devoted to you and yours as we always have been, but more committedly so than ever. For your virtues and those of your friends cannot fail to bring more kindness from you to us. And so, persuade yourself that I shall serve the honor and prosperity of you and your friends with the greatest warmth. Please commend me to them all. Farewell and love. January 1492.

XLI

To Girolamo Campagnola

On attempts to stimulate one's talent with a variety of studies.[41]

If you ask what I'm doing, I will say studying the law. For whose sake are you doing this, you will ask. For the sake of a weak, fragile, and meager talent.[42] Why? So that this talent can deal with creditors and—I want to speak frankly—since talent is dependent on credit due and debts owed.[43] For it is a very sweet victory indeed to outstrip men of eloquence, and a further reason is so that one will not present oneself as uncorrected, unimproved, and unschooled. This, however, I believe is no absurd thing to demand.[44] Besides, you know, my Campagnola, how my meager talent responds to correction. Certainly the various and difficult fields of letters ensnare crowds of learned men. Nor am I talking about trivialities.

"For what place is there for genius?[45] Unless our hearts are afflicted by poetry, they are said to not give their cares over to the lords of Cyrrha and Nisa."[46]

Those who simultaneously take on diverse tasks seem to excel most in human affairs. From your last letter I learned that long ago a young boy put his talent to the test, which is something I approve of greatly and admire very much.

All that's left to say is that you should know that my loving brother and all the rest of our family send you greetings. Farewell. [Undated.]

XLII

To Jacopo Gennaro

She thanks him for the pleasing praises of her he has collected.[47]

Your admirable and singular virtue demands that I answer you in the speech of the Romans. For we are accustomed to pay our respects to learned and important men. Therefore, greetings, sweet glory of the virtues! For who would not hope for your well-being, you who abound in eloquence and virtue. How richly endowed you are in these qualities can be guessed from your elegant rhythms and beautiful verses, and all the more so because your beloved Lodovico Gatulo has praised you highly for your character and erudition in a lengthy oration at my house. Although you have praised me highly thanks to your generosity, I cannot give you equal praise and thanks, and if I could I would be afraid that I would fail to praise you for the qualities I should be praising you for. You should know one thing: all your works have seemed all the more pleasing to me, the more praiseworthy they've been. Know then that I am always prepared to serve your honor and utility. Farewell. [Undated.]

XLIII

To Jacopo Aurelio Augurello

Fedele extols the power of his eloquence and poses the philosophical question of whether the human will is capable of rejecting the good when it is put forward in an eloquent speech.[48]

*E*ven though I have often read that it is our legacy as humans that one man can impart his knowledge to another if his speech is polished and elegant, now that I have read your beautiful and sensitive poems, I have come to see this more easily for myself. Indeed, the power of your eloquence and the gravity of your speech have persuaded me of that which I certainly thought I could not be urged to do: to leave my friends, my relations, and my sweetest native city, to go to the invincible queen of Spain to whom I am eager to fly—I even beg to go—because of your most eloquent persuasion. So great is the power of sweet speech, O immortal gods, for it renders those things easiest that seem to the human mind most difficult. Since I have been very much amazed by this process, the following question has occurred to me: can the will refuse the good if it is offered to men in an elegant and beautiful oration? If one concedes that this is possible, then the will might be shown to desire the bad rather than the good, which no philosopher has dared to affirm. But if someone should say that this is not possible, is there anyone who can deny that the will is free? This would be an absurdity; and it is violently at odds with the truth. While I often brood a great deal about these things, my learned Aurelio, I have recently been more disturbed than usual. And so, because of my unusual feelings of friendship and warmth for you and yours for me, I am telling you openly the things that have come to mind as I waver back and forth. And if it is shameful to be ignorant, I can be easily reproved. But if it is a beautiful thing to seek the unknown so that we may be instructed by those who are more learned than we, then I rejoice at being instructed by you. Farewell. [Undated.]

XLIV

To Giovanni Antonio Zabarino

She praises his poems.[49]

Yesterday evening when my teacher gave me your poems to read, which display every elegance and merit the highest praise, I realized you were a man of learning and consummate eloquence. Therefore, I salute not only your learning, for which I have the highest esteem, but also your native city, which itself makes you similar to my teacher. For that region can deservedly be called fortunate that abounds not only in fertile lands and rich produce but that nourishes and fosters men of virtue and erudition. O fortunate, rich country, O felicitous Flaminian land, which I believe pays tribute to both Mercury and Jove. The delicacy, however, of your poems and your extraordinary oration strikes fear in my heart since I am nothing but a poor novice.[50] For the meager powers of my mind fail me, though I want and burn to respond to you. My tongue clings to the roof of my mouth,[51] my voice dares in vain to speak. Nonetheless, relying on your kindness, I have taken up my pen with trembling hand so that I may send you a sample of my writing, though far inferior to yours, lest you call me negligent and slothful. Criticize rather this letter as deficient in learning.

You praise me so highly in your poems and call me one of the Muses— surely this is the doing of your virtue, not mine. "Praise that comes from those who are worthy of praise is a sweet and pleasing thing since, as you know, this is the handmaiden of virtue."[52] If there is anything that would bring pleasure to you and honor to me, you have only to command it. Therefore, my most learned man, I shall bring this letter to a close lest I should seem to you verbose. Take care and be well. [Undated.]

෨

THE VENICE-UDINE CONNECTION[53]

XLV

Marcantonio Sabellico to Cassandra Fedele

He sends his Enneads *to her.*[54]

*Y*ou will say, Cassandra, that my *Enneads*[55] are finally coming to you tardily. But better late than never. As to our agreement, I preferred to risk the date promised rather than the project itself. In the latter case the plan can be blamed; in the former, chance. As you know, all duties should be judged not by their outcome but by the spirit in which they are done. You should pay attention to necessity, not delay. While the leaves are being placed in order, while the capitals are being illuminated with the slow guiding of a scarlet-inked brush, while the volume is being sewn to its roller ends, its shape perfected on dowels and lined with gold, one and then another month has gone by without my noticing it. But what if this delay results in profit? We rolled an abundance of these for you in two days' time. Unless these *Enneads* of mine are so heavy that you could not even carry them in two days' time, they could stay with you in your lodgings for more days, and they could not be anywhere more contentedly than there.

Nor should you think that the work that is coming to you is of little importance, though it contains ineptitudes. For many things are going to occur to you as you unroll the work—things that should not escape your careful attention. You should be able, then, if it is not burdensome to pour over the work for hours at a time. I will think you will have done enough by seeking out not a long series of things, which would be foolish, but a small number of passages, as though having scanned through the whole. Thus in coming to know the work in parts you will not be oppressed by it. Farewell. When you know a part, judge it against the whole. Minerva cannot be deceived by that. [Undated.]

XLVI

To Marcantonio Sabellico[56]

I received your *Enneads*, most learned man, with scarcely any trouble when they finally arrived. You should not be blamed for any delay, which should be forgiven in any case since so great a work—so great a monument—has been produced. Indeed, he who reflects on the life of the man who composed it would think that it had been a very long life. I have read much of it now, but not so much that I can judge it. Asking someone else to critique it is better than relying on my opinion. But if you are only asking what my sense of the work is, I think that nothing more useful, more beautiful, and more absolute has been done in our time. I would say that the work rivals that of the ancients were it not that I would fear that you might be suspicious that my motive was to flatter you rather than to say what I really think. But because you believe in me enough to entrust me with such a great work, I owe as much to you as the matters you treat in this volume owe to you. Farewell, O glory of literature. [Undated.]

XLVII

To Filomuso of Pesaro

She proclaims the erudition of a noble poet.[57]

P lease hear what I am doing. I am admiring your wonderful letters. Why, you ask? Are you not a Peripatetic? Still, this school seems to me to have been neglected by you. For these letters of yours indicate that you do and do not study, and that is the same as affirming and denying something at the same time—a method all the Peripatetics oppose. Perhaps these things will seem to be my *Enigmas* until I have probed them more analytically.[58] What? What do I hear, you Cicero basher[59] (to use your own term), when Aristotelian solutions are what one believes in.[60] But let me speak the truth: I rejoice if it speaks to your words; but I fear that you say false and untrue things. What are you glad of, you will ask? Except for you, I'm not afraid to enter into disputations with anyone. But really I am glad to enter into constant debates with the Muses, the Ciceros or the Sabinuses[61]—and most importantly, with Galeazzo, who is distinguished in every sort of learning and adornment, and with eloquent Benedetto,[62] whose praises I would sing as eloquently as I can. But I am afraid of muddying their praises with my proclamations.

But let me come to the *Enigmas*. Your elegant writings have eschewed the study of this work because of the lack of books.[63] You affirm, however, how polished and charming the *Enigmas* were and that the work could not have been written except by a serious scholar. What do you say, Cassandra? Are you failing to pay attention to the divine Filomuso, a man of Greek brilliance and Roman gravity whom no one in our country can surpass in the liberal arts? But enough about this. I want you to know that I am applying myself to my studies with all diligence. Have good thoughts about my health and my father's, and be mindful of your own. Farewell, glory of our century. [Undated.]

XLVIII

To Filomuso

Cassandra agrees to study Aristotelian philosophy.[64]

*Y*ou will both laugh and be appalled when you read this ignorant letter. You will laugh that I, a mere girl, aspire to things extremely difficult, even for a man. And you will be appalled that, due to the weakness of my mind, I am not capable of understanding these things. But to probe more searchingly,[65] sometimes I am angry because Aristotle's beliefs don't want to be understood by me and like a brilliant ray of light they scorn me as if I were darkness itself. It is not clear to me that I should adore him with honey-sweet compliments or regard him with disgust. Nor is it necessary for me to fashion myself after your little work, even if without it I could do nothing. Therefore, what I shall do I don't yet know. But let me speak the truth: while the literary men do not hesitate to count this philosopher both among the critics of Cicero and the greatest of the Peripatetics, they also are aware that I am completely deficient in the Aristotelian method. Therefore, I shall not cease to beg him by expression, gesture, and the sweetest words and to say, "O charming leader, I beg you to allow me, Cassandra, to understand you, even though you are considered the prince among philosophers, still you are known to be humane and kind to those who wish to be your pupils, and this is permitted to each whether great or small." You ask what cares keep me up all night? What's this I hear? What cares, you ask? Ah, you ask, as though you were my host, how I have worn myself out in strange silence, in darkness, and constant diligence, wholly fixated on studies in the Peripatetic philosophers. Farewell, paragon of all the virtues. [Undated.]

XLIX

To Filomuso

She celebrates his poems.[66]

"What are you doing, Cassandra? Do my letters and erudite rhythms not please you?" you ask. On the contrary, your works are quite pleasing, but they have been written in so elegant a style that I have been unable to read them. But I cannot cease to thank you, for I am aware that in the composing of such long letters you have done painstaking and elaborate work with poetic schemes. Why do I not read these, you will ask? How much human feeling there is in these works, how sweet they are, how eloquent, how delightful! This much I confess. For really, you have composed every work beautifully, but you keep me from sleep, and I am here, in constant fog; neither have I any light nor doorways out of here, and what is worse, I cannot rouse anyone from sleep. From this time on, I grieve strangely. For I think the world is going to collapse. Really, I sleep, lest ghosts should assail me while I lie sleepless. When all humans are in their beds, I—as if alone in the light opposite innumerable bodies of the dead—see all the more that I must go to sleep since not only your Cicero but also my Aristotle abandons and scorns me. Therefore, don't write to me until the apostle calls us, saying: "Now is the hour for you to awake from your sleep."[67] In the meantime, you will triumph in earnest, as you are used to doing. Farewell. [Undated.]

L

To Filomuso

She praises Filomuso's poetry and thanks him for his poem praising her.[68]

Having read your verses, you should know how much intellectual pleasure and sheer enjoyment I have received. I realize this is not possible. For such erudite and refined polish seems to flow from the beauty of your diction and the gravity of your thoughts that they bubble up not as from a new spring but as though from an ancient one, moss-covered and full of every charm; and it is to these ancient waters, whose antiquity itself is canny, that your poems should be compared. Therefore, I would be afraid to praise and celebrate in these numerous letters of mine the brilliance of your mind, the authority of your most excellent family, and the renown of your name not only in Ferrara but also throughout all of Italy, since you and your poetry deserve to be extolled not by my homely Minerva but by a very famous orator.

Thus I know for certain that I am indebted to you in every way, not only because of your lofty erudition and the integrity of your virtues but also because of the praises you lavished on me in your poem. How deeply these undeserved praises have touched me you can easily guess. Farewell. Venice.

LI

To Giovanni Battista Scita

She disparages her own talent and thanks him for his visit.[69]

At last I have had the time to send you some brief letters. "But you've had problems writing, Cassandra," you'll say? Good gods, what do you want? Have you not noticed the lack of cultivation of my mind, thanks to whose limitations not only have I barely touched on my own not wholly impenetrable studies in dialectics (as you well know) but also your own, despite constant efforts to the contrary. Alas, my dear Scita, you who are possessed of a superior mind, surpassing judgment, and the flowers of learning and who have listened to the speech of one who is uncultivated, are unaware of the learning of which I am capable. But of this, even if the powers of my mind have never appeared weak, you, not I, must be the judge. For when you have visited me you have brought with you such an aura of brilliance that I myself was so imbued with it that those who came to me were rendered dumbstruck. Finally, I have received from you, Scita, letters beautiful in their eloquence and worthy of the highest praise, about which I would say more were it ever to appear that your keen and agile mind should desire a more prolix essay from me. Farewell, O flower of literature.

LII

To Giovanni Battista Scita

She agrees on the defense of a poet.[70]

Be well, you who are the glory of the Virtues. I have no idea what you are engaged in since I've been away so long. But I have heard from the Muses that you are consumed by great protestations and that they are getting the better of you, my Scita. Once I get the information from you, you will know, by heaven, that I will demonstrate that they are the guilty ones, and I shall make them regret their own thoughts. Indeed, I believe one's friends should be protected—you especially, since I think of you as not ordinary but unique in your good qualities. Because of the enormity of your learning and the fertileness of your virtues you ought to be honorably loved and venerated by me. You know, then, my seer[71] and Muse, how many months went by when I wrote letters that were meant to be sent to you and how many times you and I stood at the same threshold. But I don't know what accident kept the letters from being delivered to you; I think that surely the mice devoured them. But let me think of something sweeter. Here, then, is a little letter from which you will learn of all my doings. I beg you to provide the same for me. Vale, and if it is necessary for me to protect you, you will be protected. Farewell again. Venice. June [Undated.]

᠕

THE VERONA CONNECTION

LIII

To Matteo Bosso

She promises to serve him.[72]

Have a look at these letters, most learned Matteo, which you so zealously demanded of me when we spoke face-to-face, though they are not of the sort that might seem to be able to confer any honor or advantage upon you. Still, it is very gratifying to us that you ask us to perform the duty of writing to you, who are a man of the highest virtue and eloquence. And so, the main purpose of this epistle is to say that I shall never be wanting in any matter of your honor and utility. Farewell. [Undated.]

LIV

To Panfilo Sasso

She praises his poems.[73]

I have always thought all illustrious men and those similar to you were happy. Such men delight in exercising that faculty of the mind, which is unchanging and is theirs alone, with complete concentration and engagement. But I praise you above all others and admire you, not only because you desired to surpass the men of this age, but also because you wished to equal those of the ancient world as well. And when I read and reread through your poems I seemed to hear the gravity of speech and the sweetness of the ancient bards. Since you have celebrated me in these poems of yours with such kindness, I shall praise you, lest I should be afraid to lionize you because of these poems of yours, for which I owe you a debt of thanks. Rest assured then that I shall honor you with extraordinary goodwill because of the innumerable gifts from your heart and mind. Farewell. [Undated.]

LV

Panfilo Sasso to Cassandra Fedele

On his age, life, and mind. An encomium of the city of Verona and the hopeless illness of Laura Donata.[74]

Hello, Cassandra, flower of fearless virginity and golden trophy of the liberal arts and letters. You have charged and convicted me at the same time, lazy man that I am, of the crime of negligence. I would only like you to know, veritable mother of learning and wisdom and dearest daughter of age, that my love for you—no, I should say my loyalty—is so great that although your name resounds throughout the whole world, I, of all the learned men I know, am the greatest and most untiring herald of your praises. And since I, Panfilo Sasso of Modena, who have lived on a street by the name of Rapha within the precincts of this land of Verona for thirty-eight years, cause men to stop and marvel (an effect you also have with your good letters on the subjects of philosophy and theology), beguiled by my extemporaneous poems, which are sung in meters and accompanied on the lyre or kithara, I also have sent you praises of yourself in addition to my prior eulogy of you. This man has written the two enclosed epigrams in your honor, and having done something previously through my writings, he has voluntarily chosen himself from among the many literary men as your adoptive father.

Look, Cassandra, at what fame I am going to pursue among mortal men before I die, insofar as the stars will smile kindly upon me. This happy circumstance would be still more favorable to me if I were to engender children of genius[75] naturally, but would also kindly do the same in the willing adoption or arrogation, if you will, of the children of other parents, in the way that you and Panfilo, stars on earth yourselves, are related. Therefore let there be everlasting thanks to God, the greatest and best of all celestial beings. We, who are inhabitants and sojourners here, pray not only that we obtain the shelter of His protection, but also that Giulio[76] may pursue those virtues that are especially agreeable.

This city is indeed a celebrated haven for literary men and great artists, but the rest is all womanish and ritual consolation.[77] We intellectuals behave foolishly and are at a loss and shaken by the grave illness of magnificent Laura Donata, whom, though we hoped she could be cured by the doctors at the beginning of spring with the changing of the seasons, we fear all hope (so we have heard) is in vain. But even if we are untiring and do not desist from our oblations to God and our secular orations, still we hope we may apply in our grief to the cloistered sisters who are sympathetic to our pleas and to you whom we do not hesitate to portray as a heavenly being. For we know your own loyalty and that of your family to both spouses. Farewell and greetings to all our mutual friends and to your parents; tell everyone else to be well. Verona. March 1493.

LVI

To Panfilo Sasso

Cassandra acknowledges their mutual affection and is pleased. She too recognizes Julius's talent. She mourns the death of Laura Donata.[78]

I have read and reread your beautiful letters again and again. They strike me as no less amiable than they are elegant, and from reading them I have received a great variety of benefits. Especially when you declared in every part of these letters that you loved and, what is more, esteemed me, it made me happiest. But it should please me more that the same has become true for me about you, and for a long time. You also suggest that I should be surprised that our Giulio is making such progress on the path to virtue? Well, I am not in the least, for I am acquainted with his mind and memory. No more about this then.

I am in very great pain. For it has been announced, even as I sit here writing, that the light and glory of our life, Laura Donata, has passed away and left us to mourn her. Farewell, and please do greet all our friends and love us.

LVII

Girolamo Broianico da Verona to Cassandra

He praises her intellect and charm and also the exercise of her womanly skill, and he exhorts her to decide upon the study of virtue and letters.[79]

A common maxim that the Greek Isocrates[80] addressed to Demonicus is this: to the end that every man who possesses virtue may be loved and respected, let him embrace it with the greatest zeal. With this in mind, after Francesco Veronese,[81] my compatriot—who is young, modest, sincere, adorned with virtue, and on whom I so depend among my friends that I esteem none more dearly than him, and who is half my soul—had been at my house the other day, it could be said that he makes resound that maxim, and is one whom I so love, esteem, and respect that Orestes, Phythias, and Laelius would not proclaim to history that they had loved Pylades, Damon, and Scipio[82] with as much mutual love. He has wondrously extolled your learning, virtue, wisdom, and beauty to me. And so, I am impressed by the grace of your virtues—such honors must be praised in whatever manner it is permitted to do so. Yet I am accustomed to admire exceedingly such traits in a woman when we see her so very cultivated in the pursuit of letters that she—you—seem to be a second Minerva[83] descended from heaven. And I could do nothing but offer you these paltry words in exchange.

I have seen that you alone have been graced with the venerable character of the noble Roman women of the Cornelii and Porcii and the daughters of Pisistratus.[84] Your name is Cassandra, but I say, truly are you Cassandra in your demeanor and beauty. For you are second neither to Lucretia, the purest of women, nor to Helen,[85] whose beauty you possess, and whom no one wished to gaze upon lest they should fall madly in love with her. Your shining blue eyes are like divine stars. . . . your heart, . . . the way you walk, which . . . is so graceful[86] that you are declared to be not a mere girl but a goddess. You differ from the goddess in this respect, however: she herself was unchaste, whereas you truly are a most pure girl. Your hands, on which there is no stain, so sparkle with the art of Arachne and Pallas[87] that it is more than credible that they should be said to weave and to paint with a needle. But why should I compare you with ancient women and those descended from noble stock? Since you bear the name of the Fedeli and are a true member of the Christian faith, you should strive to imitate Catherine, Agnes, Lucia,[88] who did not hesitate to expose their very beautiful and alluring bodies to tortures for the sake of their passion for the Lord Christ. It is to the emulation of the most honorable lives and the sacred mores of these women and the devotion with burning desire to the study of literature that I urge you. And with this I shall bring to an end this letter, for I know that the powers of my meager mind are being sadly weakened, such as they are, by the work of describing your lofty virtues. And though I have said much, very many things remain unsaid. Do not in any sense leave off from the things you have begun, do not abandon the study of letters, and conserve and increase the great virtues you possess, if they can possibly be increased. Farewell. [Undated.]

LVIII

To Girolamo Broianico Veronese

She responds with thanks and reciprocates with praises of him.[89]

*H*ector, according to Naevius, said the following: "I am very happy to be praised by you, father, who are the object of praise; for praise is pleasing if it comes from one who lives by praise."[90] Do not be surprised, most eloquent one, that I thought I ought to embark upon such a theme in this simple and uncultivated letter since I am extremely happy to be commended by you, a man whose life deservedly has been crowned with every sort of praise. For what is more elegant than your celebrated and brilliant ideas? What is more admirable than your letter, which gleams with the sheen of its style? Your letter is written so eloquently and is so beautifully arranged that I can think of no one I would esteem more highly since it is not possible to write more elegantly.

And though you are in possession of the precious gift of eloquence, the mistress and queen of human affairs, for my part I do not think such things are worthy of our admiration: on the other hand, the degree to which you are dedicated to the service of God can easily be seen from the very letters you have sent me. For I praise the former virtue; however, I respect most the latter.

And affected by that, I cannot fail to be very much in your debt, even if I have never seen or had the opportunity to know you. When I have considered that I ought to esteem people I have never seen on account of their virtue and honor, I give great thanks to you for the accolades you have showered upon me, which in my opinion are worthy not only of a chaste young girl but also of a goddess. The immense kindness and virtue that is yours, which impels you to speak in this way, has brought this about. Would that it had been my good fortune to be worthy of this good opinion of yours.

You write, however, that you consider no one more warmly and love no one more dearly than your compatriot Francesco Veronese. I rejoice exceedingly and in particular because you dared to honor him with such love as Pythias had for Damon and Laelius for Scipio. Oh, blessed and almost immortal are those who enter into such an elegant and spacious lovers' chamber of friendship and so superb a portico and temple.[91] What else? I hope you will think it worthwhile to convey my greatest thanks to my

Francesco and yours on behalf of his services to me, which have been very great and which, as long as I have breath in my limbs, I shall not forget. I, however, will strive with all my strength not to abandon the study of literature. And if you will send your letters to me, I will know that you welcome my friendship and keep them as witnesses to our mutual goodwill. Farewell. [Undated.]

LIX

To Girolamo Bentacordo da Verona

She apologizes for the brevity of her praise.[92]

If you read this very brief letter, you will hardly be gripped with admiration. For I shall imitate the philosophers who extol brevity above all else in writing and also those epistolographers who are particularly noted for their epistolary economy. Therefore I shall appear to have abandoned my own precepts. For I had decided to praise and celebrate you, as is right. But it would seem that this is not possible with a long oration. For so great is the field of your virtue[93] that I must turn my attention to myself, for I am in agreement with the philosophers. About myself, however, one can make only the briefest statement: indeed, one cannot be too brief. I am not qualified to speak from a position of talent or learning; my task is to put my trust in others. These are my virtues. Hear, I beg, how meager they are, how I tell them all with a single word. Nor can I tell all your virtues. My job, then, is not to write about your many virtues but to talk about my few virtues. Besides, I shall answer your excellent man Paris all the more gladly because his request pertains especially to the philosophers. For it is the poets' burden to seek glory; the philosophers', however, is to unravel the causes of things.[94] But you will recognize this yourself in our sluggish Minerva.[95] Farewell. [Undated.]

ᗢ

THE VENICE-MILAN CONNECTION

LX

To Bonifacio Bembo

She apologizes to him for her delay in writing.[96]

If you remonstrate loudly with me, my Bonifacio, you can rightly be blamed by me, for "we ought not to complain about friends, especially when they have done that which they are supposed to do."[97] To what purpose will you say these things? Am I not sending you my tardy little letter? I admit this willingly. For our singular custom demands this so that I can strive for the friendship of others and work energetically on those things that will pave my way to everlasting fame. Even if "I judge that it is more satisfactory to do one thing with distinction than many in a mediocre manner,"[98] still, although I had not simply tasted the sweetness of eloquence and the sublimity of the liberal arts in the manner of the dialecticians—to use your word—but being skilled, I had immersed myself in them, I attempted to acquire them both to the best of my ability. Nor do my perennial duties and services in fact vanish in vain day after day. I truly rejoice, and why not? For who does not desire to strive for glory and a reputation for virtue? I am inspired to write to you because I take very great pleasure in your mind, yet being far away, I cannot enjoy this pleasure face-to-face.

For you do not begrudge giving praises to anyone since you have people fawning on you on all sides, and yet you are supportive of my paltry compositions. Recently I received your letter given with an oration to my father, who reported that you are much visited, are living your life, and are triumphing in earnest. And this has been a source of great happiness to me because of my unmitigated goodwill toward you. Your letters were finally received by everyone with great enthusiasm, with the exception of Valdora, who is away.

What remains is for me to beg and beseech you above all to give greetings from my father and me to the Venetian orator, a very brilliant man and my compatriot, who some years ago performed a rhetorical duty for the duke of Milan in our Senate. Farewell, and greetings to you. I entrust myself to you. [Undated.]

LXI

To Bonifacio Bembo

She congratulates him.[99]

Greetings, glory of the virtues. We are all well, and we have heard that you've triumphed in earnest. For you are praised publicly and magnificently, and you are even sometimes celebrated in my presence. At that time, I may become a chattering magpie, as is my wont, stuttering over an awkward oration. Now you know it all, O most fortunate man! I follow you with the greatest devotion so that I may also appear fortunate. Don't you approve of my idea? And why not? For "everything prevents us from hoping for happiness."[100]

Finally, it is right to esteem a man who is zealous about the lesser virtues and devoted to you, and who loves and courts you so that a mutual friendship may develop. For our friends should be allowed to love us. Farewell.

I send you greetings from my parents. You should know that I not only entrust myself to you but to everything else that is full of virtue. Again, farewell. [Undated.]

LXII

To the very learned Bonifacio Bembo

Cassandra thanks him for his encomium of her and praises his poems.[101]

It should come as no surprise to you that my response to your poems is tardy. For I see that I have performed the duty of a true friend. If I had responded to your poem before I answered the letter that has now been delivered to me from you (though its contents were previously unknown), I would have completely trusted in our friendship. For this friendship has long existed between us and is one that I think should be tended to with honor and respect as though we were joined by kinship, to the end that nothing is closer than the bond we share. And even if the envious think otherwise, I in any case think little of their opinion. For you have long been aware of my honorable respect for you; moreover, it is so venerable that the envious cannot weaken it. I would like to persuade you of this, my Bembo: I would expend the greatest effort defending whatever pertains to the increase of your honor and fame—if they ever could be increased, for they are already so great. But I ought not to promise things that involve unending thought and anxiety for me. For your virtues are so great that they would receive the highest praises from all men anyway.

But I shall return to your poems so redolent of antiquity. How much they pleased me you can well imagine, even if I were to say nothing at all. Nor should we wonder that among the ancients, men believed that poets were possessed of divinity. Of this Ovid himself sang as follows: "The god resides in us: the deity comes to us. These are heaven's gifts."[102]

Since you are endowed with the power of the art of the poet, I believe and am convinced that you among the most consummate poets will be perfect and superior in your art, and as I shall say specifically, I think you already perfect in this and believe your wondrous intellect and superb learning are worthy of a crown of laurel. And when you celebrate me in your verses, you do so as is the custom of all the poets; but because you so easily surpass them does not in itself endow me with any power. For I am well aware how strong my meager talent is. Be well.

LXIII

Bonifacio Bembo to Cassandra

He mentions his praise of her and promises to reciprocate.[103]

*H*ello, my darling[104] and my jewel. I am well, Cassandra. I have been absorbed in my own solitude for some days now. I had charge of those sweet, pretty, delicate, and gentle little boys without their parents. So to my great annoyance, I could not write until today. I wanted you at least to receive greetings from me for our Testa.[105] Consider now what I have been doing and that my life has been entirely without solace for so many days. Now I am beginning to take stock. You will have a letter every day from me if I receive one from you—longer and more gentle ones every day. I long to hear what you are doing with your studies, what Gasparino[106] is doing and has been doing if he's back. Farewell. Poisolo at Castelfranco. August. [Undated.]

LXIV

To Bonifacio Bembo, most worthy man

Cassandra praises him and invites him to come to Venice.[107]

I received your letter. It was delivered by the most excellent doctor Giovanni[108] who is bound to you in fraternal love, but it is not possible for me to praise your eloquence though it should be clear to everyone that no one equals you in talent and intellect, elegance of speech, or in your moral virtue. Truly, no one is considered more distinguished than you, and all sing, as though with a single voice, your innumerable praises. But you yourself, take stock of your virtues, and take a look at the panegyrics about you, and you will recognize that all men think in the same way about your worth. But if I were to describe in detail everything I know about your virtues and everything other people think, it would be long enough. May you consider this one message wherever you are: may you consider that your virtues will be your guides wherever you are and your praises will be celebrated especially because you are bound to me in unique and holy benevolence since I have been imbued by the fertile creativity of your mind. Therefore you yourself will understand how sadly I have endured your departure ever since I have been away from your teaching.

Therefore, take care to return as soon as possible. Your return is awaited not only by me, believe me, but by everyone here, particularly my teacher Gasparino[109] of the Order of the Servites who has necessarily benefited from your virtue and impeccable character, who commends himself most enthusiastically to you. We have heard nothing about our most reverend Prior Girolamo,[110] but we are anticipating his arrival almost immediately. But enough about all this.

I shall come now to what you wish to know—whether I am excited, as I am accustomed to be, about my literary studies. Know this: I am passionately engaged in these studies. Indeed, I am becoming more and more involved each day thanks to the diligence and earnestness of my teacher, and I take great pleasure in my studies. I would say more, but I trust I will see you soon. I send you my own greetings and those of my very earnest father. Take care, and be well. Venice. September 1487.

⁓

THE FLORENTINE CONNECTION[111]

LXV

Angelo Poliziano to Cassandra Fedele, the most learned girl in Venice

An encomium of her.[112]

O maiden, glory of Italy, what homage could I prepare to pay you or say to you that you would dismiss as not worthy of the honor your letter brought me? It is amazing to think that such a letter came from a *woman* (but why do I use that word?): I should say instead: a girl and one not yet married.

Earlier times no longer have the right to boast about their Muses, Sibyls, Pythian prophetesses, Pythagorean women philosophers, Socrates' Diotima, or Aspasia.[113] Nor should Greek monuments show off the names of their women poets: Telesilla, Corinna, Sappho, Anyte, Erinna, Praxilla, Cleobula, and others. We can now easily believe the Romans and their stories of the eloquence of Laelius's and Hortensius's daughters and of Cornelia, mother of the Gracchi. We know this much; nor do we believe that the female sex was naturally consigned to stupidity and dimness. Your sex has been praised down through the ages, just as we find among the lowest slaves who have reached the pinnacles of literature and philosophy. But in our own time when few men have achieved much in literature, only you, a girl, exist, who would rather comb a book than wool, paint with a quill rather than rouge, stitch with a pen rather than a needle, and who would rather cover papyrus with ink than her skin with white powder. And this is no more odd or less strange than if violets were to grow in ice, roses in snow, or lilies in the midst of frost. But if the attempt itself is seen as a miracle, what shall we say of such great advances in scholarship? You will, Cassandra, write subtle, elegant, articulate Latin missives, and although with a certain girlish grace, a certain virginal simplicity, they will still be very sweet and also serious and prudent. I have also read your oration, which is erudite, eloquent, sonorous, brilliant, and full of felicitous talent. Nor have we heard that you lacked the ability to compose extemporaneously, a gift that even great orators sometimes lack. You are also said, when you practice dialectics, to tie knots that cannot be unknotted and to explicate mysteries that others have never before solved. Thus you so comprehend philosophy that you quickly and vehemently defend all questions posed and formulated and you dare, though a maid, to run with the men. Thus it was in the playing field of scholarly studies that sex did not stand in the way of your mind, nor mind in the way of modesty, nor modesty in the way of genius. And though no one would fail to praise you, still you restrain your own and your audience's opinion of you modestly and respectfully when you cast your virginal eyes down on the ground. O, who will stop me right now, so that I may gaze at your pure maiden's face, admire your look, manner, gestures and, as if with thirsting ears, drink in your words, which come to you as though dictated to you by the Muses, and finally so that I may step forth suddenly, a poet made perfect by your presence. May no Thracian Orpheus or Linus win me over with their poems, although Callopea was Orpheus's mother and beautiful Apollo was Linus's father.[114] I used to admire Giovanni Pico Mirandola[115] in the old days, nor did I think there was anyone more handsome or more superior in every realm of scholarship than he. But now I have begun to respect you, Cassandra, next after him, and perhaps even already right beside him. May God Almighty grant you good fortune in all your undertakings. And when you leave your parents, may you have a supporter and consort worthy of your virtue, so that, just as now the flame of your natural genius sparkles on its own, so may it later gleam nourished by tinder and the winds, so that night and the chill of all ignorance and boredom with letters may be dispersed from the hearts and minds of the men of Italy. Vale.

LXVI

To Angelo Poliziano

She invites Poliziano to write to her and to participate in an edition of her works.[116]

Even if I confess, glory of our age, to being slow in answering your letter, still it is not just of you to accuse me of negligence, for I shall accuse you of the same injustice, especially since you promised me you would deluge me with letters. In any case, I believe there has been no negligence; you all the same have been forgetful of our friendship—a more serious offense in my view. I was very pleased to be loved by you and counted among the circle of your friends. If you are careless about our friendship, remember at least your promise: don't say you will foster that same relationship and then deny it. See to it that the end of the friendship agrees with its beginning. And since I love all your friends on your account, it is only fair, indeed for your sake, to ask you to produce the piece of writing you have long been contemplating; to prevail on you to write something that is worthy of you so that I can enjoy it and profit from reading it. Your gift to me is this: your encomium of me, your Cassandra. Alas, why have I said Cassandra rather than your city, the flower of the whole world? Everyone in the whole world not only expects this, they demand it. Enough on this, since I know you already know all about it. Other than that, I beg you likewise to greet in the same way Marsilio Ficino and Bartolomeo Scalo,[117] the most learned men in your city, on behalf of me and my whole family, and do not forget to send my regards to my most excellent sister, Alessandra. July. [Undated.]

LXVII

To Angelo Poliziano

She excuses the lateness of her letter.[118]

I hear that you want to take me to court because I took too long to answer the letter I owed you. ". . . harsh act . . ."[119] For as many times as you accuse me I shall deny your charges, especially considering that no one would dare to testify that I am your debtor. Enough joking. I am in your debt; still I pay you, though the payment is tardy. Better late than never, however. To make an end of this, you should know that a man highly accomplished in the liberal arts, Magister Pizamano,[120] has declared that I am much loved by you and also by Alessandra,[121] about whom he told me many things when I saw him. For this I will continue to owe a double debt, and also to her most excellent father. Do send him my best wishes. Farewell, O happy wind. April 1494.

LXVIII

Angelo Poliziano to Cassandra

He excuses his silence.[122]

*Y*our letter seriously charges that after I left you, I neither sent you letters nor did any of the things I promised you when we were together. My dear Cassandra, I will explain the reason for this—as if to admit to your charges—so that you will not be offended at my lapsed duty. When I came to Venice to visit and pay my respects to you, which was the primary reason for my coming to Venice, and when you appeared like a nymph from the forest wearing a beautiful gown and so beautiful yourself, having long expected me, and when you addressed me with your flowing and, as I would say, elegant words intoning a divine music, it was then that my mind became paralyzed with wonder (I believe you remember this) by the extraordinary nature of the meeting. As Aeneas said about himself, being disturbed, my mouth gaped open, and I could only stammer, struggling to get a few words out.[123] This could scarcely excuse my speechlessness to you. The rest later. [Undated.]

LXIX

To Bartolomeo Scala

She congratulates him for having brought up a daughter educated in literature.[124]

I congratulate and thank you, O man of virtue and honor, for having dedicated your daughter, who is the soul of virtue, to the study of literature. But why? From her letter I recognized that dry kindling had been added to a fire because of which rewards have been offered to you of the sort that all prudent men of genius usually hope to receive from the gods, and that bring fame and a reputation for virtue to you. I confess that I am in your debt, for this much the weight of your virtue exacts and asks. Farewell. [Undated.]

LXX

To Bartolomeo Scala

The geniuses of our own time are in no way inferior to the ancients;
therefore the study of true virtue is necessary.[125]

*W*e say that the race of men is defined by our Peripatetic as a rational animal,[126] for we surpass the rest of living things in that we
possess reason. In this way we are similar to the gods; we read in Plato that
we differ from them only in our mortality. It is no wonder, then, that with
reason as your guide you have equaled the ancients whom you greatly extol.
If this reason thrives in us as we hear it flourished in the ancients, we also
shall be added to those who apply themselves to study. There are times of
ascent and times of decline, and even the stars and the poles of heaven are
changed. Nor for my part will I cease to imitate antiquity, so that if I am
able to attain the virtues of the ancients I shall burn with a desire for true
goodness.

Finally, you should consider that a very pleasing thing has happened to
me, namely, that I came to know the same thing about our Alessandra from
your letters that I had learned from your dedicated friend Matteo[127] when
we spoke face-to-face, and I can see that this matter was highly gratifying
to you. The feeling is mutual because of my extraordinary esteem for you,
and it has made me all the more appreciative of you to be made much of by
you and, still more, to know how much I am esteemed by your family and
friends. Thus I want you to know that I will never cease to love you like a
father. Farewell. January 1492.

LXXI

To Pico della Mirandola[128]

I rejoice that you desire my letters. I am not really surprised since I
know I have always been respected by you. And so, to satisfy you I
write simply to say that I have nothing to write about. Ever since I have
dedicated myself to different kinds of studies it has been hard for me to
speak a word much less compose an epistle. In addition to this, I beg you

to give my and our whole family's greetings to Bartolomeo, his daughter Alessandra, Marsilio Ficino, Angelo Poliziano, and Cristoforo Landino, the most learned of men. April 1494.

NOTES TO CHAPTER 4

1. Though only a small sample of her correspondence is extant in Tomasini's edition of her *Epistolae*, it is clear from Tomasini's testimony regarding the piles of Fedele correspondence he originally worked from and from the letters that do survive that her network was extensive. On his sources see the introduction in Tomasini (44–46).

2. See Margaret King, *Venetian Humanism in an Age of Patrician Dominance* (Princeton: Princeton University Press, 1986), 224–25. King notes that in the fifteenth century the University of Padua "became Venice's university." Venetian subjects were allowed to study nowhere other than this "flourishing center of Aristotelian philosophy," which in fact owed its development to Venice's close regulation of its curriculum and hiring (225).

3. On the writings of Augurello (1440–1515) see Giuseppe Pavanello, *Un maestro del Quattrocento (Giovanni Aurelio Augurello)*; Girolamo Tiraboschi, *Biblioteca Modense o Notizie della vita e delle opere degli scrittori nati degli stati del serenissimo signor duca di Modena* (Modena: Società, 1781–86), 22–24; and R. Weiss, "Giovanni Aurelio Augurello," *DBI* (1962), vol. 4, 578–81.

4. On Ramusio (1443–1506) see Pavanello, *Un maestro del Quattrocento*; and Cesira Cavazzana, "Cassandra Fedele," 250–51.

5. Sabellico (1436–1506) was in Udine 1472–83 and in Verona in 1484–86 where he finished thirty-two books of his history of Venice. He taught at the School of San Marco in Venice, see King, *Venetian Humanism*, 425–27. On Filomuso (c. 1440–1506) see G. Pavanello, *Un maestro del Quattrocento*. Filomuso was born in Pesaro; he served as *preposto* (canon) at the cathedral there. Sabellico got him his post as maestro at Udine in 1489; he came to Venice as an *arciprelato* (bishop) in 1505 (both suggest high ecclesiastical titles).

6. On Bosso (1427–1502), abbot at the Badia in Fiesole through the 1480s and early 1490s, see Giovanni Maria Mazzuchelli, *Gli scrittori d'Italia*. He was a famous Veronese humanist who taught Ermolao Barbaro, later patriarch of Aquileia and ambassador to Duke Lodovico Sforza of Milan. Bosso's correspondents included Cassandra Fedele, Giovanni Pico della Mirandola, Bernardo Giustiniani, Francesco Gonzaga, Lorenzo de' Medici, among others. He taught at Padua in 1451 and again in the late 1490s. See also C. Mutini, "Matteo Bosso," *DBI* (1971), vol. 13, 341–4.

7. On Panfilo Sasso see Pavanello, *Un maestro del Quattrocento*, 180–81: Sasso was born in Modena in 1455 and was a poet and close friend of Augurello. He left Modena to live in Rafa on the outskirts of Verona in 1494 and there met Bosso. Sasso was well versed in philosophy, dialectics, and oratory and wrote in Latin and the vernacular; he wrote a eulogy of Brescia. On Cendrata see King, *Venetian Humanism*, 366, 411. Cendrata was sent in 1491 to Venice by the city of Verona as its orator to

argue his city's case against Venice. He met Fedele that year and heard her speak. Nothing further is known about Fedele's Veronese friends Bentacordo and Broianico.

8.   See Fedele's correspondence with Alessandra in letters XI–XIII.

9.   On Poliziano (1454–94) see *Il Poliziano e il suo tempo*. After Ficino, Poliziano was the most brilliant of the Hellenists of his generation. In addition to the sons of Lorenzo de' Medici, he tutored Alessandra Scala; he also composed numerous poems in Latin and Greek, edited Latin and Greek texts, published his learned Latin letters, and composed two volumes of literary critical essays.

10.   *Respublica litterarum*: the standard humanist phrase to denote the informal associations of learned men who met together or wrote to one another to discuss literary and philosophical questions.

11.   On Negri (1452–1515) see King, *Venetian Humanism*, 413–14. Negri had a brilliant reputation as a scholar of Greek philosophy. He taught in Padua, Rome, and Hungary. On Tancredi and Gennari see Cavazzana, "Cassandra Fedele," 250, 251, 256.

12.   On da Schio see Cavazzana, "Cassandra Fedele," 253.

13.   On Campagnola see E. Safrik, "Girolamo Campagnola," *DBI* (1974), vol. 17, 317–18.

14.   On Tomeo (or Tomei) see King, *Venetian Humanism*, 432–33. Tomeo was born in Venice in 1456, the son of a Greek emigrant, and died in Padua in 1531. He earned his doctorate at the university in Padua under Chalcondylas in 1485; he occupied the chair of Greek at the school of San Marco in Venice from 1494 to 1506. He was an important figure in the development of science at the University of Padua and a key participant in the controversy over the relationship between Plato and Aristotle, whom he saw as compatible.

15.   On Bonifacio Bembo see Mazzuchelli, *Scrittori d'Italia*, 728–29. Born in Brescia in the 1460s, Bembo opened a humanist school near Castelfranco. After some years at Pavia, Bembo was hired in 1493 by Pope Innocent VIII as professor of rhetoric at the Studio in Rome. Mazzuchelli gives no dates for his life. See also A. Baldino, "Bonifacio Bembo," *DBI* (1996), vol. 8, 111–12.

16.   See Tom. 98, 144–46. See Cavazzana, "Cassandra Fedele," 253. Tomasini spells this addressee's surname "Scledeus," but as a general rule I have followed Cavazzana's italianized versions of Fedele's addressees' names.

17.   Famous woman orator, daughter of celebrated Roman orator Hortensius; in 42 B.C.E. in the Forum she successfully argued against a luxury tax the Triumvirs had levied against wealthy women.

18.   Virgil *Aeneid* 4.12. Tomasini sets off quotations in the letter texts by switching from italic to roman type.

19.   "Desinat ad Coelum iam laude extollere Vatem / Mantua Virgilium taceat Verona Catullum / Graecia nec docti memoret monumenta Platonis / Magnaque iam sileat Ciceronem Roma disertum." The source of this quotation is unknown to me.

20.   He refers here to Fedele's praise for the faculty at the University of Padua in her oration for Bertuccio Lamberti.

21.   "Non mihi sunt fulvi radiantia dona metalli, / Mitto igitur parvo munere poma tibi." The source of this elegiac couplet is unknown to me.

22.   See Tom. 99, 146–48.

23.   In Greek mythology the Hesperides (the "daughters of evening") guarded the golden apples that Hera received as a marriage gift. It was the last of Hercules' labors to get possession of the apples.

24.   Tom. 100, 149–51. On Tancredi see introduction to this chapter and n. 10 above.

25.   Fabius Pictor (254 B.C.E.), the earliest known Roman historian. Livy drew from Pictor's chronicles in his history of Rome.

26.   In Greek myth a whirlpool off the coast of Sicily perilous to sailors; Charybdis stands opposite the other danger, the reef Scylla. Both are personified in classical literature as female figures.

27.   Favorinus (fl. 120 C.E.) was a famous Second Sophistic Greek orator and philosopher under Domitian; he was a contemporary of Plutarch and taught Gellius and Fronto.

28.   On Negri see the introduction to this chapter and n. 11 above. One of Fedele's friends, Negri was considered an important Hellenist scholar by her circle in Padua. He taught Plato, Aristotle, and Greek philosophy. Cyllenian is an epithet applied to the god Hermes whose birthplace was Mount Cyllene in Arcadia.

29.   "Nescio quid maius in tot nascatur orbe." The source of this quotation is unknown to me.

30.   "Surely you are divine, maiden, etc." Though not set off in roman type by Tomasini, this is a close paraphrase from Virgil *Aen.* 1.327–329 that her readers would have easily recognized.

31.   The Sibyls were ancient soothsayers and thus were considered repositories of knowledge and truth.

32.   Antenor, in Greek myth, was the Trojan elder who counseled before the city was sacked that Helen should be returned to the Greeks; in Italo-Roman myth he is credited with the founding of Padua (ancient Patavium).

33.   A moutain in Sicily famous for its volcano.

34.   Pliny the Elder (23–79 C.E.), a Roman writer much admired in the Renaissance for his encyclopedic *Natural History,* a monumental attempt to catalog all knowledge.

35.   Tom. 3, 5–6. On Tomeo see the introduction to this chapter and n. 14 above.

36.   Laelius Gaius (b. 186 B.C.E.) and Scipio Aemilianus fought together in the Third Punic War. Cicero (106–43 B.C.E.) immortalized their friendship in his dialogue *De amicitia.*

37.   According to Tomasini (*Epistolae et orationes,* 212), the gift was a commentary to Aristotle's *Parva Naturalia.*

38.   This man is unknown to me.

39.   Tom. 44, 66–67. On Campagnola (1435–1522), a correspondent also of Bosso and Tomeo, see introduction and n. 13 above; also Guiseppe Vedova, *Biografia degli scrittori Padovani*, vol. 1 (Padua: Minerva, 1832), 192.

40.   Tom. 52, 78–79.

41.   Tom. 4, 6–7.

42.   "Imbecillo et fragili ingeniolo": Fedele writes using her favorite diminutives. These are impossible to translate literally every time in English. In this case "meager" conveys her self-deprecation more idiomatically than "little."

43.   Note here that Fedele is sprinkling her letter with legal terms: *flagitare* (to demand or summon before a court of law), *facere periculum* (to make a trial of someone or something, or put something or someone to the test), *creditor* (creditor), *faenus* (interest on a debt: the legal language of money lending and banking), and *obiectio* (an objection, a charge).

44.   On *flagitare* (to demand): see n. 43 above.

45.   *Ingenium* (which I have here translated "genius") is one of Fedele's favorite words: it is difficult to convey in English since it has many meanings in Latin, all of which may be simultaneously suggested in a Latin passage; *ingenium* can also mean: talent, mind, intellect, intelligence, genius, inborn ability, nature, or character. As we have seen Fedele frequently uses its diminutive form, *ingeniolum*.

46.   Cyrrha was a town in Phocis where Apollo was worshiped (Lucan 3.172); Nyssa, the legendary birthplace of Dionysus (Diodorus 3–4); the verses are a paraphrase of Lucan *Bellum civile* 1.16–66. Tomasini erroneously identifies the passage as indebted to Juvenal, see *Epistolae et orationes*, 212.

47.   Tom. 42, 64–65. Gennari was abbot at the Seminary at Padua, see Cavazzana, "Cassandra Fedele," 250–51.

48.   Tom. 10, 15–16. Augurello (1440–1515) belongs to the Paduan circle of humanists; see introduction to this chapter and n. 3 above. Augurello had sent Fedele a poem praising her (in Tomasini, *Epistolae et orationes*, 13–15). This letter is Fedele's response.

49.   Tom. 83, 119–120. Zabarino (b. 145?) was a friend of Fedele's teacher Gasparino Borro and belongs to her Paduan circle.

50.   "Tyrunculam": note Fedele's extraordinarily sophisticated use of Latin technical vocabulary; here the diminutive, gendered female form of *tiro* or *tyro*, the masculine noun for an inexperienced soldier.

51.   Note the paraphrase from Catullus 51 (itself a paraphrase of Sappho's ode *Phainetai moi*). Tomasini's text erroneously reads *linguas*; the text should read *lingua*.

52.   The Latin text reads: "Ea profecto laus dulcis ac periucunda est, quae ab his proficiscitur, qui in laude vivunt, quae ut scis ancillula virtutis est." The source is unknown to me.

53.   On the Venice-Udine circle see my introduction to this chapter.

54.   Tom. 73, 102–3; on Sabellico (1436–1506), historian and leading humanist in Venice in the 1480s, see introduction to this chapter and n. 5 above.

55. Fedele refers to Sabellico's world history, *Enneades sive rhapsodia historiarum* (Venice, 1498–1504). Sabellico also wrote two histories of the city of Venice.

56. Tom. 74, 103–4.

57. Tom. 6, 8–9. On Filomuso (born Gianfrancesco Superchio; 1440–1506), poet, cleric, and protégé of Sabellico see the introduction to this chapter and n. 5 above.

58. "*Aenigmata* (enigmas) fortasses haec mea videbuntur, quoad *enucleatius* (analytically) proferam." In this letter Fedele uses *aenigmata* both here as noun and in her next paragraph as a book title; she seems to be referring to the *Problems* (*Problemata*), a fifth-century C.E. compilation spuriously attributed to Aristotle. Both *aenigma* and *enucleatius* tend to be used in philosophical works and are rather rare; they lend an erudite cast to the letter that should not be lost in translation. *Enucleatius* suggests a probing to the core of a thing; it is found in Gellius 19.8.14; 7.3.47; also Cic. *De or.*3.9.22; *Tusc.*4.14,33; 5.8.23.

59. *Ciceromastix* was an epithet denigrating Cicero found in Gellius *Attic Nights* 17.1.1. Literally, it means a scourge of Cicero.

60. "Hem quid audio cum Aristotelea facta [sint], tu Ciceromastix (ut tuo utar vocabulo), quid hoc vult." The Latin is not quite complete as it stands; I've added a *sint* after *facta*. *Velle (vult)* is a philosophical term: to "believe."

61. Figures known for their powers of speech: the *Camaenae* (the Muses), the *Cicerones* (Cicero, the most famous of all the Roman orators, d. 43 B.C.E.), the *Sabini* (Sabinus, was a first-century C.E. Roman orator and jurist).

62. It is not clear which Galeazzo and which Benedetto she refers to here. Tomasini (*Epistolae et orationes*, 213) refers us to Giovio's *De Galeotio Martio* and Toscano's *Peplo Italiae*.

63. "*Librorum penuria*" (the lack of books), *librorum calamitas* (the disaster of books). The "loss or tragedy of books" was a common trope in Renaissance literature; the humanists, as lovers of classical antiquity and participants in the classical revival, constantly decried the destruction of most of the ancient legacy through wars and conflagrations.

64. Tom. 7, 9–10.

65. "Ut enucleatius omnia aperiam": she will literally open up everything going to the very core of ontological problems. Again Fedele introduces language and terminology demonstrating her acquaintance with Cicero's philosophical works. See the previous letter to Filomuso.

66. Tom. 40, 61–62.

67. The source of this quotation is unknown to me.

68. Tom. 35, 53–54.

69. "Schuta" in Tom. 54, 80–81. Cavazzana, in "Cassandra Fedele," identifies Scita as a member of the circle of prominent humanist in the Venice-Udine-Padua circuit who were admirers of Fedele. See also King, *Venetian Humanism*, 271.

70. Tom. 25, 38.

71. Fedele uses the potent term *vates* rather than *poeta*: the Augustan poets' favorite word for a poet, which suggests the prophetic, sacerdotal, inspired, otherwordly qualities of the poet.

72. Tom. 51, 78. Bosso (1427–1502), a native of Verona, taught Ermolao Barbaro. Bosso was abbot at the Badia in Fiesole near Florence but also produced a large humanist correspondence. See introduction to this chapter and n. 6 above.

73. Tom. 119, 183–84. On Panfilo Sasso (1455–1527) see G. Tiroboschi, *Biblioteca Modenese*, 22–34. Sasso left Modena to live in Verona; he was a close friend of Matteo Bosso and published epigrams, lyric poetry, and *rime*. See introduction to this chapter and n. 7.

74. Tom. 120, 184–86. "Laura Donata" is unknown to me.

75. Tomasini reads *genium*; the text should read *genii*.

76. It is not clear who Giulio is.

77. "Tripudiaria et effeminata quaedam solatia": Fedele uses the word *tripudaria* to modify *solatia* (=*solacia*, consolations), which is not in the OLD but appears to be an adjective formed from *tripudium* (a sacred ritual dance).

78. Tom. 121, 186–87.

79. Tom. 114, 174–76. Nothing more is known about this Broianico other than that he belonged to the humanist circle of Bosso, Panfilo Sasso, and other friends of Cassandra Fedele. Each of the letters in this pair demonstrates the full-blown rhetorical Ciceronianism of the high Renaissance.

80. Isocrates (436–338 B.C.E.), whose letters, orations, and encomia became popular in the Renaissance. One of his literary letters was addressed to a certain Demonicus.

81. The identity of Broianico's friend is unknown to me. This highly ornamental letter combines the humanist recommendation letter form (for Francesco) with a formal encomium of Cassandra replete with classical exempla.

82. Three famous pairs of friends are the mythological Orestes and Pylades and Phythias and Damon and the historical figures Laelius and Scipio made famous by Cicero's dialogue *On Friendship*.

83. The Latin equivalent for Athene, goddess of wisdom and reason.

84. One Cornelian daughter, Cornelia, was the famous mother of the Gracchi brothers. Though a noblewoman, she educated them herself. Another daughter of the Porcian clan (*gens*) was the prudent wife of Julius Caesar's assassin Brutus. The daughters of Pisistratus, a sixth-century tryrant of Athens, are unknown to me.

85. Three women in classical myth who exemplify ideal womanhood, either because of female beauty and allure as was the case with Helen; or through feminine chastity as in the case of Lucretia, who killed herself rather than live after being raped; Cassandra is the example of hyper-chastity because she successfully defends her virginity against the attempted rape by a god.

86. The ellipsis dots are Tomasini's.

87. Arachne challenged the goddess Pallas Athene to a contest of weaving. Both are emblems of virginity in Greek mythology.

88. These three women are models of Christian purity and sainthood.

89. Tom. 115 (labeled letter 114 in Tomasini), 176–78.

90. Gnaeus Naevius of Capua (fl. 266–40 B.C.E.), Roman writer of tragedies, comedies, and epic, prior to Plautus. Only fragments of his work survive. Naevius is associated with the "good old days" when Romans were brave and virtuous.

91. Note her striking images: "in huiusmodi amicitiae ornatissimum thalamum spatiosissimumque porticum tamque excellens templum inciderunt." *Thalamus* is the Greek word for bedroom, lovers' couch, or marriage bed. The language seems surprisingly sophisticated and even cunningly erotic for Cassandra who is everywhere described as *castissima, virginalis, innocens;* the reference here seems to be to Plato's theory of love and friendship.

92. Tom. 9, 12. Bentacordo, a professor of literature, was a correspondent of Matteo Bosso and a member of Cassandra's Veronese coterie of admirers.

93. "Tam enim magnus tuae virtutis se nobis offert campus": an agricultural metaphor is unusual for Fedele.

94. "Philosophorum vero causam enodare": *enodare* means to unravel (literally, free from knots); it is a term used by a favorite author of Fedele, Gellius, *Attic Nights* 13.10.1.

95. For the source of the colorful expression *pinguis Minerva*, see again Gellius 13.21 (20), 4.

96. Tom. 33, 50–52. On Bonifacio Bembo (146?–95) see n. 15 above: Mazzuchelli, *Gli scrittori d'Italia*, 728–29. Born in Brescia in the 1460s, he established a humanist school at Castelfranco near Venice. He was appointed by the duke of Milan to a chair at Pavia (1489–93). Called to Rome in 1493, he died there two years later. See also A. Baldino, "Bonifacio Bembo," *DBI* (1966), vol. 8, 111–12.

97. The source of this quotation is unknown.

98. The source of the quoted text is unknown to me.

99. Tom. 37, 58.

100. The source of this quotation is unknown to me.

101. Tom. 81, 113–14.

102. Ovid, *Ars amatoria*, 3.549.

103. Tom. 88, 125–26. Note that Bembo sent this letter from his humanist school in Castelfranco near Venice.

104. *Deliciae* (here *dilitiae*): a playful address with erotic overtones, as in Catullus 2.1 to Lesbia.

105. Their mutual acquaintance "Testa" is unknown to me.

106. Gasparino Borro, the Servite monk who was Cassandra's teacher and mentor throughout her adolescence.

107. Tom. 89, 126–27.

108.   No clue is provided by Tomasini's notes as to the identity of "Giovanni."

109.   Gasparino Borro: see n. 108.

110.   There are no notes on this "Girolamo" in Tomasini.

111.   Fedele's longtime friend from Verona Matteo Bosso who was abbot of the Badia near Florence through the 1480s and early 1490s was probably the connecting rod to the Poliziano-Ficino-Medici circle. See the introduction in this chapter and nn. 6 and 9 above.

112.   Tom. 101, 155–58. On Poliziano (1454–94) and his circle see the introduction to this chapter and n. 9 above. This famous encomium of Cassandra by Poliziano was reprinted in Poliziano's own *opera omnia* and was circulated widely.

113.   There follows a standard list of illustrious ancient women, most of them from Boccaccio's *On Famous Women* or Plutarch's catalog of famous Greek women. Note that in the Renaissance seers and prophetesses are equated with learned women. Diotima is famous for having taught Socrates in Plato's *Symposium;* Aspasia was Pericles' consort; the list of Greek women poets is standard in the Renaissance. Roman women figure similarly. Hortensia is a Roman woman orator, and the brilliant Cornelia taught her sons the Greek classics. Laelius's daughter is an unknown figure.

114.   Orpheus is a legendary pre-Homeric poet and son of the muse Calliope. Linus is another poet of lesser fame than Orpheus in Greek mythology. Apollo is the Greek god of music, medicine, archery, and prophecy.

115.   Pico della Mirandola (see the introduction to this chapter) was a longtime friend of Poliziano, a well-known philosopher, and member of Ficino's circle.

116.   Tom. 102, 158–59.

117.   Ficino, Scala, and Scala's daughter Alessandra all members of the Medici circle. Fedele may have corresponded with Ficino, although no letters to or from him are included in Tomasini.

118.   Tom. 103, 159–60.

119.   ". . . *chalepon pragma* . . .": Tomasini's ellipsis dots seem to indicate that the Greek quote is incomplete.

120.   Mentioned as Fantino Pizzamano in Fedele's letter to her Paduan friend Girolamo Campagnola.

121.   Alessandra Scala.

122.   Tom. 104, 160–61.

123.   The famous tag from Virgil's *Aeneid* recurs in various versions throughout the poem as at *Aen.* 3.48: "obstipui steteruntque comae et vox faucibus haesit" (I was stunned, my hair stood on end, and my voice stuck in my throat).

124.   Tom. 109, 165. On the Florentine chancellor and Medici client Bartolomeo Scala and his daughter Alessandra, see the introduction to this chapter.

125.   Tom. 110, 165–66.

126.   Fedele refers to Aristotle's famous formulation from his *Nicomachean Ethics*, "man is a rational animal."

127.   Matteo Bosso of Verona, abbot of the Badia.

128.   Tom. 80, 110–11. This is the last of the Ficino-Medici circle letters. It is from the philosopher Pico della Mirandola. See the introduction to this chapter and nn. 8 and 9 above. Cristoforo Landino, mentioned in the last sentence of this letter, was another well-known member of Ficino's Neoplatonic circle.

V

MEN OF THE CHURCH

Cassandra Fedele's correspondence with men of the Church includes letters exchanged with popes, cardinals, the heads of monastic orders, friars, and priests.[1] Though elegantly Ciceronian and studded with learned literary allusions, these letters differ from the correspondence with her academic and literary friends in their formality and sheer opportunism.[2] The majority of her letters to and from clerics are encomia and patronage letters. Gone is the easy camaraderie, the literary puns, and banter with her university friends that we saw in the preceding chapter.

To her contacts among the clergy Fedele sends elaborate eulogies. In turn she expects a stipend, a court appointment, a letter of recommendation for herself or a friend in the form of an encomium, or an outright gift of cash. Her letters to the Spaniard Alexander VI (Rodrigo Borgia; pope, 1492–1503) and the abbot de Cervato are part and parcel of her courtship of Queen Isabella and King Ferdinand. Her correspondence with them exposes her near obsession with securing an appointment to the Spanish court. Her letter to the Florentine prelate Leo X (pope, 1513–21), in which she recalls her connection to his father Lorenzo de' Medici's brilliant literary circle in Florence, asks the pope point-blank for assistance: she has just been widowed, she heads a numerous family, and she urgently seeks "the shade of his wings," she writes. Her letters to two clerics whom Alexander VI would soon make cardinals, Pier Dabuson, who expelled the Turks from Rhodes, and Sigismondo Gonzaga, brother of the Marquis of Mantua Francesco Gonzaga, are full of flattery. Her letters to the friars Francesco, Jacopo, Stefano, and Marcello emphasize the importance of combining religion and the values inculcated by the Church with humanistic studies.

LXXII

To Pope Leo X

Cassandra Fedele, most humble servant, wishes him perpetual happiness.
She beseeches him for financial assistance.[3]

When I first set sail at a tender age on the sea of letters, a gift for writing and the duty to write were given to me, either by the power of the stars or the councils of men, for the benefit of all humankind. For this reason I dared send my letters to Your Holiness. Someone looking at me will perhaps ascribe it to the meagerness of my talent that I did not hesitate to write to you, pontiff and chief of all priests, for you are a man of wisdom, learning, singular sanctity, and the font of all virtue.

Many things, however, summon me to the work of writing: indeed, your incredible clemency toward all righteous men and your divine charity toward those whom you think worthy of embracing in the bosom of your pious compassion. Therefore, although it pleases me to partake of the gifts of your intellect, your mind appears to me to be so daunting and difficult a fortress that it would seem incapable of being shaken by strength of mind or the power of silver-tongued oratory. For after you had been elected to the office itself by divine council (not to mention the other) and with consensus of all even in these volatile times, then more with your divine than simply human authority you calmed the turbulence left in the wake of years of brutal war to such an extent that tranquil peace came to all. And once peace was concluded under your aegis, you strengthened that peace with your liberality, magnanimity, and justice toward all the peoples of Christ to the end that we shall fear not even an unforeseen attack by the enemy.

The weight of circumstances overcomes our weakness of mind. The same thing happened to me in the presence of your father's greatness, Lorenzo Il Magnifico, whose memory awakens such awe in me that nothing would seem greater to me and whom, because he was a being divine rather than human on earth, we were forced to let go. The name of each, most blessed father, will shine like the sun among the stars and mortal men, whose greatness compels me, being not only a woman but an uncultivated woman, to be silent. Even with this silence inspired by your father (whose memory I have always cherished), still I shall not cease to make known Your Holiness's extraordinary magnanimity toward me. For you, a prince and a man of such fame and greatness, who did not think it unworthy to answer sometimes my inelegant letters, were willing to gratify my request, though

I am a woman and was unknown to you, and to honor, in response to my recommendation, the Florentine citizen, Latantio Teodaldi, with a favor.[4]

Because of your goodness I trust that I can accomplish this very objective when I recommend a person who is neither a kinsmen nor a member of your household, namely myself. On May 1,[5] Holiest Pontiff, my husband, who was dearer to me than life, passed away, filling me with such pain that I can find pleasure in nothing but tears, sighs, cries, and lamentation. Alas, so unexpected, so untimely was his death that I see myself as one already dead who remains among the living. For he was so powerful in his probity, religion, and learning that having lost a husband such as he, I feel I have no life left to live. In this tragedy, then, I am in need of your protection. It is as a supplicant that I humbly beg Your kind Holiness on my knees to shelter me under the shade of your wings, and since there are innumerable mansions in your house and since all things are subject to your power, I ask you to provide assistance to my family and me (for we are quite numerous) so that we can at least devote ourselves, if not to honor, then at least to the problem of making a living. But, most pious Father, should I accomplish with the help of your generosity what I hope for, then you will have helped many people. And ignorant though I am, I shall concentrate with such intellectual dedication that I will be willing to be everlastingly in your debt and to owe everything to your magnanimity, holiest father.

May you prosper most happily, most blessed holiness, and may God Almighty, whose dominion you hold on earth, so protect your rule that you may serve the interests of the holy church and the Christian people over which you wish to preside. April 1521.

LXXIII

To Pope Alexander VI

She gives praise for she has experienced his magnanimity.[6]

That mercy was the source of much of the benevolence that was shown by ancient men no one doubts. But if all their benevolence were collected in one place, most blessed Father, I know that it could in no way compare with the munificence of Your Holiness. For even if those ancients who dispensed such benevolence were also to have been endowed with other virtues, still they should not have been thought morally formed since they lacked the faith in whose defense Your Holiness strives together

with the holiest fathers of the church. And if they had been in competition
with this one man, they would of necessity be considered inferior due to
your celebrated acts, since you bring to the deliberations of your sacred
heart a formidable consortium of all the virtues. Thus, most blessed Father,
I must give praise to two things that my words and the failing powers of my
mind might otherwise diminish: first, your exceptional virtues, by whose
light and splendor every nation and all memory of excellent men are over-
shadowed and eclipsed; second, the divine gift that you have bestowed
upon me with such piety and generosity and the most excellent carrier and
herald of your praises, a worthy attorney and devoted servant of Your Holiness, Benedetto Missolo Pagano,[7] for he is an outstanding knight and one
endowed with every gift of mind. Therefore, what words should I use to
give thanks to you? They come not easily to mind, and how can I promise
to say a few things in my own behalf when I have nothing? Rather, I shall
ask Almighty God to bless prayers for your prosperity, to protect your life
and body from all uncleanliness, to keep it untainted by immorality, and to
make it perennially strong. [Undated.]

LXXIV

To the holy pontiff Alexander VI again

She gives thanks for his gift.[8]

When I ponder the magnitude of the honors you have conferred
on me, I have not considered it beyond my capability to demonstrate my gratitude to you in these letters, especially as I do not wish to be
in any way deficient in virtue. For gratitude of the mind and soul is a virtue
of particular importance (as I see it). And I am all the more appreciative
because I prefer no less to be grateful than I am to appear so in your eyes,
who are our most worthy protector and the highest authority among all
men. Moreover, no one is so devoid of human kindness, so hard-hearted, or
so made of iron that he might appear, after accepting the kindness, not to
have deserved it, but to be overwhelmed by it or unmoved. Such is the
weight of your services to me that I confess I owe my life to you. For you
thought it a worthy thing to bestow this sacred office upon me from you,
blessed Father, since you trusted so wholly in Benedetto Misolo Pagano's
testimony about me. If you rightly inspect his very great and innumerable
virtues, you will see that he is considered a man not only of integrity and

learning but also a most excellent knight and attorney adorned by the emblems of virtue; and he has extolled to the skies your excellence, dignity, temperance, virtues with the highest praise and glory. He is worthy of your love and embrace. Other than this I only wanted to say that I hope you will think Cassandra desirous to respond to your kindnesses and your good opinion in so far as she is able, given the meager powers of her mind, nor will she at any time fail to sing your praises. Thus the memory of your kindness will remain with me forever. I entrust and give myself wholly over to the magnitude of your mind. Farewell.

LXXV

To Pope Alexander VI[9]

I a lowly woman, would not dare to write to you, pillar of the Roman Church, unless I had been forced to do so by the urgings of the distinguished attorney and orator of the very Christian king, Maynerio.[10] He has extolled your virtues and dignity at my house and everywhere else in a marvelous oration in which he has declared that you are extremely kind, gentle, and generous. Because of his constant declarations, I have dedicated myself to you as your most devoted servant. Nor I am able to hide my devotion and enthusiasm, since I shall always celebrate your fame to the best of my ability and I shall pray that the supreme Lord will vouchsafe you in felicity and grant a happy outcome for my prayers. Farewell.

LXXVI

To Domenico Grimani, the cardinal patriarch of Aquileia

She congratulates him on his appointment to the cardinalate.[11]

Even if it is later than is fair that I have written you, most reverend father, I have lacked only the ability to write, not the wish to do so. For what could I do more happily than rejoice and congratulate you whom I have always served and respected so highly and whose goodwill toward me and my meager virtue I have sometimes known. But poor health, by which I have always been grievously afflicted in the past, has slowed me down in my writing at the present time. And now, feeling somewhat better, I have thought that I should do nothing until I send you this letter so that you will know how much joy and happiness I and my whole household have had since we heard that you were appointed patriarch of Aquileia by the distinguished Venetian Senate, which the whole city believed done before it was actually announced. Thus your extraordinary virtues seemed to demand this, to insist on it as though you were their own and as if they could never find anyone comparable to you.

Since you then are the richest source of doctrine and every virtue, and you are, as it were, the most splendid star of our age, fortune and felicity have worthily embraced you. Thus I congratulate you no more than I do the city that is no less the recipient of your honor than are you. It only remains for me to mention that which I can do for you and do frequently, namely, to pray to the Almighty Lord that He may preserve and protect you for our sake for a long time to come. Vale, and consider yourself greeted by me, my father, and entire family who are and have already long been yours. Farewell, glory of our age. Venice. October 1497.

LXXVII

To Sigismondo Gonzaga, pronotary

She predicts that he will receive ecclesiastical honors of the holy purple.[12]

I believe that, in eulogizing the greatness of your mind and your great excellence, most worthy prelate, no one should consider me reckless or overly bold. Those who initiate a correspondence themselves take on this responsibility for the writings. Even if I recognize that my powers are meager and unequal to the divine gifts of those men and especially in my eulogies of you, whose brilliant talents, great eloquence, the long ancestral lineage, and innumerable wonderful deeds I heard about from many people. I heard a great deal about you from a priest by the name of Leonardo[13] who is a man of character, goodness, and virtue and who is very solicitous of you since you are his primary sponsor. At his suggestion, I resolved to send these brief little letters to you, even though they are not worthy of you. Now, I was somewhat timid, not because I was afraid to converse face-to-face with you, who are a serious youth and of noble rank, nor was I in awe of your elegant letters and your eloquence, which indeed are very great next to mine. For I deal on a daily basis with very learned men. Still, although everyone agrees that you rise to greater heights each day, still I fear you may think that I have been a little too bold in daring to write you, who are a pronotary and the brother of a prince; true dignity and majesty of power demand a eulogist far more eloquent than I. Nor does this Cassandra, who is to be trusted more than Priam's daughter,[14] prophesy in vain. For it was madness that stimulated that Cassandra's predictions. But I who have pious thoughts conjure up visions of a lofty tiara for your holy head. May the gods grant such a thing and soon! Therefore if in spite of their ineptitude and audacity, my little letters are ill-suited to your dignity, I would like you to attribute them not to Cassandra but to the man who persuaded me to write to you, who is most powerful and able. Venice. October 1487.

LXXVIII

The illustrious general Pier Dabuson, master of the Holy Order and the Militia of San Giovanni of Jerusalem

An encomium of Cassandra.[15]

An unprecedented marvel has given our age a subject that has to be debated prudently and with profound discretion. It has demonstrated that a manly mind can be born in a person of the female sex and that women, though their sex be unchanged, can acquire traits that clearly belong to the male. The Spaniards admire, praise, and respect Queen Elizabeth[16] who is famed for her celebrated virtue; the French feel the same toward Anna,[17] the king's sister who is noted for her wisdom and generosity; and the Venetians adore you who are their most learned female citizen. It is also relevant to mention that I, too, admire erudition in ancient women. But I am already in enough pain, my Cassandra. When I was in Venice again, I failed to merit an invitation to see you—who are a second Terentia,[18] another Eustochia, and whom I only know from second-hand reports. Your epistle praises me in a declaration of esteem that I by no means deserve. Certainly I am unlike the man you extol; nonetheless I should like to resemble the one you suppose me to be. Alas, how I lament my grave and sorry fate to be bereft of such consolation. Indeed it has been a gratifying task to address the pontifex maximus,[19] the vicar of Christ, the very Christian king of France,[20] and other great personages. But to see and speak with you, a woman so reminiscent of antiquity, will be even more pleasurable, and likewise to hear the brilliant arguments of Cicero from your own sweetest lips. And so I bless you, my devout Cassandra. I bless your parents as well, because they raised such a daughter. And may God, the nurturer of wisdom and the Graces, imbue your mind with brilliance in order that He may extend His influence through a human spirit and so that, in that manner, the splendor of His being may become brighter each day. You too can soothe crude and ignorant minds with the sweet erudition of your conversation. But I do not waver in urging you, who combine purity of body and soul with a knowledge of literature, to follow the example of the sanctity of Demeter's daughter[21] as St. Jerome urges.[22] Farewell, happy and devout Cassandra, glory of our age, splendor, and marvel: may you know that I, ignorant and a foreigner, am utterly devoted to you. And fare you well again, lest you fail to think it important that you pursue me with the Christian love that unites us. Now I shall bring to an end my rambling speech so that I won't injure your learned ears with my simple-minded praises. Again and again, I bid you farewell. Rhodes. February 1487.

LXXIX

To the illustrious leader Pier Dabuson, general of the Sacred Militia of San Giovanni of Jerusalem

Fedele congratulates him on his successful campaign against the Turks, and she commends him on his praise of Giulielmo Caorsini.[23]

Since I have recently been thinking about your virtues, most illustrious chief, it has occurred to me that it could be seen as a sign of ingratitude if I did not publicly praise you in some sort of eulogy. Since I have often written encomia for celebrated princes and since your own people acclaim your virtues as not simply human but divine qualities and with clear proof, I too wanted to make such a presentation to your grace. Still, since you are noble, generous, and kind and superior to other men in every facet of goodness, had I even dared to publish an encomium for you in my letters, I knew I would have taken on a heavier burden than I was capable of then sustaining. And so, I have abstained up to this very day from that privilege.

But since then, plans have evolved as though according to their destined direction, and the very eminent Giorgio Chiaro,[24] who has every interest in your singular honor and who himself is the image of modesty, has offered me—though I had not expected it—the opportunity to speak about you. He told me of your many marvelous deeds in the course of quite a long speech, all of which kindled my desire to write about you all the more though I was already fired up about it. From him and others we learned of the chaos and crisis the Christian religion has undergone there in recent years, though when it was almost toppled you have raised it up with your energy, your intellect, and your divine prudence. For not only have you felicitously crushed all the impious attempts of the Turks in a reversal of the times but you caused the enemy to retreat from your walls slaughtered and disgraced, with the result that others were free from harm.

All these beautiful things were related by your legate Giulielmo Caorsini,[25] who is a worthy subject of your history not only because of the singularity of his integrity but also because of the sincerity and elegance of his speech, and a man who should win a place among past writers rather than contemporary ones and who deserved to be praised by such a great man. Thus I congratulate you on your good fortune, most clement prince, and all Christians who say that you should be publicly and privately congratulated salute you. I am afraid, however, that I may begin to weary you with a speech that is too long. Therefore, I shall end this letter with a brief concluding passage—one I often use in addressing the greatest princes. I solemnly pledge my devotion and service to your honor. May Almighty God vouchsafe your prayers and bring you prosperity. Venice. October 1487.

LXXX

The Reverend Abbot de Cervato to Cassandra

He complains about the disdain for literature and offers an encomium of Cassandra worthy of her.[26]

I have heard, divine Cassandra, and many have told me, of your extraordinary virtues, the pure and chaste conduct of your life, your beautiful writings, and of all the rest of your excellent gifts of mind and body. And so I have attributed as much to you as one hopes there is in any woman of our time. For alas, we have descended to the worst of times when the study of literature is as much an object of contempt for women as it is for men. No honor is earmarked for the poet's labor and his plow, and the fields of wisdom grow dirty from disuse while the ploughmen have been removed. Who would have believed that another Cassandra, a poet after King Priam's daughter (the girl Apollo made learned,[27] said Homer), would be given to our time? But when I call to mind again and again the beautiful speeches you made and how your divine lips, your animated face, and your firm speech and lungs contradicted nothing at all in your maidenly purity, and when I think of how we all stared in amazement at this unaccustomed act of nature and the miraculousness of the thing, I am firmly convinced it is thanks to God's divine hand that you have been preserved for our times so that, in an age when virtue itself has been weakened and is under attack, you will be a very powerful example of virtue. You will be a defender of learning and a champion of letters both human and divine at a time when literature is ignored and all wisdom is regarded as nothing, so that at your urging and by your example, men at least, if not women, may blush at being ignorant and may free themselves from luxury and sloth. I rejoice because I am allowed to see you, to speak to you, and to enjoy your most pleasing conversation. Certainly there have been many things I have said about the city of Venice and, while words fail me, my resolve is firm. But in this one way you are an obstacle to your city, because I now must relinquish it to turn to your praises, lest I should fail you both. Come now, most learned maiden and last hope of literature, pursue the role our redeemer has designated for you with unceasing efforts: "Why have you hidden from the wise and revealed yourself to the improvident?" But now to come to my own role: while others may sing your praises with greater eloquence, I can be useful to you in this one way: that I shall lay open my whole heart to praising you. And if my poems are still capable of anything, then I shall certainly display them everywhere and at all times so that I may fill all Spain with your praises. Farewell, glory of our age. [Undated.]

LXXXI

To the Reverend Abbot De Cervato

An encomium for the abbot, Spain, and the king and queen of Spain.[28]

I thought it only right for me to respond to your kindness and your letter so full of wonderful charm and elegance, and when I read it I was buoyed up with the greatest happiness. For when I read your letters and think about my delightful friendship with you—even if I could actually experience it far from your presence—still since a friendship is renewed and refreshed by letters it will shine more brilliantly, now that I have seen your complete commitment to honor and to praise me. You have done me such a great number of favors, I have thought, that not only could I not magnify or grace them with an oration of my own, but I could neither reciprocate nor even count them. So much indebted am I to you, therefore, that I find it difficult to find the words to thank you. Still, in whatever manner your blessed benevolence is to be obliged, I shall spare nothing in glorifying your praises and name, if it is possible that they can be glorified since they already are glorious by themselves. Besides, I have derived no small amount of pleasure from the eloquence of your letters. For the gravity of your words, your gift for oratory, and your use of the abundant style are worthy not of silent appreciation but should be publicized with open admiration. For nothing can be found that is more delicate, prudent, or sacrosanct than your letters. Indeed who is superior to you in goodness, modesty, and studies in the liberal arts and who surpasses you, then, in every kind of praise? Given that you are endowed, then, with such virtues, with what benevolence, with what studies shall I follow you? How then shall I sing your praises? For whom, O immortal gods, and with what blessed love am I inflamed?

But no wonder, for who does not know the climate of your kindly country? What a lovely place is your land, how excellent are its cities, how cultivated its citizens! In comparison to whom would your citizens not only not appear more pleasing or more sublime but not be construed as such by hoping or wishing? I would say something grandiloquent and noble about the majesty of your empire and king if only I weren't terrified by the magnitude of such a project. For there is no river of talent so great, no elegance of oratory or writing that would not, I would say, enumerate its praises point by point or that would not even celebrate it in passing.

I don't hesitate to assert this, however: there is no ruler among the Christians who can be compared in power or energy or the other royal virtues to your king. I cannot, however, omit the praise of your most splendid queen herself, to whom I am so devoted that I wish nothing more than that it might fall within my province to obey Her Highness and carry out her commands. For the great fame of her virtues is so widespread—and even you confirm this—that I think of nothing else day and night. But the queen herself has subdued a nation of savage barbarians, an innumerable horde, protected by the nature of the countryside, a people abounding in an excess of all things and an almost incredible wealth of provisions. More-over, what place, what city, what region has not been increased and become illustrious under her patronage? Therefore, since nature and fortune have brought you so worthy a gift as to be born in that region, rejoice, my priest, in your superb lot and enjoy your good glory and good luck.

Other than this, I would just ask you to remember our most respectful goodwill. Your friendship delights me very much, but most of all because of your loyalty, steadfastness, and seriousness: for if we possess these virtues, no forgetfulness, no distance, no separation of time or place will ever de-stroy the extraordinary bond between us. The rest is related to your promise on behalf of your loyalty to me and your diligence and our not just recently begun but clearly confirmed friendship. I would like you to take charge of my encomia, as you have shown, and I would like, while we live, to enjoy the fame that comes to us from you. Be happy. In the meantime do not cease to take care to preserve the foundations you have laid, and convey my greetings and those of my kinsmen. Farewell. Venice 1487.

LXXXII

To the Florentine priest Michelangelo

She praises his poems and thanks him for them.[29]

Even if I have hesitated to send you (who are so eloquent) this plain letter, which is without any grace or vestige of artistry, still when I received your poems a few days ago, which were filled with scholarly culti-vation and elegance, I resolved to write you a short note about them so you would know how greatly I esteem you. For your poems make manifest the brilliant mind and unassailable character that is clearly yours. Not only do I see that you have touched and tasted the waters of Aganippe[30] with your lips but I also believe you have immersed yourself in the springs of the Pyrenees and every river on Mount Parnassus[31] as well. Therefore, you can deservedly be called unique, blessed, and fortunate by all men since not only do you redound in all virtues, but it is also evident that you come from a most ancient and noble family of Etruscan stock. For this city of yours is truly the flower of Italy, and thus for virtuous men and those whose inclina-tion is to seek the good, it far surpasses other cities, as does the rain when dark clouds menace above. Indeed, it can be judged more brilliant than the sun (according to the testimony of Dante, whose remains are preserved in the illustrious tomb erected by the magnificent lord and knight Bernardo Bembo near the home of the divine Francesco;[32] for in recent years Bembo served as *praetor* there, and he did so with justice that was mingled with great clemency, according to the reports of many others whose names we do not mention because of their great number and the tedium of reciting them.)

But you are kind and generous to say that I should be garlanded with laurel, ivy, and olive leaves. And now, by Pollux, I believe you are indeed a kind and gracious soul to wish to bestow on me the title of poet laureate with your verses. It not only inspires me: it kindles and inflames my spirit to pursue virtue. Therefore, venerable priest, I give everlasting thanks to you for your exceptional magnanimity toward me in every decorous matter that is yours to administer, and if only my meager abilities can be demonstrated, may you know that I am prepared. Farewell. [Undated.]

LXXXIII

To Brother Francesco

She apologizes for her diminished eloquence, which has been affected by her studies in dialectics and philosophy.[33]

Although an abundance of evidence caused me to recognize your incredible goodwill long before now, when I received your letters elegant in their Ciceronian eloquence, your confirmation of our friendship brought me enormous joy, and their cumulative effect on me has been enormous. For I knew you were a man of religion and singular learning and that you looked forward to receiving my little letters so that you could adorn, magnify, and recite my meager eulogies in all places, and so that these would provide testimony in conjunction with later writings which I would hope would be of such a sort that they would merit being read in all the schools and sought after by learned men. But every vestige of my former eloquence seems to have been kidnapped by some fate or other. Dialectics and the study of philosophy have done it in. Therefore, since a genre of literature harsher than anything else and one akin to dialectics has been bequeathed to me, I think my letters should be shown to no one. Still, whatever the case may be, I took care that my writings should be sent to you so that you might easily see how much I esteem you. This is no surprise not only because of the merits of the entire church and above all your own merits, but also because of your holy offices and the perfectness of your knowledge, which only religious men possess at this time. Farewell. Venice. May [Undated.]

LXXXIV

To Magistro Stefano, member of the Servite Order

She urges him to produce an edition of the Dialectics.[34]

Since I want very much to retain your exceptionally kind disposition toward me, I thought it would be appropriate for me to write you not to show you that my honorable affection for you has increased, a thing not possible in the least since my love and regard for you are already enormous. Indeed, may I offer an explanation as to why I esteem you from my heart and venerate you? In addition to your extraordinary integrity and the innumerable gifts of your mind, what gravity you have, what fortitude and constancy! To what studies and sciences have you devoted yourself since childhood! All these things are now flourishing in you. Therefore, I beg you to think not only of what other men have done but of that which you yourself have produced by dint of your own talent and enthusiasm; but most of all I want you to be mindful of the work you have begun that contains praises of me. And so, I see that I should be bolder in making it clear in these little letters of mine that embarrassment has kept me from saying these things to you face to face; for letters don't blush.[35] I am afflicted with a strange desire that you should do what was promised to me, and even though you said you certainly would do it, still I hope you will forgive my being in a hurry, for to tell the truth what motivates me is not so much the desire for immortality as it is the authority of your testimony, the benevolence of your information, and the sweetness of your nature.

I must admit that I am more than greedy enough to be immortalized by so great a man as you, and I beg you not to blame me for my avarice and ask that you allow me this little bit of glory since my nature and our friendship demand it. If you complete the work you have begun, believe me, nothing will in my view be more magnificent, more celebrated, or more solid than the study of the *Dialectics*.[36] The same has been said to me by my tutor, the worthy teacher of theology and beloved Brother Gasparino, a man of singular temperance, pure morals, and divine virtue, in whose character there seems to be no room for improvement, for in him every kind of virtue and goodness already flourishes, and finally nothing can be found which is wanting for his immortality. Therefore, on behalf of his and my honorable esteem for you, if this appeal has any weight with you (and I trust that it does) so that you have cause to complete what you have begun, it is necessary that you do this, nor would it be harmful to your honor. Nor do I have any doubt that I, a young girl immersed in the study of literature, am pursuing my own glory in praising you.

That is all I have to say. I see that you can in no way deny me this. And our friendship, because of its immortality, will be an ornament to both orders of Servite brothers, a source of encouragement to your friends and of everlasting glory and utility to me. Take care and be well. Master Gasparino, the greatest jewel and glory[37] of the Servite Order, sends greetings to you. Lastly I commend my father, myself, and all of us to Your Holiness. [Undated.]

LXXXV

To an unnamed correspondent

She recommends her teacher, the Servite monk Gasparino Borro.[38]

I know—because of your extraordinary esteem for me and all my family—that it's not necessary that I write a letter to your most reverend authority since my father, who is more dear to me than life itself and entirely devoted to you, has decided to talk to you face-to-face. And so, in order for me to summarize this matter in as few words as possible yet satisfy nonetheless my sense of obligation to your authority and so that then I may make clear how important the matter is, it has seemed best in this brief note to beg and beseech your authority to show and make available to me in this concern of mine the support of which you are capable—no, utterly capable—of giving, so that this man,[39] whom I recommend in this note and whom my father will examine in person, can take on and pursue a duty that is by no means small. I hear that one man, Giovanni Capello,[40] the chief steward of San Marco Magnifico, can do a great deal; indeed, he is the pivotal figure in the whole matter, and I am aware that nobody in this city can overturn his opinion, unless it is you, given the prudence, the eloquence, and finally, all the persuasiveness and the strong faculty of reason that is yours. Regarding this matter, I beg and beseech you not to burden yourself—though you have often promised me many things—with letting me know the outcome by letter. This man, whose virtues and learning are so well known that these attributes would serve as references by themselves, is a priest who was once my teacher. Ever since then, I have been so concerned about him that I would not hesitate to lay down my life, my health, and my good name to ensure his well-being. He now should succeed the deceased preceptor of clerics at San Marco and obtain that position. What more should I say? The time now seems right to press on with your most frequent promise so that I can at last be in a position to collect on it. I entrust myself to your authority. [Undated.]

LXXXVI

Jacopo Ponzano, humble professor of the Order of the Servites, to Cassandra Fedele, a most virtuous maiden

He urges her to pursue wisdom.[41]

May I greet you in the name of the Lord, wisest maiden, sending ahead this letter of praise. When I landed at Vicenza on my return and recalled your goodwill toward me, while I scarcely had time to take pen in hand, I have taken it up and have submitted these letters to your prudent judgment, even if they are not learned, to convey my affection for you and to make it clear that my goodwill toward you is indeed very great. A passage from John the Evangelist expresses this for me since I hoped what I would write to you would be very powerful: "To him who has, goods will be given, and from him who is lacking, even that which he seems to have will be taken away."[42]

I have thought continuously of you alone, and even if I say I have thought of you as unique, I do not think I err. You will direct your mind to that wisdom that, when it looks down upon terrestrial affairs, makes men true. Nor will I consider it labor to summon you with my little letters to wisdom of this sort, which makes men gods. For you know, and you know well, how many philosophers who have dedicated themselves to the study of literature have wandered through many regions and have undertaken many labors so that they could render you so learned in knowledge and wisdom. For with what do the gymnasia resound? With what various and diverse debates and controversies of scholars and men of every religion live in the universities lest they should seem to profess ideas that have already been said? For you certainly know that which I know you know well: that all men differ from animals, for they differ not in that which is characteristic of animals but in that which belongs to rational beings. For what, as Bede asks, is more bestial than a man who abounds in reason yet fails to use it? Just as knowledge causes all rational men to differ from the other animals, likewise it causes men who devote themselves to the study of literature to differ not only from those who are ignorant but also from those who do not wish to have knowledge. It is right to declare those men bestial about whom the Lord said to the prophets: "Because you turn away from knowledge, turn yourself away lest you occupy yourself with my priesthood."[43] Our savior also chastised the disciples, saying: "Up to now, you had no intelligence."[44]

Therefore, my most prudent maiden, strive for that wisdom about which I have spoken and embrace it with a joyous face and mind. Strive so that sleepless days and nights do not keep you from attaining wisdom, but rather so that all bitterness may become sweet with the love of wisdom. For knowledge is a noble tree, as our ancestors have said, whose roots are bitter but whose fruit is the sweetest. Hear, then, what is said in John, in the Apocalypse: Avoid the false flattery of this world, and appear to tread the path you have taken.[45]

It is my hope that with the acuity of your intellect and God as your leader you will distinguish yourself with the knowledge and learning of your teachers so that men will believe that you belong among the Sibyls. Farewell then. Greet your parents and uncle for me and show that you are not forgetful of me. And garland yourself with knowledge and wisdom so that . . . the virgin. . . .[46] [Undated.]

LXXXVII

To Professor Jacopo Ponzano

She congratulates him on his monastic dignity.[47]

I am glad you are well. I, too, am well. You yourself can judge how happy I was to receive your letter, which was full of every adornment. Though I do not seek you out with the ordinary friendship of people who find it not at all odd to have taken their time to answer your letter, for during the last few days I was in the country to rest my mind. But enough of this. Whether I should congratulate you or be sad that you have been made head of this monastery is not an easy thing for me to judge. For I understand that you have been crowned with the highest honors and praise, though I do miss your presence. But whenever I think about this, the bond of our mutual goodwill comes to mind; nor will forgetfulness brought about by any distance in terms of space or time ever destroy this bond. Therefore all of us rejoice that you have attained this honor. But because of your piety and dignity I hope that you will achieve yet greater things. Thus I beg God almighty to preserve you until you reach the ripe old age of Nestor. Farewell. [Undated.]

LXXXVIII

To Brother Marcello

She apologizes for the paucity of her letters.[48]

I confess that I have been a little slow to respond to your letters. But to be slow to respond is better than doing so on the "Greek Kalendae."[49] Therefore, since I now have some free time, I wanted to seem agreeable in your eyes. And so I have written to you as often as I have received your letters, and they have brought me great pleasure. For they glistened with every eloquence and shone with a bright and unending fountain of words and thoughts. But enough about this. Your virtue is not without testimony from me, though everyone celebrates it. Nor have I forgotten the mandate you delivered to my father and me as you were departing. You should know that we have managed our duties with great goodwill, care, and diligence. My feeling is unchanged, nor has it ever been otherwise, for it is most loving of you. No man who has a noble mind has ever done something that could not be redeemed by prayer. I do hope, in any case, that we shall never be without your virtue. Farewell. [Undated.]

NOTES TO CHAPTER 5

1.   For an overview of the church in Rome, its clergy, and its patronage networks during Fedele's lifetime see Charles L. Stinger, *The Renaissance in Rome* (Bloomington: Indiana University Press, 1998); see also Peter Partner, *The Pope's Men. The Papal Civil Service in the Renaissance* (Oxford: Clarendon, 1990); and Barbara McClung Hallman, *Italian Cardinals, Reform, and the Church as Property* (Berkeley: University of California Press, 1985).

2.   Some of Fedele's academic and literary friends (see chapter 4) like Bonifacio Bembo and Matteo Bosso were priests, but were first and foremost intellectual comrades.

3.   Tom. 123, 189–92. Leo X (pope, 1513–21) was the son of Lorenzo de' Medici.

4.   Tomasini spells his name Lactantius Tedaldus; he is unknown to me.

5.   Her husband, Gian-Maria Mappelli, a physician from Vicenza whom she married in 1499, died May 1, 1520.

6.   Tom. 84, 120–21. Pope Alexander VI was the Spaniard Rodrigo Borgia (pope, 1492–1503) and a nephew of Pope Calixtus III.

7.   "Missolo," a correspondent of Fedele (see chapter 6), is unknown to me.

8.   Tom. 85, 122–23. Fedele does not name the pope but by the context of the letters it has to be Rodrigo Borgia (Alexander VI) who occupied the papal throne 1492–1503.

9.   Tom. 77, 107. On Missolo see n. 7.

10.   See Fedele's letters to Louis XII, king of France, and his orator Maynerio in chapter 3.

11.   Tom. 70, 98–99. In 1497 the Venetian Senate secured permission from the pope to appoint Grimani, a learned historian and philosopher, as the patriarch of Aquileia. Grimani's name is not given in Tomasini's heading.

12.   Tom. 2, 3–4. Sigismondo (1469–1525), the brother of the Marquis Francesco Gonzaga, was elevated to the cardinalate in 1506 under Julius II.

13.   This "Leonardo" is unknown to me.

14.   Cassandra, daughter of King Priam of Troy, rejected Apollo's love. The god punished her by giving her the gift of prophecy and condemning her never to be believed since she appeared to be raving mad.

15.   Tom. 97, 142–44. Tomasini (219) records that Dabuson (whose first name Fedele writes as "Petrus"), a Frenchman who was the General of the Order of San Giovanni of Jerusalem, defeated the Turks at Rhodes. For this victory he was elevated to the cardinalate by Pope Innocent VIII (1484–92).

16.   Dabuson must mean Isabella (1451–1504), queen of Spain and Castile.

17.   Anne, sister of Charles VIII.

18.   Terentia (fl. 50 B.C.E.) was the faithful wife of the Roman orator Cicero, and later Sallust. "Eustochia" is unknown to me.

19.   At the time of the writing of this letter the pope (pontifex maximus; the vicar of Christ) was Innocent VIII.

20.   The king of France in 1487 was Charles VIII.

21.   Demeter's daughter Persephone, who was abducted by Hades, king of the underworld, and later returned to her mother.

22.   St. Jerome (347–419 C.E.), the early church father and famous misogynist. Fedele uses here the Latin version of his name: Hieronymus.

23.   Tom. 15, 25–27.

24.   "Chiaro" is unknown to me and not mentioned in Tomasini's notes.

25.   "Caorsini" is not mentioned in Tomasini's notes nor is he otherwise known to me.

26.   Tom. 93, 133–34. As noted in the introduction to this chapter, this encomium of Cassandra and her response to the Spanish abbot must be considered in the context of Cassandra's quest to win an appointment to the court of Isabella and Ferdinand, the queen and king of Spain and their courtship of her in the years 1488–97. See the exchange of letters between Cassandra and Queen Isabella in chapter 1.

27.   By giving her the gift of prophecy.

28.   Tom. 94, 135–37. See n. 26 above.

29.   Tom. 82, 115–17. The Florentine priest "Michelangelo" is unknown to me.

30.   In Greek myth Aganippe was a spring in Boeotia sacred to the Muses and Apollo. See Ovid *Metamorphoses* 5:5.312.

31.   The Pyranees and Mt. Parnassus were the dwelling places of Apollo and the Muses.

32.   The poet Dante (1265–1321) is said to have died in Florence. It is not clear who the "divine Francesco" ("Divi Francisci") is; it seems not to be the poet Petrarch because of the Ravenna connection. The father of Cardinal Pietro Bembo, the Venetian humanist Bernardo Bembo (1433–1519), serving as captain in Ravenna, ordered Dante's tomb in that city restored in May 1483 (see King, *Venetian Humanism*, 336–38).

33.   Tom. 16, 27–28. "Friar Francesco" is unknown to me.

34.   Tom. 14, 23–25. Brother Stefano was elected General of the Servite Order, of which Fedele's longtime teacher Gasparino Borro was a member.

35.   "Literae non erubescunt." Tomasini identifies this tag as Cicero.

36.   By the title *Dialectics* Fedele is surely referring to Aristotle's handbook on the subject, which is entitled the *Topics*.

37.   The Latin nouns *ornamentum* (adornment, jewel) and *decus* (glory, honor, grace) belong to the obligatory palette of flattering epithets in humanist encomia. Poliziano in his ecomium of Cassandra addresses her as *decus Italiae*.

38.   Tom. 39, 60–61. Fedele writes a letter of recommendation for her beloved teacher the Servite monk Gasparino Borro. The addressee of the letter is unknown.

39.   See Fedele's letter above (Tom. 14, 23–25) to Brother Stefano of the Servite Order on Borro. This is another letter of recommendation for Gasparino Borro, her longtime teacher for a position at San Marco.

40.   "Capello" is unknown to me.

41.   Tom. 117, 178–81. This encomium to Cassandra and her response suggest that Brother Jacopo is either responding to the reports of her oration for Bertuccio Lamberti at Padua (in 1487) or that he attended the ceremony himself.

42.   Mk 4:25 and parallels (Mt 13:12; Lk 8:18).

43.   "Quia tu scientia repulisti, repella te ne sacerdotio fungaris mihi." The source of this text is unknown to me.

44.   "Adhuc, et vos sine intellectu estis." The source of this text is unknown to me.

45.   "Blandienta tandem mundi huius falsa devita, et ut capisti calcasse videaris." This must be a paraphrase since it is not set in roman type. Clearly Ponzano is quoting scripture throughout.

46.   The ellipsis dots are Tomasini's. The letter is unfinished.

47.   Tom. 18, 30.

48.   Ibid., 19, 31.

49.   The *Kalendae* was for Romans the first day of the month, and traditionally the day when the bills were paid.

VI

UNKNOWN CORRESPONDENTS AND HUMANIST FORM LETTERS

Fedele's correspondence in this chapter includes letters from unknown correspondents. The majority of these letters either lack an addressee or give the addressee's first name only. The remaining letters address correspondents whom Fedele's biographers and editors have been unable to identify. Some of the letters that Tomasini has labeled "addressee unknown"[1] may be form letters—boilerplate pieces—produced for ready use as the occasion demanded. Other unattributed pieces appear to be early drafts for future letters. The letters in this chapter fall roughly into three categories, though there is some overlap among the categories: lengthy, formal encomia and shorter letters of praise; friendship and patronage letters; and letters of apology for her slowness to respond. The encomia include everything from formal eulogies down to the briefest notes in which she praises colleagues on their Latin style or encourages fledgling writers and scholars to persevere in their work. The friendship letters encompass a similarly broad span of writings: they range from breezy, impromptu notes to close friends to stiff, mannered letters of introduction. They also include the odd piece of special interest: a plea to an unnamed high official, couched in the language of patronage friendship, for leniency in a court case in which a cousin of hers was charged with a felony; and a miniature yet thoroughly Ciceronian essay on *amicitia* (humanist friendship), portrayed here as a lifelong bond between intellectual and moral peers that confers honor and utility on those who engage in it and is based on a sense of mutual obligation.[2] Her letters apologizing for her tardiness as a correspondent have a greeting card quality about them. She offers three pat and unvarying excuses: she has been suffering from a chronic, but unspecified illness; she has been wrestling with difficult philosophical texts and has had no time for pleasure; and, finally, she is painstakingly slow at composing letters.

〜

LETTERS OF PRAISE

LXXXVIII b

*An unattributed encomium from a legation at Bergamo addressed to Cassandra
in which her virtue and erudition are celebrated.* [3]

*S*ince there are today no interpreters of dreams and no divine oracles
in the temples, springs, groves, and mountains of Apollo and Aesculapius,[4] I have long asked myself, O eminent Cassandra, whether we
ourselves are not occupants of an iron age.[5] And for this reason I have wa-
vered and dithered anxiously over whether I should worshipfully follow the
time-honored precepts of the Latin language, which once led divine minds
to everlasting glory, since I had not at all convinced myself that a humanist
program could be practiced in so ignorant and dull an age. But the integrity
and excellence of your character and learning so lifts me out of the bog of
my uncertainty that I seem to hear the call of the Sibyl, who in ancient
times brought true hope and succor to the human race. Therefore, in my
avid desire for you, O most learned of maidens, Apollo and the Muses (such
is my guess) have brought me to you as to the one true idol and sole refuge
for mankind and the revered avenger of the groves of Aonia, to gaze upon
the light of eternal truth and the sacred path of virtue in the image of your
true and divine glory and at the true sweetness of your character. And this
has come to me as ordained. And because of this I have partaken of the
sublimity of your virtue and I have felt in my heart the continuing fire of
my passion for you, so much so that I have nothing sound and whole in
myself except to give thanks to the Lord Almighty for having allowed me
to be born in your lifetime. For through the contemplation of your virtue, I
hope to touch your being and I beg you, wisest of maidens, on this account
to show us the glory of true immortality in your guidance of us. And if you
will do this, as I hope you will, I shall have believed neither Sappho nor
Priam's daughter has come to us but instead the divine Cumaean Sibyl,[6] and
I shall always endeavor to offer up all the virtue that is in me, if there be
any, to the altar of your goodness. Farewell, O glory of letters. [Undated.]

LXXXIX

To the delegation from Bergamo

Cassandra Fedele thanks the orators from Bergamo for their beautiful encomia.[7]

The day before yesterday, most excellent doctors, when I received your letter, which is informed by the gravity of your thoughts and the melodiousness of your words, yet has a certain grandeur, I read it, first delighting in the letter for its own sake, and then enjoying it all the more, for, though absent from you, I seemed still to drink in the elegance of your speech and the abundance of its sweetness which it fell to me, a mere maiden, to enjoy face to face a few days ago, thanks to your generosity and kindness. That it happened this month was all the more gratifying, let alone, by God, on that day. For you not only delivered a brilliant oration about me in my presence at my house, but I saw that what[8] it said brilliantly was believed. But what occurred before? I always knew this after you came here to the house, but now I know it more clearly and with more assurance. And thus I confess I shall always be wonderfully indebted to the very distinguished and well known orators of Bergamo. As to your being saddened, however, by the ignorance and coarseness of our era, I would trust you on this point if the men more learned in every branch of knowledge were not also considered the most accomplished men of our time (this is my limited view anyway), and if there were no men more learned now than those who lived three hundred years ago. Therefore, we should not lament things that are easy for every man, or certainly for an educated man, to recognize and demonstrate with a number of arguments. I do not see why you would want to happen to be born in our time unless you could be of use to nature in guiding scholars and particularly me since if I (who am much superior to others, you say) were to be endowed with talent, then I would demand nothing so gladly as your praises, O magnificent orators, whose words are disseminated throughout the world. Your commendation of me and your exhortation to me to pursue virtue remain most pleasing. But lest the question of obligation should arise between us—whether I might be indebted to you, having shown you how very young a girl I am, or whether you might be indebted to me, having thought me worthy of your presence and favor—if I were to owe you more, I would cease writing. But I confess that, in concurring with you in most things I am much indebted to you. Take care and farewell. [Undated.]

XC

Ambrosius Miches of Dalmatia and Sebenica to Cassandra

A commendation on the nature and fortune of her gift.[9]

*D*on't be surprised, Cassandra Fedele, that I, a stranger, should write to you whom I've never seen. The rumor of your talents that has spread abroad and reverberates in our ears, forces me, among others, to impose upon your erudition, the result being that you will have at least learned that your fame and celebrity are talked about everywhere and have even penetrated into the distant reaches of our province; nor can they be contained within the walls of your own city. The reports that are being spread abroad about you and your scholarship would be a source of wonderment whether they were found in the feminine sex or the masculine one. Great is the power of virtue and learning, so that wherever they reside, your name cannot remain obscure.

Many things commend you to us, extraordinary maiden: the renown of the city of your birth in the world, the famed city of the Venetians, your mind, your parents, and the gods have given you beauty as well as riches of the spirit. But such riches are the common property of many men; in mind and learning in the liberal arts, however, few men are your equals, and because of these things you illumine your native city and bring fame to your parents who, if they have hitherto been relatively unknown, will now shine the more through your eminence.

"The Muse has given you your voice, Mercury your skill, Jove your mind, and great Apollo your lyre."[10]

You have, however, increased these gifts with ineffable study, you have surpassed your sex, you have overcome nature, and you have equaled not only the most illustrious maidens of our time, as for example, the divine Constanza Varano, Ippolita Sforza, Battista Malatesta, Isotta Nogarola of Verona,[11] all of whose brilliant orations and letters in poetry and prose have been widely circulated. But in addition, you have attained the fame of those women of antiquity who were the glory of their age, as for example, in Roman times Cornelia,[12] mother of the Gracchi, who bestowed upon her sons not a little of the elegance and charm of her oratory; and Hortensia, daughter of the consummate orator Hortensius—who learned her art at her father's knee—who surpassed all others in her eloquence and espoused the cause of the Roman matrons in the Senate winning the admiration of all who heard her. To this list the poet Sappho must be added, who proclaims in her poems that all future ages will celebrate her. One cannot fail to mention Aspasia who was the most learned woman of Socrates' time. Nor, I believe, will future generations be silent about you who have trained your mind in the fine arts, not for womanish wool production or manual labor. For such persons will consort with Lactantius (also known as Firmianus) in the underworld, who neglected the arts of the mind and embraced those of the body.[13] There have been warrior women, such as the Amazons and the maiden Camilla, who dared to compete with men on the battlefield in war. Still, I believe that merit is greater when men rival one another not physically or manually but intellectually and in training in the liberal arts, just as you, most fortunate maiden, are accustomed to seek fame not with physical prowess but with the virtue of your mind. For excellence in these things, as our Cicero[14] testifies, we think beautiful and praiseworthy. Certainly nothing is more profitable than to strive hardest to attain the summit of the virtues and the things fortune can never destroy, relegating the advantages of the body to second place. Therefore, whoever fails to praise you or to number you among the world's illustrious maidens, is unworthy of praise himself. Come, then, loyal maiden, and take care, as you have begun to do, to see that the name that belongs to your family and kinsmen is a virtuous name and that you are truly loyal, both in name and in fact, and add the treasure of the sacred scriptures to the good books that you possess. Take care that there is oil in the lamps you now have, as is said in the sacred proverbs, and be counted among the virtuous maidens so that you may be received by the Lord. Vale, blessed in the Lord and pray for us. Sibenix. 14 January 1487.

XCI

To the most excellent Doctor Ambrosius Miches

She has been busy with literary obligations, she apologizes for the tardiness of her response, and she relays her greetings.[15]

I am certain, O most worthy man, that you will accuse me of neglect, since I was forced to be a little tardy in responding to your very beautiful letters. But I prefer to own up to the sin of tardiness rather than to have you suspect me of being neglectful. I came to the study of literature at the tenderest age, and ever since then I have received so many letters that I was not able to have any respite from writing. What is more, I have been continually surrounded in my own home by learned men who wish not only to visit with me but to enter into disputations with them. These things, then, have caused me to be a little slow to respond.

Therefore, I beg you not to think that Cassandra spurns your goodwill; rather, I seek it with the greatest love. Nor is it of little concern to me to be able to display the strength of so great an obligation. Therefore I pray that you will want to count me among your friends. Why have I been talking about my pursuing your goodwill? So that I might seek your friendship, or because of your maturity and the magnitude of your virtues. Therefore, I pray that you will pursue me with a father's love, for I love and respect you just as I would my own father. Command me, therefore. Give orders to your daughter Cassandra: it will be your daughter's task to execute your commands. That you extol me so to the skies should be no surprise whatsoever. I recognize here the performing of a father's duty: your daughter has already become excited about her literary studies, and you spur her on with praise. 'Is it true, my little daughter?' you will say. Your praise has always inspired me. Therefore, I thank you hugely and beg you to love me with a father's love. Farewell. Venice. May 1487.

XCII

Giovanni Mangonio Cosenza to Cassandra

He praises her wondrously.[16]

The writings of orators and poets from almost all over the world have come together to praise you (and they already fill a volume), Cassandra, now that the winged fame of your name has flown to so many places. But nowhere have you been too highly praised or praised enough. For, in my opinion, nature has done so many great things for you that she has set no limits for your praises, and she herself was unable to stop herself from going further. It is necessary for mortal minds to proceed only so far that they attain the goals set by nature. And although they have written many things about you, it is not a matter of doubt that still greater texts survive near at hand. Alas, gods above—may I, with your permission, speak out, Cassandra?—I who unwillingly and invincibly grieve that you so elevate the feminine sex and so stand at the apex of the world that you alone (whom only envy outstrips) have in some way either destroyed our sex or seem determined to destroy it. But when nature wished to put her own powers to the test through you alone, she spent her own might on your genius. More willingly and gladly though, I congratulate you and I am delighted to find that in the above-mentioned volume the genius of Angelo's daughter has still never been properly praised and appreciated; in just the same way, I have read, no one believed the prophecies of Priam's daughter.

Farewell, O radiant light among priestesses and initiates.[17]

Farewell again, and among your own friends, praise your Mangonio. Venice. 5 January [Year not given.]

XCIII

Camillo Napolitano to Cassandra

He desires a letter from her.[18]

Although I always had a very high regard for you and thought of you as a person of great learning and eloquence, now that I have heard the honey-sweet oratory with which you spoke publicly, no eloquence could possibly express how greatly I admire you—though it was that gift that made me acquainted with the superiority of your mind and your learning in comparison with our other contemporaries. I have heard that when an oration is perfectly presented, a like rationale is offered to everyone to speak. And so the result is, and rightly so, that while all men seek some learning or other in you, they also love, admire, and respect you. And so it is that, even if I esteemed you of my own free will prior to this time, now I am forced to love and respect you with every possible loyalty. Moreover, may I beg that you not find it too tedious a task to write to me. And if you do this, as I hope and desire, not only will this be the beginning of a friendship between us, but it will be your task to command me to extol with the highest praises that eloquence of yours that is divine rather than earthly (and this proves that you were born not of this world but came down from heaven), and mine to carry out your commands with good cheer. [Undated.]

XCIV

To Francesco Camosi

*Cassandra urges Francesco, the son of Francesco Camosi,
to emulate his father's virtue.*[19]

Even if my extraordinary goodwill would seem to need no further confirmation or proof, still I thought I should write to you, not to make
that clearer but to show proper respect to your and my most beloved and
learned Franciscus Camosus, Knight Magnificent, since he insisted that I
send you something literary. And his command, I decided, should be willingly obeyed so that he could judge for himself how much I esteem him
and how great my love for him is, and also so that I could with my writing
spur on you who had already been spurred on by your own desire to study
literature. Indeed I have seen that you by heaven have been endowed with
a powerful intellect and a formidable memory. What is more, I believe that
not only are you well suited to the pursuit of knowledge, but you were born
for it. And not only will I urge you on in this pursuit; I will insist on it. For
there is nothing sweeter, more excellent, or more pleasurable to human beings than this. But there is also something else that should inspire you to
study literature, since you happen to have inherited the wisdom of your
most excellent father, that Knight Magnificient, whose prudence in every
circumstance, not to mention fortitude and skill in the administration of
martial affairs, is so great that we seem to be gazing at an Achilles; Indeed,
I beg you not to fall short of your father whose glory you should imitate,
embrace, and magnify. If I weren't absolutely sure that you would and should
praise and agree with my thoughts, I would write at greater length about
this matter—but I see that you yourself have got the fever. Whatever I have
done, it has not been to incite this fever in you but rather to show my love
to you, your father, and your most excellent mother, to whom you will send
greetings from me. Farewell. [Undated.]

XCV

To a correspondent unnamed

She thanks him for the praises.[20]

Even if I am not in the habit of answering all those who write to me because of the difficulty I have in writing,[21] still, when I realized from your works, composed in continuous prose with both gravity of diction and a highly polished literary style emanating from nothing if not the most learned sources,[22] I decided to send these brief letters to you so that I could show you how much I esteem you and so that you would know this. And so at last I have received your praises of me, and as surely as I may think I have not deserved these, just as vehemently would I hope I shall deserve them. In the meantime, you will continue to prosper, and you will consign your name to immortality. Farewell. [Undated.]

XCVI

To an unnamed addressee

She thanks her correspondent for the honorable speech and delivers an encomium of the city of Verona.[23]

Your long-awaited letters were finally delivered to me. I've read them, and I've been very delighted with them. I have also had my parents, who have always been completely devoted to you, share in this pleasure. For from these letters I have easily seen that I have always been eager for you to love and esteem me and for you likewise to become very important in my life. Nor was I wrong, for you are a very capable man because of the persuasiveness of your speech and the seriousness of your ideas. To these qualities, one should add prudence, magnanimity, and moral and religious probity, which I have perceived in you not only from your letters but in seeing you in person when you fulfilled your obligation at this most sacred senate, together with your colleagues, the demarchs—for this is what I call them, but, according to Plautus, they called the men of this era *comites*—and the splendid knights and attorneys so knowledgeable in the law. And because of the virtues and kindness you showed me when you thought it worth your while to visit me at my humble abode, I do not deny my debt to all these men and likewise to myself.

For I confess that I am indebted to Verona and still more to the Veronese. Verona is considered the little flower of the whole state, for she flourishes among excellent men of virtue and goodness, and she is opulent in arable lands. I have enjoyed Verona's great dignity and charm, and the greatest longing for your city persists in me. Perhaps we shall fulfill your wish at some point if God is willing.

Besides, I hear that you continue to extol my name in assemblies where the most eminent men gather and especially in the presence of the praetor and most excellent knight Marco Mauroceno, a man distinguished by his ancient lineage and his luminous presence in this noblest of cities in our time. But I would be happy if I were wholly able to satisfy your eminence. And so you should know that I want very much to keep my honorable promises to you. For your abundant virtues not only invite me to love and adore you but also to entice and attract you to me. Farewell. [Undated.]

XCVII

To Bernardo Pino

She promises mutual service.[24]

As I read and reread the ornate phrases and charmingly wrought conceits in your poems and letters, I began to reflect on ancient times—times when men of genius used most readily to flourish. And you, I believe—can I speak with their indulgence—are by no means inferior to them. One delights in the last of your praises of me as a little gem among women,[25] and one believes that those praises ought not be dismissed since they come from the pen of a most excellent man. And so I would want you to recognize and believe that you are treated with importance in my work and that you are cherished and honorably loved by me. Therefore, I am making so vehement a pledge to you regarding my goodwill toward you that you will believe that I shall happily show that which I am capable of showing. Farewell. [Undated.]

XCVIII

To Pino again[26]

*N*ow I shall pay my debt to you, who have repeatedly asked for and eagerly await a little letter from me, for I have owed one to you. From your letter I have easily guessed that you are a man endowed with the fluency of genius and a fertile mind from which comes extraordinary eloquence.

Therefore what should I expect from you, and what should I know for certain? Concerning your immortality, I eagerly long to have this declared by me; I trust that you are already destined now to live for all eternity, and I trust too that from your praises of me I, too, will attain this gift of immortality. Therefore, convince yourself that it is with extraordinary goodwill that I have devoted myself to you. Farewell. [Undated.]

XCIX

To Giovanni Basilio Agostini[27]

I received your letter on April 22 wherein I could easily see the traits that are so typical of you: your superior learning and your kindness, because of which I have thought so highly of you and always shall. I only wish that the gods had endowed me with the powers of mind to shower praises upon you in equal measure, but "we ought to hope for that which our fortune has brought us." Besides, I am well aware that you have praised me too much. You have done this so that others will also celebrate my name, but these things are of less importance in comparison to what you promise me: that you will consign my name to immortality with your elegant poems. O marvelous and divine reward! I hope you will do this effortlessly with your sublime eloquence.

Anything further I should say about the world's opinion of your poems should be left to the literary men. In my view they are all very beautiful. Farewell. The priest Stefano and my parents salute you. April 1494.

C

To Paolo Fiscare, the excellent companion of Agellius

She confesses herself unequal to the praises of the companion of Agellius and sends greetings from herself and her family to him.[28]

*B*ehold, here is the very energetic and persistent herald of your praises, Giovanni Battista di Grande, a very fine youth and an eager servant of the virtues, who delivers Cassandra's little letters to your eminence. He urged and persuaded me to write you, and I became very hopeful. I felt I should obediently heed his advice. For you have clearly realized when we have talked face-to-face how much I defer to you and esteem you, and now from this letter you will realize this even more clearly. Therefore, lest you should think it not worth your time to read this letter with your usual kindness and natural generosity, you will see in every part of it my respectful love and unceasing sense of duty toward you, and you will realize that I have not been unmindful of you. Alas, why did I say "unmindful"? I would like you to know how much gravity and loyalty there is in Cassandra's esteem for you and how greatly that esteem has grown. For I believe that the duties of this esteem of mine are to cherish and venerate your greatness, your singular liberality, your incredible magnanimity and not only to praise and surpass its own innumerable gifts but also those of your men as well. And I have not been in the least wary of taking on this duty of celebrating your name. For the field of your praises is so wide that the finding of material to write about is easy for me but—and may I speak the truth?—ending the work was difficult and there were never enough words for me to celebrate you adequately in terms of the merits you have, and I was never able to achieve moderation in my encomia of you. But what more is there to say? Because of my verbosity I have become a chattering magpie. When I think about it, Cassandra says, smiling, "O immortal gods, how great and unique is my service to this most excellent companion. For when I commemorate his distinguished works, I seem like a magpie. Nor am I angry on this account but rather I rejoice all the more because an unheard of profit can be attained by celebrating with song the immortalization of a magpie!" Hear, then, why my parents are most dedicated to you, and why Cassandra, a most respectful girl, rightly asks of you please, that I may entrust them to your care. Farewell. Venice October 1490.

CI

To an unnamed addressee

An exhortation to pursue virtue.[29]

See how great the excellence of your mind is and how many of the rest of the virtues are yours. Your letters, after all, inspire me—who am daunted by the difficulties of writing—to write you whom I don't even know; but, what is more, they draw me toward you. And the preachings of the noble Ludovico Capra, who is wholly devoted to you, have not only made me an admirer of yours in your absence, but I have become a proclaimer of his praises myself. For famously adorned with these praises, you will be celebrated even more famously if you work energetically with all care and diligence on your studies in literature. And even if I do not doubt that you are doing this, still I am all the more driven to persuade and urge you to strive after virtue because I have heard that you have been endowed by nature with the highest intellectual acumen and talents. And therefore I hope that you will be counted in the very short roster of excellent men, and I hope that you will not only equal your famous forebears but that you will far exceed them. In the meantime, I'd like you to know that I am dedicated to your splendid parents, to you, and to all your kinsmen on account of their virtues and honorable goodwill. I shall be a bastion of singular loyalty and constancy toward you, insofar as your virtue has desired this. See that you recommend me to everyone there. Farewell. Venice. July 1492.[30]

CII

The Venetian protonotary apostolic priest to the maiden Cassandra Fedele

He apologizes for his writing.[31]

Most people might be surprised that I am writing to you, a maiden worthy of great public acclaim. The same people are surprised that Jerome wrote to Paula, Eustochia, Marcella,[32] and other women. But the work itself should be less the object of our attention than the intention behind the writing, lest we should seem, deservedly, to have hired the vineyard of the lord in vain.[33] Etc. [Undated.]

꒰

LETTERS OF FRIENDSHIP

CIII

Addressee unnamed

The institution of friendship.[34]

*I*t is not my intention to prove wrong or refute Empedocles' idea that love is the first principle in nature.[35] Because of it the human race was born, is continually replenished, and will be sustained for all eternity. All things in nature are subject to its power. If we agree that this bond of good-will[36] is the founding principle of humankind, then love belongs all the more to those on earth. Since the first principle of love[37] is that the powers of minds may be united for the sake of virtue and honor and so that one person may embrace another with goodwill,[38] I honor you with the love due a father. Ever since I came to know your modesty and gravity, heard your wonderful eloquence, and saw your erudition praised by the most distinguished scholars, I am more inspired every day by this pure and sacred friendship of ours, and I have realized in talking with you face-to-face that you love me as a father loves his daughter, and as Lodovico Balangino[39] also does, a most uncommon friend. Thus it is usual that in this one bond alone we should find consolation for the many cares and woes of the world. Etc. [Undated.]

CIV

To a correspondent unnamed

She praises her friend and promises to make the effort to write.[40]

*A*ristotle holds that every individual who acts does so to serve some end.[41] This axiom should, I think, be accepted by me as it has been by other thinkers. For it is the habit of a philosopher to ponder at length the result of things. For "after an event has occurred, it is the habit of the uneducated man to say, 'I had not thought of this.'"[42] And so, I have considered for a long time what caused me to write to you, who are so gifted, and I have found nothing, except that your beautifully embellished letters have roused me to take on the onus of writing, and I thought I would oblige you with this letter. I have thought it would be strange for me to write you: first, since your eloquence, learning, and innumerable virtues would require greater elegance and fluency of speech than is mine. For what eloquence is there in me for you? What sweetness of speech ? All writers rival one another in praising you; still, they struggle equally in their rivalry since your oratorical style is so multifaceted: you are a master not only of everyday speech but also of highflown, noble oratory as well. Therefore, this age comes to flower though you alone, and it revives antiquity. Second, our honorable goodwill seems not to demand proof. For not only is this already proven by our letters but also I promise now in the presence of Ludovico Gatuli,[43] a most excellent man who is like a father to me, that I and all our family will never fail you in matters of honor. [Undated.]

CV

To Pietro

She postpones fulfilling her obligations.[44]

*E*ven if I have many impediments that keep me from being able to write, much less compose letters, still it seems only right, when I think of your many kindnesses to my brother and his wife and also your virtues and the excellence of your whole family, to send these very brief letters to you since your praises are so ardently proclaimed and sung at my house by your godfather and godmother that I am marvelously drawn to loving you. We ought only to confess to you how much your virtue and service to us seems to demand of us in return. Therefore, if there is anything that can bring our honorable works to you and yours for both honor and utility,[45] please know that all of us are prepared to serve. I commend us all and especially my charming[46] sister-in-law and my brother, to you, and your consort. [Undated.]

CVI

To an unnamed correspondent

She petitions on behalf on behalf of her kinsman.[47]

*Y*ou should not be surprised that I am writing to you, a man of authority, whom I have neither met face to face nor spoken with. For I want you to know that I am indebted to you, and all the more so since I have received no small favors through your influence, while I myself have done nothing for you. Thus I have felt not simply moved but compelled to write you. Besides, I would like to show you that our goodwill is mutual, and indeed I am happier in my life because I have won your friendship than I was before. For I am loved by you, most excellent man, worthy of all praises. Therefore if you love me as much as I esteem you, will you not take into serious consideration the petition of my kinsman Ludovico Nicheta, who is most solicitous concerning you. I know that you will respond satisfactorily and quite generously in the matter that you learned of from Ludovico about Rudio, for it is right, and the matter must be legally addressed so that the debtors can satisfy their creditors. And so I would clasp your knees in supplication if I did not already trust in the bond of friendship and obligation that justice and your influence demand. All that is left to say is that you should know that I will never fail to show my respect for your name and honor. Farewell. Venice. March 1493.[48]

CVII

To Cypriano

She apologizes for the meagerness of her talent.[49]

I would like to obey your honorable request that I should write to you frequently, but Minerva scarcely permits it. For she says that the place where my genius dwells is so unrefined and uncultivated that she herself cannot live there with me. Unlucky me! What should I do? I am criticized and I can't defend myself. But please hear what I'm thinking. I'm going to blame you if I don't receive letters from you on a regular basis. Minerva is pleased with you and reveals her eloquence to you in abundant measure. I speak now from experience. For what gravity, what elegance of expression, and what sweet words are there in your letters, and these are the qualities people admire in you! I am pained, then, to receive nothing new from you. Have I not shown that I love you? O good gods! This is strange. Have I been considered too old? Do I not respect you as a daughter would a father, between whom there should be mutual love? Farewell. [Undated.]

CVIII

To Lepido Pierio d'Antichi

She praises him.[50]

Were I to write you, I might be afraid I'd be wasting my time. But you will say, "Aren't you indebted to me for my declaration about your virtue?" I had been considering not writing to you at all, for it is impossible for me to thank you adequately. Therefore I shall praise your virtues—and I shall admire them, I would add—since the act of expressing gratitude seems beyond me. But those who are ignorant can still admire, as the example of the prince of the Peripatetic philosophers indicates. In fact, I know that you, because you are eloquent and articulate, are wonderfully effective in both modes of speech. For I speak from experience; for me, both your poems and erudite letters are proof positive. Your name should—so help me God!—be celebrated by me, and I believe I ought to extol your virtues. All that remains to be said is that you should know that I am forever indebted not only to you but also to your good man and our extraordinary friend, Lancio. Farewell. [Undated.]

CIX

To a friend

She congratulates him on his patron.[51]

Your archangel (though truly ours as well) has come to us with the sweetest letter from you, and he is clearly a man who is thoroughly erudite. We could have hoped for nothing more, for we all longed to know something about you, your health, and your situation. Now with such letters and such a messenger our prayers have been well satisfied. Now we all rejoiced together about you, and we are most glad and congratulate both you and ourselves because your exceptional character has been recognized, and great men, whose lot it has been to be the recipients of rank and good fortune, have taken an interest in you with the result that through you alone our family may achieve fame. Go forth, therefore, as you have done, and when you have reached your goal with great virtue, look for greater things. You could find no better or more powerful patron than your Ascanio.

Therefore, we congratulate you again and again. If I did not dispatch my letters to you until I had yours, as it was always my intention to do, it was because of the persistently poor health that has tormented and weakened me for a long time now. For this reason I won't write more. When you have the opportunity, greet the very great papal deputy and viscount Ascanio[52] for my father and me. Consider us yours. Farewell, and love us.

CX

To Andrea Campagnola[53]

Please know that reading your letters has given me the greatest joy, for it has been easy for me to see that all things regarding our friendship are confirmed and settled, and especially that therefore you would not hesitate to extol my meager accomplishments—something I very much appreciate. For you may certainly expatiate on them with the master Fantino Pizamano, among others, a man of the highest virtue and repute. For whatever I do, I would like his approval. The only thing left is that you should know that I love you as I would a father. I send greetings from me and my parents to my godmother and all the rest of your family and friends. Vale. Venice. January 1492.

CXI

To an unnamed addressee

She concludes a pact of friendship on the basis of virtue.[54]

I want our friendship to be perennial. Why am I uneasy? For when I recognized from your eloquence and learning that your fertile mind lent such luster to learned men that the waters and rivulets of your elegance could be enjoyed, I hoped that I too could be counted among the number of those you praise. Your venerable virtue, however, which itself served as the starting point and origin of our friendship, will scarcely fall short of my opinion. Added to that is the fact that our Luca, your kinsman, who is un-usually accomplished and learned, is loved and respected by me. What more should I say? We cherish all those in your family, but then they are all con-sidered men of great ability by everyone. Since this pact of friendship has been entered into by us I therefore beg you to perform the duties of a friend: to use and treat my works honorably and rightly, as though they were yours. Farewell. [Undated.]

CXII

To Arnulfo Arculani

She offers her service.[55]

I think that you may perhaps be surprised at how often I have written to you, but when you reflect on my perennial service to you and the bond of our friendship,[56] you should not consider it in the least surprising. For since you are a man of wisdom and integrity whose qualities I wholly cherish, I love you as I would a father. But indeed, I do not think that any of my letters have been delivered to you in the past few days, alas. But I believe what I said, I deeply believe it. In sum, may I add this one thought, that I shall subject myself to your venerable authority rather than to my own will? Whatever I think will be to the good of your honor and advantage,[57] I shall willingly do. Farewell.

Please accept greetings from my parents, my whole family, and above all, from me, Cassandra. Again, farewell.

CXIII

To an unnamed prince

She offers her services and sends him greetings from herself and her family.[58]

E ven if, when my letters were sent to you before, Fortune refused to open up the great expanses of your heart and mind to the place where I am and always have been—for I knew they had not been delivered to you, and whether this happened through foul play or negligence is not at all clear to me—nonetheless, she was not able to bar my incomparable regard for you from your mind. You must only trust, by heaven, that Cassandra is so attached to you that she does not believe that any evil can result from anything you have commanded. For your clemency, loyalty, your magnanimity toward all and the enormity of your virtues would seem to demand this from me, especially since your praises are sung at my little school with absolute regularity and, above all, by your distinguished herald and excellent orator Sigismondo. For this man saluted me in your name—and this I found delightful and in no way displeasing—since I, Cassandra, seem to be esteemed thanks to the gentility of a very magnificent prince, by whose efforts it is possible that not just one human but humankind itself can be fostered and brought together from all parts of the world. Therefore I entrust myself to your magnanimity. What else? I am called Cassandra no longer, but instead, your little servant. All that remains is that I should commemorate the facts of your ancient lineage and of your illustrious founder. But these topics wend their way into every place and are often sung by the most learned men, and so they seem not to require my uncultivated oration. Therefore, though I may intentionally omit including such works, nonetheless I and my whole family send greetings to you. Farewell. [Undated.]

CXIV

To a certain unnamed prince

She invites him to emulate the example of his ancestors.[59]

First of all, while I was debating whether to send you some sort of letter or not—an act which I seemed utterly unable to carry out because of my lack of skill in such things, the magnitude of your exceptional virtue kept me from writing. Pietro Paolo Venancio, my sister's husband, who is very solicitous of your wishes, has urged me—though against my will—to write to you. For he so well described the magnificence of your mind that I was able to confess to you that I was addicted to the reading and writing of little epistles, and whenever I received them I felt that these times were happier than prior times. And so it occurred that in and through these epistles you came to be the rescuer of culture and magnanimity, the promoter of Latinity, and the patron of artists and writers. But why do I ramble on and on? In the eyes of the most illustrious prince, your father, these works of yours are no less distinguished in their wisdom or luminous in their felicity and immortality than their unique and novel results: for not only do these works themselves gleam and shine, but it is due to you that antiquity has at last been revived and the era of the ancients flowers once again. And since so sublime a gift from the gods has been proffered to you, I congratulate you on your good fortune and I rejoice that the Macarean god of poetry[60] and the art of rhetoric, whom no one denies must be worshiped and adored, is present in you. But I return now to you. I shall pray to the almighty and omnipotent Lord that, just as you place your efforts and aspirations in literature and in the doing of great works, He may assign a fortunate outcome and long-awaited prosperity to your works and heirs. Farewell. [Undated.]

∽

LETTERS EXCUSING TARDINESS[61]

CXV

Cassandra Fedele to an unnamed correspondent

On the difficulties of philosophy.[62]

*I*n this letter you will hear how slow I am at writing. This I blame on my deficient talent. But why, you will ask? Because, I say, I have dared to set sail on the vast sea of philosophy. Ah, what have I said about its powers? But, and this is more important, in the most excellent men, daring is compounded with more daring. They are not afraid to debate even the most erudite matters with everyone. O good and best God, when I think about such things I smile and think I will be laughed at. And so, if you think a lot of me and my honor as you insist you do, then you should urge me in the most vehement terms to give up the task I've begun, and I'd like you to testify that it will be difficult. Farewell. [Undated.]

CXVI

To a correspondent unnamed [63]

*Y*ou thought that your letters were delivered to me some time ago? You are mistaken since I only received them in the last few days. And worse still is that I have scarcely read them. . . .[64] But since I was able to learn from them that you were hoping that I would add laudatory verses of my own to your work, I would have done so, by Hercules. For not only should good work receive praise, but I should have wanted to oblige you anyway, even if by providing what I now think would be superfluous. I do not doubt that the most learned men have already satisfied your desire. Other than that, I only want you to know that this friendship of ours is no less a source of pleasure to me than to you. Certainly I have derived more from it than you, for I am esteemed by a man of virtue, modesty, and moral integrity whereas you are loved by a woman of little ability toward whom, since she is honorable, I pray you will continue to have goodwill. Farewell. April. [Undated.]

CXVII

Correspondent unnamed

She thanks him for his epigrams.[65]

I had decided to abstain from the business of writing since I have been kept away by a variety and number of impediments from my literary interests. Still, knowing your virtue, I could not help but write to you, particularly since someone whose advice I have freely decided to follow has urged me. . . .[66] to do the thing that should be done so that you will know how greatly I respect your character.

From this letter you should know that I hold your virtues in extraordinary esteem, that I shall praise and celebrate them as much as it is in my power to do so, and that I shall pursue our friendship with the highest order of goodwill and service that I promise always to observe and to commit myself to again and again. Farewell. May 1494.

CXVIII

To an unnamed correspondent

She thanks him for the little gift.[67]

I see that your are surprised at the lateness of my letter. Please don't be, for I have been gravely ill ever since your poems were delivered to me by Lodovico Nicheta,[68] my beloved kinsman and yours. Even if I should be distressed by this illness that torments and causes me daily pain, still I thought I must sometime indicate to you how much I have admired and continue your epigrams. Because of them I know the power of your mind and learning. In addition, you have acquired goodness in respect to other areas in your life since you have dedicated yourself to the sanctity of religion, and finally, may I not pass over in silence the kindness with which you have extolled my little-known name. For a long time, by Hercules, I wondered whether to attribute this to your eloquence or your extremely gentle nature. Clearly, I view it as the product of both. Therefore, I think I will have done the right thing when I take care to recognize those things that pertain to your honor and utility. Farewell. Venice. April 1495.

CXIX

To an unnamed correspondent[69]

After I had learned of your kindness and virtue and the excellence of your wife and sons from my brother and his wife, who are very devoted to you, I wanted urgently to send you a letter. But I have continually struggled with ill health to the point that I have been reduced to being practically bedridden. For this reason I have not been able to satisfy my own desires. Still, impelled by your very special goodwill and my debt to you, I was determined to write to you, though only to the extent that I am able and not as much as I would like. For my illness is the greatest impediment to the task of writing, and so I hope you understand my thoughts about you from this letter. I received the roebuck from you a few days ago, and I thank you since it pleases me very much. Farewell, and greet all your family from all of us. April 1495.

CXX

To an unnamed correspondent

Fedele praises him for his eloquence.[70]

Sometimes I am angry, and it isn't clear to me whether I should be angry. I am irritated that I had taken a long time to answer your letters since I don't know whether it was fair for me to have used the excuse of slowness as a cover for my own laziness and inertia, which are the things that have kept me from answering you promptly. Putting all these considerations aside, I decided to spell out my thoughts to you, not only so you would not think me ungrateful but also since I am in your debt because you have lavished such praise on me—far more than my scant merits deserve. Then, too, I write so that you may know that I find your letters beautiful and I admire your elegant poems. For these writings abound in so much eloquence, loveliness, and charm of expression, that I should be allowed to delight in them rather than give praise and to examine them as the most worthy gift the gods have given our age. It is my privilege, then, to celebrate and praise you to the best of my ability. Now enough of this. You know from this very brief letter that we follow you with the highest and most honorable goodwill. Farewell. [Undated.]

CXXI

To Benedetto Missolo Pagano, attorney

She apologizes for the lateness and brevity of her letter.[71]

I was waiting for more of your letters so that you could read mine as well. But I think I have waited a long time, and it seems right to me to answer your lengthy and elegant letter. You have shown me the greatest kindness in sending me letters so frequently, since they remove any impediments in my writing to you, nor is the subject matter for my writing you just left up to me.

For it has been necessary for you to send me almost countless numbers of letters. Perhaps you will say, "Why, when the copiousness of my letters assists you, would you not write me back? What do you say? For I have been thinking that it's pointless to write you. Nor should I, by heaven, I have embarked on a friendship with you."

But this friendship between us is so unique that nothing can be added to it, nor is it possible for me to praise you. Your most ample and divine gifts—I call heaven to witness!—would exhaust the most consummate orator. From these thoughts of mine, you will easily understand the lateness and economy of my letter. But now the great and copious works of the Peripatetic call me away. Farewell, and we would put ourselves in your hands. September 1490.

NOTES TO CHAPTER 6

1.   "Incerto"; literally, to someone unspecified or undetermined.

2.   I refer to Cicero's famous essay on the subject, *De amicitia* (*On Friendship*).

3.   Tom. 91, 129–30.

4.   This letter's mythological allusions center on Apollo, the Greek god of prophecy, poetry, and the healing arts and his agents: his son, Aesculapius, the god of
medicine; the Muses, goddesses of poetry and literary inspiration; the mythological
Cassandra, a mortal to whom Apollo gave the gift of prophecy; and the female seers
known as the Sibyls, the greatest of whom Aeneas consulted at Cumae in Italy.

5.   The Greek poet Hesiod (8th century B.C.E.) wrote of a golden age when humans
lived without war or injustice; after that age ended things went downhill. A silver
age and a bronze age came and went, and at last came the worst time of all, the iron
age. See *Works and Days* 90–180.

6.   He refers to Sappho (the 7th century B.C.E. female Greek poet), Priam's prophe-
sying daughter Cassandra, and Virgil's Cumaean sibyl suggests the preference of at
least some Italian humanists for the figures of local myth over Greek.

7.   Tom. 92, 131–32.

8.   In the clause "verum [quod] magnifice dicebat ratum esse perspexi" an obligatory *quod* must be understood in order for the sentence to parse.

9.   Tom. 95, 138–40. After 1487, with the publication in Modena, Nuremburg, and
Venice of her *Oratio* for Bertucci Lamberti's baccalaureate at the University of Padua,
Fedele's fame, as this letter demonstrates, spanned the literate world.

10.   This unidentified Latin quotation reads "Musa tibi vocem dedit, et Cyllenius
autem, / Iupiter ingenium magnus Apollo chelim." All Tomasini's quotations are set
off in roman type to distinguish them from the italic type of the text.

11.   This is the canonical list of famous Italian women writers from the fifteenth
century. This list appears in print for the first time in Fregosa, *Factorum Dictorumque
memorabilium Libri IX* (Venice 1483), Jacopo Filippo Foresti, *Liber de claris scelestisque mulieribus* (Ferrara 1497), and thereafter in Italian and French encyclopedias on celebrated women throughout the sixteenth and seventeenth centuries.

12.   The canonical list of ancient Greek and Roman women who serve as exempla
and as foremothers for modern gifted women such as Cassandra and who figure in
her letters include Cornelia, Hortensia, Sappho, Aspasia, the Amazons, and the warrior Camilla. Ambrogio identifies each of these women, just in case his reader is not
in the know.

13.   Lucius Caecilius Lactantius (c. 249–320 C.E.; also known as Firmianus), Christian writer born in North Africa; his *Opificio Dei*, to which Ambrogio appears to refer
here, argued that the structure of the human body is a demonstration of divine prov-
idence.

14.   Roman orator (106–43 B.C.E.).

15.   Tom. 96, 141–42.

16.   Tom. 90, 128–29. This correspondent is unknown to our sources..

17.   Tomasini has "iubar *vitatarum* atque vatum." "Light of priests" and "women shunned" is impossible; "vitatarum" must be a missprint, possibly for *invitatarum* (women summoned or called; female initiates).

18.   Tom. 87, 124–25. Tomasini speculates (*Epistolae et orationes*, 219) that this admirer of Cassandra's might be Camillo Querino, a poet who flourished under Pope Leo X.

19.   Tom. 17, 28–30. This particular Camosi is unknown. Tomasini writes only that Sansoni's book *De illustribus familiis*, should be consulted on the Camosi.

20.   Tom. 47, 69–70.

21.   She refers to her difficulty as "impedimenta scribendi" here, which may be a reference to the chronic illness of which she complains in a number of other letters that has kept her from writing.

22.   Something obviously must be missing in the Latin text: I suggest a *nil* be added before the *nisi*.

23.   Tom. 49, 75–77.

24.   Tom. 22, 35.

25.   The Latin phrase she uses is *ut mulierum gloriola*: literally, like a little glory among women.

26.   Tom. 23, 36.

27.   Tom. 61, 89. Tomasini's erroneous heading to this letter is "Carmina promittit sua." She nowhere promises to send him her poems.

28.   Tom. 30, 46–47.

29.   Tom. 50, 77–78.

30.   This letter is actually dated MCCCCLXXXII (1482). I am assuming that is a printing error since there are no letters dated that early in her letter collection.

31.   Tom. 118, 181. This is a strange fragment; it is likely the first page of a letter the rest of which was discarded.

32.   Holy women who were contemporaries of St. Jerome (c. 347–419 C.E.).

33.   See Mt 20. 1–16 on the parable of the vineyard.

34.   Tom. 97b, 167–68. Tomasini erroneously numbered this letter 97 although there is already a previous letter 97 (Tomasini, 143–44); this letter here will be numbered "97b."

35.   "Amicitiam principium esse rerum naturalium." The word Empedocles uses for friendship is the Greek *philia*, which can be translated as both friendship and love. The Latin term *amicitia* connotes friendship, accord, affinity, and purportedly nonerotic love as opposed to *amor*. But there is plenty of erotic resonance and ambivalence in humanist *amicitia*. On the vocabulary of humanist friendship see Robin, *Filelfo in Milan*, esp. 22–42.

36. "Vinculum benivolentiae": literally, bond of goodwill. *Benivolentia* can be understood variously as goodwill, friendship, benevolence, affection, accord, or understanding between persons.

37. "Et cum prima sit amicitiae *ratio* et honestatis probitatisque causa animorum uniantur." *Ratio* connotes reason, order, rationality, and is generally used to translate the Greek word *logos*.

38. "Ut . . . benevolentia alter alterum amplectatur." The notion of reciprocal goodwill between friends is fundamental to humanist friendship.

39. "Balangino" is unknown to me.

40. Tom. 46, 68–69.

41. Aristotle *Nicomachean Ethics* 1.i.1–3.

42. The source of this quote is unknown to me.

43. "Ludovico Gatuli" is unknown to me.

44. Tom. 45, 67–68.

45. The phrase *conducere et honori et utilitate* ("to employ for both honor and utility," suggesting that the position will confer both money and status on the client) is a typical humanist formula for a prospective client to use in a letter to his/her patron in the language of Renaissance patronage.

46. The adjective *delitus* (here in the superlative "delitissimos"), not in *OLD*, seems to be related to *deliciae*, substantive meaning delight, charming one.

47. Tom. 79, 109–10. See Cavazzana, "Cassandra Fedele," 82–83, for details on the case of Ludovico Nicheta, a kinsman (*affinis*) of Cassandra, who was charged with having counterfeited Venetian ducats. Invoking the stock terms of *amicitia* (she speaks of "the bond of friendship and obligation," the reciprocal "love" and "esteem," and the "mutual good will" between her unnamed correspondent and herself) she begs him to intervene on behalf of her kinsman. Nicheta was convicted and sentenced to lose an eye and a hand for the felony. Since no name is attached to her addressee this letter may represent a draft of the letter or letters that were later sent, perhaps to more than one high official in the state.

48. Nicheta was not sentenced until February 16, 1500, see Cavazzana, "Cassandra Fedele," 83.

49. Tom. 34, 52.

50. Tom. 38, 59. Though her offhand paraphrase from Aristotle would seem to place Lepido in her Paduan circle, he is unknown to me and her biographers. Lancio, mentioned in the last sentence of the letter, is also unknown to me.

51. Tom. 86, 123–24.

52. Cardinal Ascanio Maria Sforza (1455–1505), son of Francesco Sforza, duke of Milan, and Bianca Maria Visconti. He was an influential promoter of humanism and patron of humanist writers.

53. Tom. 53, 79–80. Her addressee Andrea Campagnola, who seems not to be related to her Paduan friend Girolamo Campagnola, is not referred to by her biographers, nor is Fantino Pizamano, to whom she alludes in this letter.

54.   Tom. 27, 40. The "Luca" to whom she refers is also unknown.

55.   Tom. 20, 32.

56.   "Vinculum amicitiae nostrae et observantia perennis in te." This is a stock phrase in humanist letters; it features the image of friendship as a relationship that binds (*vinculum*, chain, fetter, or link) and connects over time, place, and circumstance.

57.   "Quicquid *honorem ac emolumentam* pertinere existimabo me . . . esse facturam" (my emphasis). Her promise to do whatever is necessary to further both Arnulfo's reputation (*honorem*) and his material gain (*emolumentum*) is formulaic in humanist (i.e., patronage) friendship.

58.   Tom. 26, 39–40. This letter to an unnamed "prince" (*princeps*) could be a recyclable form letter to be sent out to any prospective patron. Note the tropes: she is his servant; he is her lord and commander; she will rely on his clemency, loyalty, and generosity (code for: she knows he will pay her handsomely and on time for the eulogy she will write about him); she will praise him for his virtue, his gentility, and the illustriousness of his lineage; she is unfit to praise such a great man, her writings are uncultivated; nonetheless she will do so.

59.   Tom. 24, 37. Like the previous letter, this too could easily serve as a one-size-fits-all form letter to a patron. She flatters the man as if he were a noted patron of the arts and an active promoter of the classical revival.

60.   Macareus was a priest of Apollo, god of poetry, music, and the arts.

61.   The letters in this group have a greeting card or form letter character. Each has a phony intimacy about it, greeting card style. By the variety of excuses provided in the group of letters that follows, one can see that Fedele had a handy template from which to pick the appropriate excuse to dispense depending on the status of her correspondent and their relationship.

62.   Tom. 5, 7–8.

63.   Tom. 62, 90.

64.   Tomasini indicates with ellipsis dots here that some of the text is missing.

65.   Tom. 63, 90–91.

66.   Tomasini indicates with ellipsis dots here that text is missing.

67.   Tom. 64, 91–92.

68.   See letter CVI and n. 46 above in this chapter. This is the same cousin Lodovico Nicheta who would in February 1500 be convicted of a felony (on the date of sentencing and documentation see Cavazzana, "Cassandra Fedele," 83). Though Fedele identifies her correspondent as a family member, the rest of the letter is a standard patronage letter that could have been sent to anyone.

69.   Tom. 65, 92–93. Tomasini's caption erroneously reads "Bellum a Venetiis cum Carolo VIII gestum attigit," since there is not a word about the war in this letter, or Charles VIII, or France.

70. Tom. 8, 11.

71. Tom. 31, 48. The attorney (as Tomasini indicates in his title to the letter) Benedetto Missolo is otherwise unknown to Fedele's biographers. Her references to his elegant style and to the Peripatetic philosophers mark him as a likely member of Fedele's Padua circle, but this flattering letter could just as easily have been addressed to most of her other academic and literary friends.

VII

THE PUBLIC LECTURES

Other women before Cassandra Fedele had delivered speeches in the fifteenth-century Italy. But these were nobles or convent women. They spoke for their family's interests or those of their religious communities, and the venues for their speeches were princely courts or monasteries. Cassandra Fedele was the first professional woman writer to speak in a public, city forum and the first to address public issues in her own voice.[1] Three of Fedele's public orations, preserved in the 1636 edition of her collected letters and orations, are presented in this chapter.[2] The first of these, delivered by the twenty-two-year-old Fedele at the University of Padua in 1487 at the graduation ceremony of her cousin Bertuccio Lamberti deals with the transitory nature of worldly goods and the true path to the good through studies in natural, moral, and metaphysical philosophy. The second of these orations, presented to the doge Agostino Barbarigo and the Venetian Senate,[3] addresses the practical question of higher education for women. The third oration, spoken by the ninety-one-year-old Fedele before the doge Francesco Venier and the assembled members of the Senate in 1556, celebrates the arrival of Bona Sforza, queen of Poland, in Venice. The first of her public lectures was published twice in Italy and once in Germany before 1500;[4] subsequent reports of her public appearances as an orator and a pundit brought Fedele fame throughout Europe.

I

An Oration Delivered at the University of Padua for Bertuccio Lamberti,
Canon of Concordia, on His Receiving Honors in the Liberal Arts[5]

Gracious fathers, officers of the academy, and gentlemen worthy of the highest honor, if it were fitting for me to be afraid, now that I have bravely plunged in and stand here in your presence in this great assembly, I would stutter and stammer, and I would gradually lose my composure. But I know that my coming here is fitting, though it is by no means very brave. So let the fear end here.

I am well aware that many of you may think it outrageous that I, a young girl to whom higher learning is denied, would come before an assembly of men so learned and so luminous and not worry about my sex or talent for speaking, especially in this city where the liberal arts are flourishing now as they once did in Athens. Nonetheless, the bonds of affection and kinship that exist between me and Bertuccio compel me, however unwilling I should be, to shoulder this burden. Indeed, I would rather be accused of audacity than be blamed for refusing to honor so close a friend as he with loyalty, devotion, and service. Moreover, the very things that at first seemed to deter me now urge and demand that I take on this duty. And so I have dared to come here to speak relying on your great gentility and leniency, which, I trust, will allow you to forgive me if I should speak inelegantly and unintelligently. Indeed, there is such power in this particular virtue of yours that I hold it as proof that you are endowed with all the other virtues. I would say more about these virtues of yours if I were not afraid of detaining and boring you with such a lengthy oration—and if I were arrogant enough to think I could do your virtues justice.

Thus I shall not launch into the one theme I was called here to address, but I shall outline it in general terms. Certainly it is more difficult to find an ending for your praises than to embark on them. Having voiced these concerns, I have decided to begin my oration with a new example. Since it behooves me to speak about my kinsman, lest I should appear to be avoiding the duty assigned to me, I shall speak briefly. I have chosen to discuss the tripartite nature of good in humans according to the teachings of Cicero, Plato, and the Peripatetics,[6] since these philosophers believe that truth and justice spring from a good that is threefold. These goods belong to the soul, the body, and to those things that certain great philosophers believe are governed by fortune.

Listen closely then, distinguished gentlemen, although I know you expect to hear nothing too learned from me, for lest you think that I might use sophisticated and facile jargon in order to impress you (a thing I always avoid at all cost) I shall do what I trust you will like. For the splendor of a noble lineage (and you know this) should be honored with praises since the virtues of such a lineage are very much in keeping with its nobility. Such virtues add glory to a family, and they alone make men noble and great. But what quality or characteristic is it more important to praise in my kinsman than his character? How shall I praise his excellent studies? How do I speak of his mind, which is capacious, alert, flexible, and open to learning? His tenacious memory? His special love of the liberal arts? It is too superficial to say he was born in the most famous marketplace in the world, in Venice, if we do not add that his education in religion and devotional literature was superb. Because of his graceful demeanor toward everyone he had many friends, many advocates, and many men were desirous of his friendship. And the more these things have added to his stature, the less self-importantly he has carried himself. Just consider his carriage and the dignity of his appearance. And it is clear to everyone how innocently and with what piety he has spent his youth. For you will not easily find a son who either is or has been more respectful toward his parents, and finally, so that I may cover much in a single sentence: you see here a man who is as mature in virtue as he is young in years. And had this virtue of his not been apparent to all, I would never have dared to extol it in so great an assembly.

I shall now attempt to progress to more important matters. I shall pay tribute in brief to Bertuccio's great wealth, his strength of body, and other things of this sort. But the achievements of the mind, like those of the soul, last forever, whereas there is a beginning and end of the goods of the body and fortune. For I have never believed that money, magnificent houses, and material goods—the things with which most men are obsessed—should be included among true goods. A hunger for things can never be filled or satisfied. For who would deny that these fragile and constantly shifting pathways are not perilous and slippery? Where is now the magnificent city of Thebes, so glorious once in its luxury and buildings? Where now are Cyrus and Darius and the extravagances of the Persians?[7] Where are the Macedonians and their kings Philip and Alexander?[8] Where are the Spartans and their King Lycurgus?[9] Where is the strength of invincible Hercules? Spurina is known less for the duration of his beauty than he is for his loss of it, when he wounded his face.[10] Who can possess such things with impunity? For Necessity by the same law apportions lots to both distinguished citizens and the rabble. For was not Croesus, king of the Lydians, deprived of his immense wealth and immense riches by Cyrus?[11] And a lowly woman robbed Cyrus of his life and kingdom,[12] and of course Xerxes, who creaked across land and sea on a massive bridge made from the branches of trees,[13] having lost his entire army, fled to his kingdom, which was now contented to see the raft that was his boat. I could go on reciting useless things: where now is Rome—the city that ruled over barbarian tribes and tyrannized the Greeks, as if she were some empress or a queen? Truly, all things wither and die. Grim death pursues all transitory things.

The advantages obtained through virtue and the intellect, however, are useful to future generations. Because our Bertuccio, even when he was a boy, always applied all his energy and enthusiasm, his superb memory and intellectual acuity to eloquence, he has now become an orator of the first order and a uniquely gifted speaker. These qualities add considerable elegance and beauty to his physical advantages and his good fortune. For it is speech that makes men superior to all other animals. After all, is there any subject that is so boorish, dull, idiotic, or uninteresting that it does not come to life when it is garnished with and framed by an oration? What is more praiseworthy than eloquence? What is more exceptional or more gratifying than the admiration of one's listeners, the hope of one's clients, or the gratitude of those one has defended? There is nothing so incredible or tangled that it can't be rendered believable and straightforward by an oration. States and their princes foster and support such training in the rhetorical arts since it enables men to become more humane, more pleasing, and more noble. For this reason this sphere within philosophy has won a place for itself under that sweetest of rubrics, the humanities, since it softens and civilizes those who are of a crude, uncultivated nature.

I come to praise a young man for his studies in philosophy and his energetic pursuit of learning that has always been considered divine knowledge by the wisest men, and deservedly so. For other disciplines provide knowledge about the world men inhabit; but this one teaches clearly what man himself is, what he should seek, and what he should avoid. And there is no rational principle, no preeminent methodology, nothing that pertains ultimately to the good life that philosophy does not pursue in its investigations. Has anyone steeped in philosophy ever died lost in the throes of error? These studies burnish minds; they sharpen and strengthen the power of reason; and when men's minds lapse into error, these anchors correct and guide them. This is why Stratonicus[14] rightly called this discipline the one safe haven. By intellectual struggle we are able to seek and understand the mysteries. Philosophy is the one craftsman and schoolmistress suited to instructing us in the good life. For what surpasses its utility? What happier pursuit is there than the quest for honorable pleasure? What is more suited to the grandeur of cities than the study of philosophy? Therefore the almost divine Plato wrote that those republics would be fortunate whose rulers were philosophers or whose governments were administered by men schooled in philosophy.[15]

The invention of philosophy, the most sacred of disciplines, has been attributed to various men. The Africans believed it was Atlas; to the Thracians it was Orpheus or Zamolxis; to the Thebans it was Linus; to the Egyptians, Vulcan; and to the Gauls, their Druids.[16] Other peoples attributed philosophy's primordial beginnings or at least some part of its beginnings to other figures. Whether its beginnings lay with Zoroaster, king of the Magi or with the Gymnosophists of the Chaldeans and the Persians, philosophy has always been separated into the following divisions: metaphysical, moral, and natural. The enormous diligence with which Bertucio has pursued his studies is difficult to capture in words. He has spent as much time cultivating these studies as others have dedicated to the celebration of high holy days, to the pleasures of the body, and to physical rest. Certainly the joy and recognition that he has now attained through his labors and his all-night bouts of study need no further testimony from me as I stand before you, most learned gentlemen, since you in your wisdom have already judged that he is to receive honors in philosophy, although it is all together certain that he will proceed each day to higher things.

I would have spoken at greater length, had I not known with certainty that Giovanni Reggio,[17] whom you heard a little while ago, had commemorated Bertuccio's accomplishments in a longer, more elegant speech. But since this is the case, most noted gentlemen, lest I should turn your happiness into boredom with a longer speech, I shall draw to the end of my speech putting aside the rest of my oration.

I turn now to that duty that I know above all is mine: to express thanks first to you, the magistrates of this magnificent city, and next to you, most excellent fathers and distinguished men, because you are deserving of my gratitude for honoring my kinsman in this beautiful ceremony with your most agreeable and honorable presence in this place. For there is no one who is possessed of so doltish and ungrateful a mind that he would deliberately wish not to sing your praises for an honor so freshly conferred. I must, however, tell you that there is neither a seasoned and prudent orator who can fully describe all your virtues (for that cannot be done), nor is there one who can even fleetingly pay lip service to them.

And so in conclusion, happy are you, Cassandra, since you were fortunate enough to be born in these times, and you, blessed era of mine, and you, famous city of Padua, graced in your bounty of learned men. May everyone now cease—yes, I say cease—to marvel at antiquities. God almighty has granted that the studies of all nations should flourish in this one place and be commended and consecrated for all eternity. Though age will consume and bring an end to all things, may these divine studies of yours grow and flourish every day more and more, and may they be preserved from all the wounds of oblivion.[18]

And so I return to this one theme on which I had begun to speak, namely, that I wish to give uncommon thanks to you because you are here today in great numbers to honor my kinsman Bertucio and me who came to praise him, and because by your most distinguished presence you have brought glory to us both. On this account, may I pledge, as I would do on behalf of a brother, that as long as my kinsman and I are alive, neither one of us shall ever flag in our service to you or in our gratitude for your magnanimity, as is fitting in remembrance of your great gift.[19] On the 18th day before the first of the month, in the Christian year of 1487.

II

An Oration Delivered before the doge Agostino Barbarigo
and the Venetian Senate: In Praise of Letters[20]

The great orator and philosopher Giorgio Valla,[21] who has thought me worthy of his presence here, has urged and emboldened me, most honored prince, conscript fathers,[22] and learned senators, to ponder what the constant and debilitating immersion in scholarship might do for the weaker sex in general, since I myself intend to pursue immortality through such study. And so I decided to oblige him and to obey his repeated demands and finally his insistence that I deliver a public oration, though I blush to do so and am ever mindful that I am a member of the female sex and that my intellect is small. Thus not only should the boorish rabble be ashamed of itself, it should cease to make trouble for me because of my dedication to the exercise of my natural skills and talents. Therefore it should not seem beside the point to anyone that my mind and heart might quail at the start and that I might stutter. For when I reconsidered the magnitude of the subject on which I had decided to speak before this elegant and grand assembly, I knew that nothing so elegant, illuminating, and polished even from a man who was the soul of eloquence could be brought to you that would not seem dry, uninteresting, and crude in comparison with the greatness of your learning and your presence. For who has the intellectual power and gift of eloquence that enable him to be equal to delivering an oration on the praise of letters or doing so before such an erudite audience as you? For this reason, mindful of the difficulty of the task and the deficiency of my powers, I could very easily shy away from this opportunity to speak, were it not that your magnanimity and kindness toward all people urged me to come before you, especially since I am well aware that it is not your wont to demand or expect anyone to take on a heavier load than the rationale for the occasion allows or than their shoulders would appear to proclaim that they can. Besides, two additional things persuade me to speak: your fitting affability, which in the beginning seemed to give me pause; and your kindness, which causes me to think no oration would be more pleasing to listen to or sweeter to men who are extremely erudite, as are the great majority of you, and also to men who are notably interested in education than an oration whose subject is (in whatever way appropriate) the praise of literature and the liberal arts. Stirred by these thoughts, since I see that you are listening to me attentively, I shall speak very briefly on the study of the liberal arts, which for humans is useful and honorable, pleasurable and enlightening since everyone, not only philosophers but the most ignorant man, knows and admits that it is by reason that man is separated from beast. For what is it that so greatly helps both the learned and the ignorant? What so enlarges and enlightens men's minds the way that an education in and knowledge of literature and the liberal arts do? These two things not only remove men far above the realm of the beasts, but they so simply and easily separate educated men from the ignorant and uncultivated that in my opinion men in paintings and even men's shadows do not differ more from real human beings than do the uneducated and untaught from men who are imbued with learning. But if men who are boorish and unlettered have a natural yet undeveloped spark of reason and they leave it unstirred for the whole of their lives, they will force it from disuse and habit to die, and in so doing they will render themselves unable to undertake great things. For wandering aimlessly they walk in darkness no matter what the circumstances, and through imprudence, ignorance, and inexperience they run headlong into calamities, and they render the course of their lives accidental. These are men who make Fortune their god. They place all things in her lap, and when she favors them they kiss her and approve, and when she opposes them they accuse her loudly and grieve.

So many times Fortune, ruler of the world and my life, is the best soldier in battle, ready with her company. No need for prayers: seek now death with your sword. Fortune brought such prosperity to the great man when he kept the faith; but even him Fortune marked for death and at the summit of his career. In one cruel day she brought every disaster on men to whom she had given years free from harm. Pompey was a man who never understood that happiness is mixed with sorrow. Happy was he when no god disturbed him, and wretched was he when none spared him. When Fortune for the first time struck him, the sands resounded with a blow long delayed.[23]

But erudite men who are filled with the knowledge of divine and human things turn all their thoughts and considerations toward reason as though toward a target, and they free their minds from all pain, though plagued by many anxieties. These men are scarcely subjected to fortune's innumerable arrows and they prepare themselves in every way to live well and in happiness. They follow reason as their leader in all things; nor do they consider themselves only, but they are also accustomed to assisting others with their energy and advice in matters public and private.

And so Plato, a man almost divine, wrote that those states would be fortunate in which the men who were heads of state were philosophers or in which philosophers took on the duty of administration. He noted, I believe, that men well endowed by fortune with physical advantages are more often drawn to vices and are more easily seduced than those who lack such advantages. But those who are born with intellectual advantages who fail to cultivate the learned disciplines and who make deficient use of their advantages he judged unlearned and unsuited to managing of affairs of state. Nor was he wrong in this. The study of literature refines men's minds, forms and makes bright the power of reason, and washes away all stains from the mind, or at any rate, greatly cleanses it. It perfects its gifts and adds much beauty and elegance to the physical and material advantages that one has received by nature. States, however, and their princes who foster and cultivate these studies become much more humane, more gracious, and more noble. For this reason, these studies have won for themselves the sweet appellation, "humanities." Indeed, those who were uncultivated and had harsh natures became more cultivated and gentle through their immersion in these studies, while those whom nature has endowed with external goods and other gifts of the body, who for the most part are arrogant and petulant, acquire modesty, gentility, and a certain miraculous amiability toward all other men through their exposure to the liberal arts. Just as places that lie unused and uncultivated become fertile and rich in fruits and vegetables with men's labor and hard work and are always made beautiful, so are our natures cultivated, enhanced, and enlightened by the liberal arts. But clearly Philip the king of Macedonia,[24] whose virtue and work increased the wealth of the

Macedonians and enabled them to take power over so many peoples and nations, understood this. In a letter to the philosopher Aristotle in which he announced the birth of his son Alexander,[25] he explained that he rejoiced still more that his son happened to be born in Aristotle's lifetime than that he had come into the world as the heir to a great empire. O excellent words and elevated sentiments, worthy of so great a prince and emperor! That king and illustrious emperor, who was affected by having spent so long a time in his own life in the business of war and conquest, knew that an empire could by no means be ruled justly, prudently, and gloriously by a man who had not been trained in literature and the best arts.

This was later born out by Alexander himself who, having become learned in the liberal arts under the tutelage of Aristotle, far surpassed all other princes and emperors who came before or after him in ruling, increasing, and protecting his empire. For this reason the men of antiquity rightly believed that all leaders who were uneducated, however experienced they were in military matters, were boorish and uncultivated.

But enough on the utility of literature since it produces not only an outcome that is rich, precious, and sublime but also provides one with advantages that are extremely pleasurable, fruitful, and lasting—benefits that I myself have enjoyed. And when I meditate on the idea of marching forth in life with the lowly and execrable weapons of the little woman—the needle and the distaff—even if the study of literature offers women no rewards or honors, I believe women must nonetheless pursue and embrace such studies alone for the pleasure and enjoyment they contain. . . .[26]

III

An Oration Addressed to the Venetian Doge Francesco Venier
on the Occasion of the Arrival of the Most Serene Queen of Sarmatia[27]

If I were able to comprehend the enormous joy evinced by the Venetian Senate on the occasion of your long-expected arrival, most serene and happiest queen, I would say on this day, which has been taken up with welcoming you warmly into the city, that your arrival has brought greater pleasure and delight and that the city has radiated more happiness and festivity than during any prior visit by a king or emperor. Therefore since by the decree of this most noble Senate the privilege of conveying to you the will of the entire populace, their affection for you, and their obvious delight has been assigned to me, I must only lament that the thoughts that first arose in my heart and mind I can now neither explain to you in words nor elucidate with an oration—because, I believe, of the very enormity of such joy. But the serenity of our faces and the happiness of our hearts are the greatest testimony to the appearance of majesty. For there you have the most reliable witnesses of our sentiments. For that which is harbored in the heart shines forth as though through a window, and that which you cannot hear because of this speaker's lack of eloquence can be perceived through comments from the populace and from the eyes of everyone here just as joy is palpable in the looks of those who are rejoicing. Thus it is that, since everyone is overcome with incredible joy, and you with your joyous gaze have brought kudos and felicity, all men think that this illustrious day should not only be marked, as they say, with a white stone,[28] but everyone thinks the day should be commemorated each year with solemn honors. For no matter how ignorant one may be by nature, is there anyone who would not embrace the memory of the queen of the Sarmatians? Who would not marvel at the greatness of her august and holy presence? Who would not worship and revere her as though she were a goddess?

In order to respond to so many distinguished and renowned women, which I can do, I shall say that the saying "the fickle herd can feed on heavenly air"[29] certainly can never be, since, while the divine beauty of your mind and body has slipped away from my heart and mind, the memory of your name will remain so deeply ingrained in everyone's mind that no age will ever obliterate it.

But to say something myself to celebrate the greatness of your fame, which has traveled to the ends of the earth while I have remained silent, I would gladly spend all the days of my life. Nor is there anything that could please me more or that I could hope for more than that, not because I think your name would be embellished by my work and industry, but so that in glorifying you I might hope that my life too might be consigned to immortality.

Now old age, which lies heavy on my shoulders, has weakened the powers of my mind and has turned me away from, and made me rudely ill-disposed toward, the settling of my debts. I believe it will be no less valued and esteemed, therefore, to promise that I will never cease to beseech God almighty on behalf of the greatness of your most felicitous reign and your daily felicity of mind and body. Thus, most sacred queen, this magnanimous republic has decreed that, as a token of its admiration for the incredible gifts of your mind, you are to receive its highest tribute, and you will be decorated most generously with the honors due you. For your singular prudence in ruling your people during peacetime and the fortitude of your admirable mind amid the winds of war, in which you easily surpass both Tamaris, queen of the Scythians, and Hysicratea, queen of Pontus,[30] merit this honor and can bring greater glory.

But why does the slowness of this tongue of mine not travel to the place where the most sublime desires of mind and genius escape, to this placid sea, this serenity of air, this sweet and lightly spiraling breeze to show favor to the wishes of our august Senate? Who does not see that your entrance in the future into the heart of this city will be happier since the heavens, the land, and the very seas themselves seem to welcome and honor this queen with joy: and not only the Senate and the Venetian people, but foreign nations and peoples all over the world attend her with every honor? I have spoken.

NOTES TO CHAPTER 7

1. I have suggested in Laura Cereta, *Collected Letters of a Renaissance Humanist* (Chicago: University of Chicago Press, 1998) that one other professional writer, Laura Cereta may have delivered lectures in some sort of public venue in Brescia, but her "public" lectures, if they ever took place, are undocumented.

2. *Clarissimae feminae Cassandrae Fidelis, venetae. Epistolae et orationes,* edited by Jacopo Filippo Tomasini (Padua: Franciscus Bolzetta, 1636). Margaret King published the first English translations of the three orations in M. L. King and Albert Rabil, Jr., eds., *Her Immaculate Hand. Selected Works by and about the Woman Humanists of Quattrocento Italy,* 2d. rev. ed. (Binghamton, New York: Medieval & Renaissance Texts & Studies, 1991), 48–52, 69–73, 74–76.

3. The date of the delivery of this oration is unknown; Cavazzana believes that Fedele presented it sometime after her Padua speech.

4. Modena (1487), Nuremberg (1488), and Venice (1489).

5. Tom. oration no. 1, 193–201.

6. These were the principal schools or fathers of philosophy that were taught at universities in the fifteenth century. By the Peripatetic school she means principally Aristotle.

7. Cyrus II the Great (590–529 B.C.E.) was the founder of the Achaemenid Persian empire, famed for defeating Croesus and bringing the Greek cities of Asia Minor, Babylon, Assyria, Syria, and Palestine under his control; Cyrus's son Cambyses's successor was Darius I (521–486 B.C.E.); he attempted to extend the Persian empire to mainland Greece, but lost decisively to the Athenians at Marathon in 490 B.C.E., which spelled the beginning of the end of Persian hegemony in the region.

8. Philip II, king of Macedon (382–336 B.C.E.), laid the foundations for his son Alexander's ("the Great," 356–323 B.C.E.) conquest of Greece, Asia Minor, Egypt, Babylon, Russian Turkestan, and parts of India. His empire did not long survive his death at the age of thirty-three.

9. Lycurgus (c. 775 B.C.E.), the legendary king of Sparta and founder of the Spartan constitution, is credited with building a culture and military machine that rendered Sparta by the fifth century B.C.E. one of the two most powerful city states in Greece and Athens's chief rival for the leadership of the Greek states at the time of the Peloponnesian War (431–404 B.C.E.).

10. Valerius Maximus 3.5, ext. 1. Spurina was an Etruscan youth who cut himself in the face to discourage women from pursuing him.

11. Cyrus II the Great, king of Persia, defeated King Croesus and took his empire from him; see n. 7 above.

12. Herodotus 1.213–15. The woman referred to is the queen of the Massagetae.

13. "Ramorum apparatu" ("an apparatus made of the branches of trees"), Fedele calls it. According to Herodotus 5–9, it was a bridge of boats that stretched all the way across the Hellespont.

14. Stratonicus (c. 390 B.C.E.) was an Athenian musician whose sayings were posthumously collected.

15. Plato *Republic* 5.471c–474b.

16. On the origins of philosophy and the role of Atlas; Orpheus; Zamolxis; Linus; Vulcan (Hephaestus); Zoroaster, "king of the Magi"; and the Druids as founders of the discipline Fedele is indebted to the very popular text in the Renaissance, Diogenes Laertius's *Lives of the Philosophers*, 1, prologue 1–3.

17. See Cavazzana, "Cassandra Fedele," 254 and Pavanello, *Un maestro del Quattrocento*, 181. Little is known about Giovanni Reggio (or Regio), only that he was a humanist born in Bergamo and that he spoke at the ceremony for Bertucci at Padua prior to Cassandra, and did so eloquently.

18. Tom. oration no. 1, 201: "Seque ab omni oblivionis inuria vendicabunt." Her imagery of the wrong done, the wound inflicted by failing to remember, is especially poignant here.

19. This concluding sentence contains the key to the oration in that here she identifies herself with Bertucio blending her own cause with his so that his rite of passage becomes in a sense a baccalaureate and passage of initiation for her.

20. Tom. oration no. 2, 201–7. The occasion of this oration, which was delivered before the doge and the Venetian Senate sometime after the Padua oration, is discussed by Cavazzana, "Cassandra Fedele," 252–53, who says only that the oration was delivered to the doge Agostino Barbarigo in the presence of the ambassadors from Bergamo, who were so impressed with Fedele's eloquence, grace, and presence that they wrote her a lengthy encomium and dispatched it to her as soon as they returned to Bergamo. Cavazzana is unable to date the oration but suggests that it must have been delivered after Bertuccio's oration (in 1487) but prior to the end of Barbarigo's tenure as doge in 1521.

21. Giorgio Valla (1447–1500), one of the most brilliant humanists of his age, was born in Piacenza. He taught at Milan's university in Pavia (1466–85), and he occupied a chair of rhetoric at the school of San Marco in Venice after 1485; he was the author of numerous editions, translations, commentaries, and Latin letters.

22.   "Patres conscripti" is the title Cicero used to address the members of the Roman Senate in his orations.

23.   The passage is from Lucan *Pharsalia* 7.250–52; 8.701–8. Pompey the Great (106–48 B.C.E.) was assassinated as he came ashore at Pelusium in Egypt. The translation is mine.

24.   On Philip of Macedon see n. 8 above.

25.   On Alexander see n. 8 above. Philip hired Aristotle to tutor his son Alexander (later "the Great").

26.   I have supplied the ellipsis dots since added to the end of the closing sentence the words "cetera desiderantur" appear, which I take to mean "etc. [et cetera]." That is, the original speech was longer than this.

27.   Tom. oration no. 3, 207–10.

28.   On the ancient commemorating of good days with a white pebble and bad days with a black one see the Roman satirists whose work Fedele knew well: Persius 2.1; Martial 9.52.5.

29.   Virgil *Eclogues* 1.59.

30.   Two famous warrior queens in Greek mythology. Fedele's readers would have known these figures from Boccaccio's Latin compendium of ancient women's lives, *On Famous Women*, chapters 47 and 76, a bestseller throughout the Renaissance and available in Italian, French, and English translations.

BIBLIOGRAPHY

PRIMARY SOURCES

Agrippa von Nettesheim, Henricus Cornelius (1486?–1535). *Declamatio de nobilitate et praecellentia foeminei sexus. Declamation on the Nobility and Preeminence of the Female Sex.* Ed. and trans. Albert Rabil, Jr. The Other Voice in Early Modern Europe. Chicago: University of Chicago Press, 1996.

Alberti, Leon Battista (1404–72). *The Family in Renaissance Florence.* Trans. Renee Neu Watkins. Columbia, S.C.: University of South Carolina Press, 1969.

Ariosto, Lodovico (1474–1533). *Orlando Furioso. The Frenzy of Orlando: A Romantic Epic.* Trans. Barbara Reynolds. 2 vols. Harmondsworth and Baltimore: Penguin Books, 1975–77.

Astell, Mary (1666–1731). *The First English Feminist: Reflections upon Marriage and Other Writings.* Ed. and intro. Bridget Hill. New York: St. Martin's Press, 1986.

Barbaro, Francesco (1390–1454). "On Wifely Duties." Trans. Benjamin Kohl. In *The Earthly Republic: Italian Humanists on Government and Society.* Eds. B. Kohl and R. G. Witt. [Philadelphia]: University of Pennsylvania Press, 1978.

Beauchamp, Virginia W., Matthew Bray, Susan Green, Susan S. Lanser, Katherine Larsen, Judith Pascoe, Katherine M. Rogers, Ruth Salvaggio, Amy Simowitz, Tara G., and Wallace, eds. *Women Critics, 1660–1820: An Anthology.* The Folger Collective on Early Women Critics. Bloomington and Indianapolis: Indiana University Press, 1995.

Boccaccio, Giovanni (1313–1375). *Concerning Famous Women.* Trans. Guido A. Guarino. New Brunswick, N.J.: Rutgers University Press, 1963.

———. *Corbaccio, or, The Labyrinth of Love.* Trans. Anthony K. Cassell. 2d rev. ed. Binghamton, N.Y.: Medieval & Renaissance Texts & Studies, 1993.

Bruni, Leonardo (1370–1444). "On the Study of Literature to Lady Battista Malatesta of Montefeltro." In *The Humanism of Leonardo Bruni: Selected Texts.* Trans. and intro. Gordon Griffiths, James Hankins, and David Thompson. Binghamton, N.Y.: Medieval & Renaissance Texts & Studies in conjunction with the Renaissance Society of America, 1987.

Castiglione, Baldassarre (1478–1529). *The Book of the Courtier.* Trans. George A. Bull. Baltimore: Penguin Books, 1967.

Cereta, Laura (1469–99). *Laurae Ceretae brixensis reminae clarissimae epistolae iam primum e MS in lucem productae.* Padua: Sebastiano Sardi, 1640.

————. *Collected Letters of a Renaissance Feminist*. Ed. and trans. Diana Robin. The Other Voice in Early Modern Europe. Chicago: University of Chicago Press, 1997.

Elyot, Thomas (1490–1546). "The Defence of Good Women." In *The Feminist Controversy of the Renaissance: Facsimile Reproductions*. Ed. and intro. Diane Bornstein. Delmar, N.Y.: Scholars' Facsimiles & Reprints, 1980.

Erasmus, Desiderius (1467–1536). "Courtship," "The Girl with No Interest in Marriage," "The Repentant Girl," "Marriage," "The Abbot and the Learned Lady," and "The New Mother." In *The Colloquies of Erasmus*. Trans. Craig R. Thompson. Chicago: University of Chicago Press, 1965.

————. *Erasmus on Women*. Ed. Erika Rummel. Toronto: University of Toronto Press, 1996.

Fedele, Cassandra (1465–1558). *Clarissimae feminae Cassandrae Fidelis, venetae. Epistolae et orationes*. Ed. Jacopo Filippo Tomasini, Padua: Franciscus Bolzetta, 1636.

————. *Oratio pro Bertucio Lamberto*. Modena: 1487; Venice: 1488; Nuremberg: 1489.

Kempe, Margery (1373–1439). *The Book of Margery Kempe*. Ed. Barry Windeatt. New York: Viking Penguin, 1985.

King, Margaret L., and Albert Rabil, Jr., eds. *Her Immaculate Hand: Selected Works by and about the Women Humanists of Quattrocento Italy*. 2d rev. ed. Binghamton, N.Y.: Medieval & Renaissance Texts & Studies, 1991.

Klein, Joan Larsen, ed. *Daughters, Wives, and Widows: Writings by Men about Women and Marriage in England, 1500–1640*. Urbana, Ill.: University of Illinois Press, 1992.

Knox, John (1505–72). *The Political Writings of John Knox: The First Blast of the Trumpet against the Monstrous Regiment of Women and Other Selected Works*. Ed. Marvin A. Beslow. Washington: Folger Shakespeare Library, 1985.

Kohl, Benjamin G., and Ronald G. Witt, eds. *The Earthly Republic: Italian Humanists on Government and Society*. Philadelphia: University of Pennsylvania Press, 1978.

Kors, Alan C., and Edward Peters, comps. *Witchcraft in Europe, 1100–1700: A Documentary History*. Philadelphia: University of Pennsylvania Press, 1972.

Lorris, Guillaume de (1225–40), and Jean de Meun (1273–80). *The Romance of the Rose*. Trans. Charles Dahlberg. Princeton: Princeton University Press, 1971. Reprint, Hanover, N.H.: University Press of New England, 1983.

Navarre, Marguerite de (1492–1549). *The Heptameron*. Trans. and intro. P. A. Chilton. New York: Penguin Books, 1984.

Pisan, Christine de (1365–1431). *The Book of the City of Ladies*. Trans. Earl Jeffrey Richards. Foreward Marina Warner. New York: Persea Books, 1982.

————. *The Treasure of the City of Ladies, or, The Book of the Three Virtues*. Trans. and intro. Sarah Lawson. New York: Penguin, 1985.

Poliziano, Angelo (1454–94). *Opera Omnia*. Ed. Ida Maier. 3 vols. Turin: Bottega d'Erasmo, 1970.

Spenser, Edmund (1552–99). *The Faerie Queene*. Ed. Thomas P. Roche, Jr., with the assistance of C. Patrick O'Donnell, Jr. New Haven: Yale University Press, 1978.

Stortoni, Laura Anna, ed. *Women Poets of the Italian Renaissance: Courtly Ladies and Courtesans*. Trans. Laura Anna Stortoni and Mary Prentice Lillie. New York: Italica Press, 1997.

Teresa of Avila, Saint (1515–82). *The Life of Saint Teresa of Avila by Herself*. Trans. John M. Cohen. New York: Viking Penguin, 1957.

Vives, Juan Luis (1492–1540). *A Very Fruteful and Pleasant Boke Called The Instruction of a Christen Woman.* Trans. Rycharde Hyrde. London, 1524.

Weyer, Johann (1515–88). *Witches, Devils, and Doctors in the Renaissance.* Ed. George Mora. Trans. John Shea. Binghamton, N.Y.: Medieval & Renaissance Texts & Studies, 1991.

Wilson, Katharina M., ed. *Medieval Women Writers.* Athens, Ga.: University of Georgia Press, 1984.

———. *Women Writers of the Renaissance and Reformation.* Athens, Ga.: University of Georgia Press, 1987.

Wilson, Katharina M., and Frank J. Warnke, eds. *Women Writers of the Seventeenth Century.* Athens, Ga.: University of Georgia Press, 1989.

Women Critics, 1660–1820: An Anthology. Ed. The Folger Collective on Early Women Critics. Bloomington: Indiana University Press, 1995.

LIVES OF CASSANDRA FEDELE WRITTEN BEFORE 1900

Alberici, Giacomo. *Catalogo breve de gl'illustri et famosi scrittori venetiani.* Bologna: Heredi di Giovanni Rossi, 1605.

Bergamo, Jacopo Filippo da. *Liber de claris scelestisque mulieribus.* Ferrara: Laurentius de Rubeis, 1497.

Betussi, Giuseppe. *Libro di M. Giovanni Boccaccio delle donne illustri tradotto per Messer Giuseppe Betussi.* Venice, 1545.

Canonici Fachini, Ginevra. *Prospetto biografico delle donne italiane rinomate in letteratura dal secolo XV fino a'giorni nostri.* Venice: Alvisopoli, 1824.

Egnazio, Giovanni Battista. *De exemplis illustrium virorum venetae civitatis atque aliarum gentium.* Venice: Nicolaum Tridentinum, 1554.

Ferri, Pietro Leopoldo. *Biblioteca femminile italiana.* Padua, 1842.

Fregosa, Battista [Campofregosa, Baptista Fulgosius, aliases]. *Factorum dictorumque memorabilium libri IX.* Venice, 1483. With a supplement by Justo Gaillardo Campo, Paris, 1578.

Papadopoli, Niccolò C. *Historia gymnasii Patavini.* 3 vols. Venice, 1726.

Petrettini, Maria. *Vita di Cassandra Fedele.* Venice: Giuseppe Grimaldo, 1852.

Quadrio, Francesco Saverio. *Della storia e della ragione d'ogni poesia.* 2 vols. Milan, 1741.

Ravisius, Jean Tixer de, ed. *De memorabilibus et claris mulieribus aliquot diversorum scriptorum opera.* Paris, 1521.

Riccoboni, Antonio. *De gymnasio Patavino.* Padua, 1598.

Simonsfeld, Henry. "Zur Geschichte der Cassandra Fedele." In *Studien zur Literaturgeschichte. Michael Bernays Gewidmet,* 99–106. Hamburg, 1893.

Tiraboschi, Girolamo. *Storia della letteratura italiana.* 9 vols. Modena, 1786–94.

Tomasini, Jacopo Filippo. *Elogia literis et sapientia illustrium ad vivum expressis imaginibus exornata* (Padua: S. Sardi, 1644).

SECONDARY SOURCES

Agostino, Giovanni degli. *Notizie storico-critiche intorno la vita e le opere degli scrittori veneziani.* Venice: Occhi, 1852.

Arslan, Antonia, Adriana Chemello, and Giberto Pizzamiglio, eds. *Le stanze ritrovate: Antologia di scrittrici venete dal quattrocento al novocento.* Milan and Venice: Eidos, 1991.

Beilin, Elaine V. *Redeeming Eve: Women Writers of the English Renaissance.* Princeton: Princeton University Press, 1987.

Benson, Pamela Joseph. *The Invention of the Renaissance Woman: The Challenge of Female Independence in the Literature and Thought of Italy and England.* University Park, Pa.: Pennsylvania State University Press, 1992.

Bloch, R. Howard. *Medieval Misogyny and the Invention of Western Romantic Love.* Chicago: University of Chicago Press, 1991.

Branca, Vittore. *Poliziano e l'umanesimo della parola.* Turin: G. Einaudi, 1983.

Brown, Alison. *Bartolomeo Scala (1430–1497), Chancellor of Florence: The Humanist as Bureaucrat.* Princeton: Princeton University Press, 1979.

Burckhardt, Jacob. *The Civilization of the Renaissance in Italy.* Trans. S. G. C. Middlemore. New York: Harper & Row, 1958.

Capelli, Adriano. "Cassandra Fedele in relazione con Lodovico Il Moro." In *Archivio Storico Lombardo* 3, no. 4 (1895): 387–91.

Cavazzana, Cesira. "Cassandra Fedele erudita veneziana del Rinascimento." In *Ateneo Veneto* 29, no. 2 (1906): 73–79, 249–75, 361–97.

Clark, Elizabeth A. *Ascetic Piety and Women's Faith: Essays on Late Ancient Christianity.* Lewiston, N.Y.: Edwin Mellen Press, 1986.

Clough, Cecil H. "The Cult of Antiquity." In *Cultural Aspects of the Italian Renaissance: Essays in Honour of Paul Oskar Kristeller.* Ed. Cecil H. Clough, 33–67. Manchester: Manchester University Press, 1976.

Convegno internazionale di Studi sul Rinascimento, ed. *Il Poliziano e il suo tempo,* Atti del 4 (Florence: Sansoni, 1957).

Davis, Natalie Zemon. *Society and Culture in Early Modern France.* Stanford: Stanford University Press, 1975.

Davis, Natalie Zemon, and Arlette Farge, eds. *A History of Women in the West. III, Renaissance and Enlightenment Paradoxes.* Cambridge, Mass.: Harvard University Press, 1993.

Dizionario biografico italiano (DBI). Rome: Instituto della enciclopedia italiana, 1961–.

Dixon, Suzanne. *The Roman Family.* Baltimore: Johns Hopkins University Press, 1992.

Ezell, Margaret. *Writing Women's Literary History.* Baltimore: Johns Hopkins University Press, 1993.

Fahy, Conor. "Three Early Renaissance Treatises on Women." *Italian Studies* 12 (1965): 330–55.

Felisatti, Massimo. *Isabella d'Este, la primadonna del Rinascimento.* Milan: Bompani, 1982.

Ferguson, Margaret W., Maureen Quilligan, and Nancy S. Vickers, eds. *Rewriting the Renaissance: The Discourses of Sexual Difference in Early Modern Europe.* Chicago: University of Chicago Press, 1987.

Ferraro, Joanne M. "The Power to Decide: Battered Wives in Early Modern Venice." *Renaissance Quarterly* 48, no. 3 (1995): 492–512.

Gardner, Jane F. *Women in Roman Law and Society.* Bloomington: Indiana University Press, 1986.

Gleason, Elizabeth G. *Gasparo Contarini: Venice, Rome, and Reform.* Berkeley and Los Angeles: University of California Press, 1993.

Grafton, Athony, and Lisa Jardine. *From Humanism to the Humanities: Education and the Liberal Arts in Fifteenth- and Sixteenth-Century Europe.* Cambridge, Mass.: Harvard University Press, 1986.

Greenblatt, Stephen J. *Renaissance Self-Fashioning from More to Shakespeare.* Chicago: University of Chicago Press, 1980.

Grendler, Paul. *Schooling in Renaissance Italy: Literacy and Learning, 1300–1600.* Baltimore: Johns Hopkins University Press, 1989.

Gundersheimer, Werner L. "Women, Learning, and Power: Eleonora of Aragon and the Court of Ferrara." In *Beyond Their Sex: Learned Women of the European Past.* Ed. Patricia H. Labalme, 43–65. New York: New York University Press, 1980.

Hallett, Judith P. *Fathers and Daughters in Roman Society: Women and the Elite Family.* Princeton: Princeton University Press, 1984.

Hallman, Barbara McClung. *Italian Cardinals, Reform, and the Church as Property.* Berkeley: University of California Press, 1985.

Herlihy, David. "Did Women Have a Renaissance? A Reconsideration." *Medievalia et Humanistica,* n.s., 13 (1985): 1–22.

Horowitz, Maryanne Cline. "Aristotle and Women." *Journal of the History of Biology* 9 (1976): 183–213.

Hull, Suzanne W. *Chaste, Silent, and Obedient: English Books for Women, 1475–1640.* San Marino, Calif.: The Huntington Library, 1982.

Jardine, Lisa. "Isotta Nogarola: Women Humanists—Education for What?" *History of Education* 12 (1983): 231–44.

Jones, Ann Rosalind. *The Currency of Eros: Women's Love Lyric in Europe.* Bloomington and Indianapolis: Indiana University Press, 1990.

Jordan, Constance. *Renaissance Feminism: Literary Texts and Political Models.* Ithaca, N.Y.: Cornell University Press, 1990.

———. "Boccaccio's In-famous Women: Gender and Civic Virtue in the *De claris mulieribus.*" In *Ambiguous Realities. Women in the Middle Ages and Renaissance.* Eds. Carole Levin and Jeannie Watson, 25–47. Detroit: Wayne State university Press.

Kelly, Joan. "Did Women Have a Renaissance?" In *Women, History and Theory.* Chicago: University of Chicago Press, 1984.

———. "Early Feminist Theory and the *Querelle des Femmes.*" In *Women, History & Theory: The Essays of Joan Kelly,* 4–28. Chicago: University of Chicago Press, 1985. First published in *Signs* 8 (1982): 4–28.

Kelso, Ruth. *Doctrine for the Lady of the Renaissance.* Foreword by Katharine M. Rogers. Urbana, Ill.: University of Illinois Press, 1956.

King, Margaret L. "Thwarted Ambitions: Six Learned Women of the Italian Renaissance." *Soundings* 59, no. 3 (1976): 280–305.

———. "The Religious Retreat of Isotta Nogarola (1418–1466): Sexism and Its Consequences in the Fifteenth Century." *Signs* 3 (1978): 807–22.

———. "Book-Lined Cells: Women and Humanism in the Early Italian Renaissance." In *Beyond Their Sex: Learned Women of the European Past.* Ed. Patricia H. Labalme, 66–90. New York: New York University Press, 1980.

———. *Venetian Humanism in an Age of Patrician Dominance.* Princeton: Princeton University Press, 1986.

———. *Women of the Renaissance.* Foreword by Catharine R. Stimson. Chicago: University of Chicago Press, 1991.

————. *The Death of the Child Valerio Marcello.* Chicago: University of Chicago Press, 1994.

Klapisch-Zuber, Christine, ed. *A History of Women in the West. II, Silences of the Middle Ages.* Cambridge, Mass.: Harvard University Press, 1992.

Kristeller, Paul Oskar. *Eight Philosophers of the Italian Renaissance.* Stanford: Stanford University Press, 1964.

————. "Learned Women of Early Modern Italy: Humanists and University Scholars." In *Beyond Their Sex. Learned Women of the European Past.* Ed. Patricia H. Labalme, 91–116. New York: New York University Press, 1980.

Labalme, Patricia H. "Venetian Women on Women: Three Early Modern Feminists." *Archivio Veneto 5,* no. 117 (1981): 81–108.

Labalme, Patricia H., ed. *Beyond Their Sex. Learned Women of the European Past.* New York and London: New York University Press, 1980.

Laqueur, Thomas. *Making Sex: Body and Gender from the Greeks to Freud.* Cambridge, Mass.: Harvard University Press, 1994.

Lerner, Gerda. *The Creation of Patriarchy.* New York: Oxford University Press, 1986.

————. *The Creation of Feminist Consciousness, 1000–1870.* New York: Oxford University Press. 1994.

Liss, Peggy K. *Isabel the Queen: Life and Times.* Oxford: Oxford University Press, 1992.

Lochrie, Karma. *Margery Kempe and Translations of the Flesh.* Philadelphia: University of Pennsylvania Press, 1992.

Maclean, Ian. *The Renaissance Notion of Woman: A Study of the Fortunes of Scholasticism and Medical Science in European Intellectual Life.* Cambridge: Cambridge University Press, 1980.

————. *Woman Triumphant: Feminism in French Literature, 1610–1654.* Oxford: Clarendon Press, 1977.

Martines, Lauro. *Power and Imagination. City-States in Renaissanvce Italy.* New York: Random House, 1979.

————. *The Social World of the Florentine Humanists, 1390–1460.* Princeton: Princeton University, 1963.

Matter, E. Ann, and John Coakley, eds. *Creative Women in Medieval and Early Modern Italy.* Philadelpia: University of Pensylvania Press, 1994.

Mayer, Thomas F., and Daniel R. Woolf, eds. *The Rhetorics of Life Writing in Early Modern Europe: Forms of Biography from Cassandra Fedele to Louis XIV.* Ann Arbor: University of Michigan Press, 1995.

Mazzuchelli, Giovanni Maria. *Gli scrittori d'Italia.* 2 vols. Brescia: Giambattista Bossoni, 1753–63.

McClure, George. *Sorrow and Consolation in Italian Humanism.* Princeton: Princeton University Press, 1991.

Migiel, Marilyn. "Gender Studies and the Italian Renaissance." In *Interpreting the Italian Renaissance: Literary Perspectives.* Ed. Antonio Toscano. Stony Brook, N.Y.: Forum Italicum, 1991.

Migiel, Marilyn, and Juliana Schiesari, eds. *Refiguring Woman: Perspectives on Gender in the Italian Renaissance.* Ithaca: Cornell University Press, 1991.

Molmenti, Pietro. *La storia di Venezia nella vita privata dalle origini alla caduta della repubblica.* 3 vols. 7th ed. Bergamo: Instituto italiano d'arti grafiche, 1928.

Monson, Craig A., ed. *The Crannied Wall: Women, Religion, and the Arts in Early Modern Europe*. Ann Arbor: University of Michigan Press, 1992.

Musatti, Eugenio. *La donna in Venezia*. Padua: Arnalo Forni, 1892.

Okin, Susan Moller. *Women in Western Political Thought*. Princeton: Princeton University Press, 1979.

Pagels, Elaine. *Adam, Eve, and the Serpent*. New York: HarperCollins, 1988.

Pantel, Pauline Schmitt, ed. *A History of Women in the West. I, From Ancient Goddesses to Christian Saints*. Cambridge, Mass.: Harvard University Press, 1992.

Partner, Peter. *The Pope's Men. The Papal Civil Service in the Renaissance*. Oxford: Clarendon Press, 1990.

Pavanello, Giuseppe. *Un maestro del Quattrocento (Giovanni Aurelio Augurello)*. Venice: Emiliana, 1905.

Pesenti, G. "Lettere inedite del Poliziano." *Athenaeum* 3 (1915): 299–301.

———. "Alessandra Scala, una figurina della Rinascenza fiorentina." *Giornale storico della letteratura italiana* 85 (1925): 241–67.

Piccioni, Luigi. *Di Francesco Uberto. Umanista cesenate*. Bologna, 1903.

Pomeroy, Sarah. *Goddesses, Whores, Wives, and Slaves: Women in Classical Antiquity*. New York: Schocken Books, 1976.

Quilligan, Maureen. *The Allegory of Female Authority. Christine de Pizan's Cité des Dames*. Ithaca: Cornell University Press, 1991.

Rabil, Albert, Jr. *Laura Cereta: Quattrocento Humanist*. Binghamton, N.Y.: Medieval & Renaissance Texts & Studies, 1981.

Robin, Diana. "Cassandra Fedele's Epistolae (1488–1521): Biography as Effacement." In *The Rhetorics of Life-Writing in Early Modern Europe: Forms of Biography from Cassandra Fedele to Louise XIV*. Eds Thomas Mayer and Daniel Woolf, 187–203. Ann Arbor: University of Michigan Press, 1995.

———. "Cassandra Fedele (1465–1499)." In *Italian Women Writers: A Bio-Bibliographical Sourcebook*. Ed. Rinaldina Russell, 119–27. Westport, Conn.: Greenwood Press, 1994.

———. *Filelfo in Milan. Writings, 1451–1477*. Princeton. Princeton University Press, 1991.

———. "Space, Woman, and Renaissance Discourse." In *Sex and Gender in Medieval and Renaissance Texts. The Latin Tradition*. Eds. Barbara K. Gold, Paul Allen Miller, and Charles Platter, 165–87. Albany: State University of New York Press, 1996.

Rose, Mary Beth. *Women in the Middle Ages and the Renaissance: Literary and Historical Perspectives*. Syracuse: Syracuse University Press, 1986.

Rosenthal, Margaret F. *The Honest Courtesan: Veronica Franco, Citizen and Writer in Sixteenth-Century Venice*. Chicago: University of Chicago Press, 1992.

Russell, Rinaldina, ed. *Italian Women Writers: A Bio-Bibliographical Sourcebook*. Westport, Conn.: Greenwood Press, 1994.

———. *The Feminist Encyclopedia of Italian Literature*. Westport, Conn.: Greenwood Press, 1997.

Sommerville, Margaret R. *Sex and Subjection: Attitudes to Women in Early-Modern Society*. London: E. Arnold, 1995.

Stinger, Charles L. *The Renaissance in Rome*. Bloomington: Indiana University Press, 1998.

Stuard, Susan M. "The Dominion of Gender: Women's Fortunes in the High Middle Ages." In *Becoming Visible: Women in European History.* Eds. Renate Bridenthal, Claudia Koonz, and Susan Stuard. 2d ed. Boston: Houghton Mifflin, 1987.

Tetel, Marcel. *Marguerite de Navarre's* Heptameron: *Themes, Language & Structure.* Durham, N.C.: Duke University Press, 1973.

Tiraboschi, Girolamo. *Biblioteca Modenese, o, Notizie della vita e delle opere degli scrittori natii degli stati del serenissimo signor duca di Modena.* 6 vols. Modena: Società, 1781–86.

Toscani, Bernard. "Antonia Pulci (1452–1501)." In *Italian Women Writers. A Bio-Biobliographical Sourcebook.* Ed. Rinaldina Russell, 344–52. Westport, Conn.: Greenwood Press, 1994.

Treggiari, Susan. *Roman Marriage: Iusti Coniuges from the Time of Cicero to the Time of Ulpian.* Oxford: Oxford University Press, 1991.

Vedova, Guiseppe. *Biografia degli scrittori Padovani.* 3 vols. Padua: Minerva, 1831–36.

Walsh, William T. *St. Teresa of Avila: A Biography.* Rockford, Ill.: TAN Books and Publications, 1987.

Warner, Marina. *Alone of All Her Sex: The Myth and Cult of the Virgin Mary.* New York: Knopf, 1976.

Wayne, Valerie. "Zenobia in Medieval and Renaissance Literature." In *Ambiguous Realities, Women in the Middle Ages and Renaissance.* Eds. Carole Levin and Jeannie Watson, 48–65. Detroit, Ind.: Wayne State University Press, 1987.

Wiesner, Merry E. *Women and Gender in Early Modern Europe.* Cambridge: Cambridge University Press, 1993.

Willard, Charity Cannon. *Christine de Pizan: Her Life and Works.* New York: Persea Books, 1984.

Wilson, Katharina, ed. *An Encyclopedia of Continental Women Writers.* 2 vols. New York: Garland, 1991.

INDEX

Note: addressees and other individuals mentioned in Fedele's correspondence are indexed under their own name

Gaspare, Fracasso, 50, 54–56, 58–59
Gasparino (brother), 82, 117, 118
Gatuli, Ludovico, 139
Genesis (creation story), xi
Gennari, Giuseppe, 64
Gennaro, Jacopo, 71–72
Giorgio, Girolamo, 49
Goggio, Bartolomeo, xix; *In Praise of Women*, xxi
Gonzaga, Cecelia, 7
Gonzaga, Francesco, 9, 43–44, 104
Gonzaga, Lodovico, 39
Gonzaga, Sigismondo, 104, 109–10
government bureaucracies, humanists in, xvi
Greece, ancient, viii–ix
Greek, humanists use of, xv
Greek philosophy, and female nature, viii–ix
Grimani, Domenico, 108–9
Guazzo, Stefano, xix

Hammer of Witches, The (Krämer and Sprenger), xix
Hebrew Bible. *See* biblical view of women
heretical movements, in the Middle Ages, xv
higher education, for women, 154
household, integrity of, xxi–xxii
humanism, xv–xvi; and Constantinople recapture, 17; debates on women, xvii–xix; effect on literary culture, 12; influenced by classical Greece, xv; influenced by classical Rome, xv; themes in Fedele's letters, 8–11; treatises on women, xviii–xxi
humanistic studies, and religion, 104
humanists, on woman writers, 7
Humors, ix
hysteria, female, ix

Il Moro. *See* Sforza, Lodovico (Il Moro)
inaction, vs. action, viii
inheritance, x, xiv
In Praise of Women (Goggio), xix

Inquisition, 11
Isabella (queen of Spain), 5, 10, 17, 18–23, 31n. 1
Islam, 17. *See also* Turks, westward expansion of
Italy, laywomen communities in, xv

Jacopo (friar), 104
Jerome, xii

knowledge, problem of, xxi, xxiv
Knox, John, *First Blast of the Trumpet against the Monstrous Regiment of Women*, xxiii
Krämer, Heinrich, *The Hammer of Witches*, xix

lactation, xiv
Lamberti, Bertuccio, 5, 9, 64, 154–59
Lamentations (Mathéolus), xiii, xvi
Latin, humanists use of, xv
law, women prohibited from entering, 4
laywomen, communities of, xv, xvi, xxii
learning capabilities, of women, xxiv
Le Franc, Martin, *The Champion of Women*, xviii
Leita, Giovanni Battista, 78–79
Leonardo, 55, 109
Leone, Girolamo, 21, 22, 32n. 14, 36
Leoni, Barbara, 4
Leo X, 104, 105–6
liberal arts education, importance of, 8, 10
literary culture of women, 12
literature, medieval, image of women in, xii–xv
Louis XII (king of France), 47, 49
love, romantic (courtly), xii

Magi, 38
Malatesta, Battista, 7, 128
male children, emancipation of in ancient Rome, x
male/female equality, in humanistic works, xix

Venancio, Pietro Paolo, 144
Venier, Francesco, 154
Verona, Italy, 63
Veronese, Francesco, 82
vice, women's inclination to, xviii
virile qualities, according to Aristotle, viii
virtue, 137, 142
Visconti (Milan ruling family), 37–39
Vives, Juan Luis, xviii, xxi; *The Education of a Christian Woman: A Sixteenth Century Manual*, xxiv

wet nurses, xiv
Weyer, Johann, xix
wine drinking, as cause for divorce, x
witches, xix–xx
woman question, xvii, xix, xx
women: Aristotlian view of, viii; barred from public speaking, xxiii; biographers of, 13n. 4; and chastity, xxi–xxii, xxiii, 7, 26, 33n. 40; Christian doctrine and: xi–xii; in civic affairs, 10; communities of, xv, xvi, xxii; costume, xxiii–xxiv; debates on, xvii–xix; deceitfulness in, ix; despondency in, ix; education,

xviii, xxiv, 11; emancipation in ancient Rome, x; equality in contemporary life, vii; in Greek philosophy, viii–ix; inclination to vice, xviii; inferiority of, viii, xviii; inheritance in ancient Rome, x–xi; learning capabilities, xxiv; lines of succession for, xi; literary culture of, 12; lower-class, in Rome, x; male/female equality, in humanistic works, xix; nature of, treatises on, xviii; patrons, xx–xxi; prohibitions against in professions, 4; prone to diabolism, xix; querulousness in, ix; responsibilities in marriage, xviii; Roman civil legislation, viii, ix–x; as rulers, xxii–xxiii; slave, in Rome, x; slavery, in marriage, 8; treatises on, xviii–xxi; volume of writing in Renaissance, xx; writers, 16th – century boom, 15n. 29; as writers, humanists view of, 7
women's roles: and the Catholic Church, xix–xv; family, xiii–xiv
Worth of Women, The (Fonte), 12

Zabarino, Giovanni Antonio, 73